THE LIFE
OF A
PROVINCIAL LADY

*A Study of E. M. Delafield
and her Works*

Other books by Violet Powell

Autobiographical
Five out of Six
Within the Family Circle

General
A Substantial Ghost
The Irish Cousins
A Compton-Burnett Compendium
Margaret, Countess of Jersey
Flora Annie Steel, Novelist of India
The Constant Novelist

THE LIFE
OF A
PROVINCIAL LADY

A Study of E. M. Delafield

and her Works

Violet Powell

HEINEMANN : LONDON

William Heinemann Ltd
Michelin House
81 Fulham Road
London SW3 6RB

LONDON   MELBOURNE   AUCKLAND

First published 1988

British Library Cataloguing in Publication Data

Powell, Violet
   The life of a provincial lady: a study of
   E. M. Delafield and her works.
   1. Fiction in English. Delafield, E. M.
   1890–1943
   I. Title
   823'.912

ISBN 0 434 59958 1

Printed and bound in Great Britain by
Richard Clay Ltd, Bungay, Suffolk

Dedicatory Epistle to Mr Jeoffry Spence

My dear Jeoffry

When we first met to discuss my plan to write a study of
E. M. Delafield, you had already kindly offered me your
assistance. At that time I had little idea of the wide range of
your researches, and of your diligence in pursuing them. As I
came to appreciate the completeness of your E. M. Delafield
archive, my admiration was intensified by respect for your
impeccable filing system. Consequently, when you allowed me
to draw on your material, my work was made far easier and
more enjoyable by your generosity.

I must, of course, emphasize that any conclusions or
suppositions are my own, but I hope that you will accept the
dedication of this book as a token of gratitude,

From your friend,

Violet Powell
Chantry, September 1987

They say books about books are profitless,
but they certainly make very pleasant reading.

W. Somerset Maugham
The Book Bag

CONTENTS

ILLUSTRATIONS

INTRODUCTION AND ACKNOWLEDGEMENTS

Half a century has passed since E. M. Delafield's most famous book, *The Diary of a Provincial Lady*, first appeared. Three more diaries followed in which the Provincial Lady moved to London, crossed the Atlantic and coped with the early days of the Second World War. Not long ago the four diaries were re-issued in one volume, when it became clear that not only were there many readers faithful to the memory of E. M. Delafield, but that new readers were finding the Provincial Lady's domestic struggles to be reflected in contemporary life.

It would, however, be a great injustice to regard E. M. Delafield as a writer of limited reputation, or solely as the purveyor of the comedy in everyday life. If this study of her far-flung literary activity is an encouragement to become acquainted with, for example, *Turn Back the Leaves* or *Thank Heaven Fasting*, it will be no more than is due to a novelist of a distinctive and remarkable talent.

To introduce one personal note; in the summer of 1936 my husband, Anthony Powell, and I spent some weeks in the USSR, under the guidance of Intourist. Simultaneously, E. M. Delafield was travelling in Russia. She published an account of her adventures in *Straw Without Bricks*. Those experiences which we happened to have shared are, I can confirm, reproduced in this fascinating book with almost photographic accuracy.

By great good fortune, Mrs Rosamund Dashwood, daughter of E. M. Delafield, now living in British Columbia, came to England on a visit soon after I had asked her for her approval of this book. She was unstinting in her help and encouragement. Since then she has patiently answered questions, and supplied details of her life at Croyle. Rosamund Dashwood suggested that I should write to Miss Cicely McCall, not only a constant visitor to Croyle, but a companion of

xiii

E. M. Delafield on holidays in France. Cicely McCall's recollections, and store of photographs, illuminated the Dashwood family to my imagination. It was Cicely McCall who put me into touch with Mr Jeoffry Spence, well known as an historian of railways. He has also, for a considerable time, researched the life and career of E. M. Delafield. In the Epistle of Dedication, I hope I have conveyed my gratitude for his generosity in allowing me to draw on a collection which covers a multiplicity of material, from press cuttings to family trees.

My husband, Anthony Powell, has been, as ever, the most helpful of critics. My further thanks are due to Jamie Hamilton, a devoted friend of E. M. Delafield; Sir Rupert Hart-Davis; James Lees-Milne; Robert Milnes, who is engaged on a bibliography of E. M. Delafield's works; Richard Milton of Kentisbeare; my nephew, Ferdinand Mount, who made me a most useful present of the novels of E. M. Delafield collected by his mother, my late sister Julia; Mrs Lorna Waite, formerly of Uffculme; Mrs Marjorie Watts, a friend of E. M. Delafield from her earliest days as a novelist, and the widow of Arthur Watts, the Provincial Lady's inspired illustrator. Mr Douglas Matthews and the staff of the London Library have been unfailingly helpful. Mrs Bane and the staff of the Frome Library have been untiring in tracing the works of E. M. Delafield. I am grateful to the Society of Authors and the BBC for allowing me to use material from their archives; and to the British Film Institute for supplying details of *Moonlight Sonata*. I would also like to thank A. D. Peters Ltd and Macmillan Publishers Ltd for their help.

If I have lapsed in failing to acknowledge any further help, I hope that my sincerest gratitude will be accepted.

Violet Powell, 1988

I

'BEGINNINGS'

'Betjeman has the 'flu,' Evelyn Waugh wrote to Nancy Mitford in October 1951, 'and has retired to the house of the Dowager Duchess of Devonshire, where he is waited on . . . while the high-church butler reads *The Unlucky Family* to him.' Waugh had no doubts that Nancy Mitford would be familiar with *The Unlucky Family*, a story for the young written nearly fifty years before. Mrs Henry de la Pasture's history of vicissitudes, always met by incompetence, has, however, continued to attach readers from succeeding generations.

It is possible that this continuing fame would not be entirely agreeable to Mrs Henry de la Pasture. In her day well known as a novelist, she might not have relished being principally remembered for a children's book, even among Dowager Duchesses, future Poet Laureates and famous novelists. She was a woman of exacting standards, not least about her own reputation. It became clear, in later life, that she had a distaste for being renowned by the reading public as the mother of E. M. Delafield, author of *The Diary of a Provincial Lady*.

Edmée Elizabeth Monica de la Pasture, eldest child of the author of *The Unlucky Family*, was born at Aldrinton, near Hove, on 9 June 1890. Until she became a published author she was called Edmée, her family continuing to use that name even after her friends had come to know her as Elizabeth. There was to be a severe disruption in her life at the age of twenty-one when she sought and lost a religious vocation. The young woman who began to write professionally a few years later was very different from the girl who had aspired to be a 'Bride of Heaven'. Although a new name for familiar use was a sign of this transformation, there was to be a long, hard road to travel before *The Diary of a Provincial Lady* became a best-seller and the daughter outstripped the mother in popular fame.

Edmée's mother chose to write as Mrs Henry de la Pasture, but her husband actually bore the title of Count. His forebears had been distinguished in the neighbourhood of Boulogne since the fourteenth century. Among these ancestors the most brilliant was undoubtedly the painter Roger van der Weyden (1400–64), who had settled in Brussels and adopted a Flemish version of his patronymic. Of the family who remained in the Pas de Calais, Pierre François de la Pasture was created Marquis and Count by Louis XVI in 1768. His son had barely been confirmed in these titles when he fled from the Revolution to England, conveniently near, in 1791. His unfortunate sister Agathe, a *chanoinesse*, failed to escape, being imprisoned in the Citadel of Calais during the Terror.

Of the next generation, the third Marquis de la Pasture grew up completely Anglicized. Educated at Eton, he married a Miss Ellen Crauford Hardie and died in 1840. His fifth child, Henry Philip Ducarel, was born posthumously, and became, eventually, the father of Edmée Elizabeth Monica. The name Ducarel was that of Count Henry's grandmother, whose own ancestry was unusually exotic. Gerard Gustavus Ducarel had gone to India in the service of the Honourable East India Company. Marriages between the servants of the Company and Indian ladies were far from infrequent, as family groups of the period confirm. 'Gusty' Ducarel had not been many years in India when, *circa* 1772, he married the daughter of His Highness the Maharajah of Purnea, which lies near the frontier of Nepal, and from whence, one hundred and sixty years later, the first flight over Everest was to be launched.

Converted to the Roman Catholic faith, the Maharajah's daughter took the name of Elizabeth. She was probably about fourteen at the time of her marriage, but she survived until 1822, having borne seven children. Her eldest daughter, Elizabeth Coltée Ducarel, had less of a gift for survival. She died at twenty-six, leaving a child by each of her two husbands, Archibald Foulkes and Pierre-Marie François de la Pasture, both of whom predeceased her. Her son by her second marriage was Henri-Pierre, third Marquis de la Pasture, who, as has been seen, died before the birth of his son Henry, father of Edmée Elizabeth. Among E. M. Delafield's works there is only one, *The Marriage of Rose Barlow*, a short novel, which deals with India, but this limits its plot to the horrors of the Mutiny. Edmée does not seem to have taken any particular interest in a half-Indian great-grandmother who had died ninety years before her own birth. Nor do there appear to have been any specifically Indian characteristics in the fourth generation, beyond, in Edmée's case, a delicacy of bone structure remarked on by many who knew her.

Although of a kindly character, charming to his children and loved by them, Henry de la Pasture seems to have made little mark in the world beyond the circle of Catholic families to which he was connected by birth and marriage. When he finally married, in 1887, he proved, however, to have found a wife not only twenty-one years younger than himself, but of a far livelier and ambitious disposition. Elizabeth Lydia Rosabelle Bonham had been born at Naples in 1866, shortly after the city had seen the departure of the last Bourbon king. Her grandfather was British Consul General at the time of her birth, Naples having a large British colony, besides a flow of visiting artists. Miss Bonham's father was also in the Consular Service, and it is possible that his posting to Boulogne brought Edmée's parents together, the de la Pastures retaining some family connections in the neighbourhood. Wherever they met, their marriage took place at the Church of Our Lady of Victories in Kensington, both bride and bridegroom belonging to the Roman Catholic Church.

The birth of Edmée in 1890 was followed by that of Bettine Marie Yolande in 1892, but the family grew no larger. Mrs Henry de la Pasture openly expressed disappointment at having brought forth female children only, but this did not prevent her from developing a possessiveness towards her daughters which manifested itself in the determination that her influence over them should be paramount. Still only in her twenties, she also started on a literary career. According to her entry in *Who's Who 1934*, her first book was published when her eldest child can have been no more than four years old.

For the next twenty years success came to Mrs Henry de la Pasture, both as a novelist and playwright. To *Who's Who* she gave details of publications and theatrical productions, but even in 1934, when she had ceased to publish for nearly twenty years, she was not prepared to mention *The Unlucky Family* among her works. There is a trace of ingratitude in this omission, as she must have enjoyed the rewards of the popularity of *The Unlucky Family*. Her own family might be called lucky in having a wife and mother who made a substantial contribution to the family income, which it seems that Henry de la Pasture made no effort to augment. This pattern of reliance on a writing wife and mother was to be repeated, even more remarkably, in the next generation.

When E. M. Delafield contributed to a volume called *Beginnings*, published in 1935, the existence of her mother as a far from extinct volcano caused her to handle her own beginnings as an author with circumspection. It was her mother who had read her earliest attempts at writing conceived in a highly tragic manner, and who gave the useful advice only to write from her own experience. Less sympathetically, it was presumably also her mother who limited the time allowed for reading to one hour in each day. This prohibition came, Edmée thought, partly from the idea that what children enjoyed must be severely rationed, and partly from the belief that a child glued to a book throughout the day would be failing to learn the amenities of human society. Subterfuge was the only way to evade this prohibition, and, though successful, feelings of guilt naturally developed.

The de la Pastures lived as a bilingual family, and although Edmée wrote that her French vocabulary was more limited than her command of English, her performance at the age of eight was far from despicable. Being set 'Fairy Wishes' as the subject for a French composition, she wrote a poem of which the first four lines expressed her early absorption in the world of books:

> Si une fée m'apparaissait
> Et me disait, 'Que veux-tu?'
> Bien sûr que je repondrai,
> 'Tous les livres qui peuvent être lus.'

At roughly the same age she could remember sitting in a meadow and, as she leant against a haystack, listening to her mother reading *The Pilgrim's Progress*. It seemed to the child that the 'pleasant land of Beulah' was a prevision of the meadow in which she sat. This recollection belonged to a period when the de la Pastures, somewhat nomadic in their habits, were spending the summer at East Butterleigh House, near Cullompton in South Devon. This temporary home happened to have a view across the Culm Valley to the house called Croyle, with which Edmée was to become so deeply associated in the memories of her family and friends.

It was at Croyle that Edmée made her home for the last twenty years of her life, gave birth to her daughter, wrote her most remarkable books, and suffered the cruellest of losses. To the little girl listening to the account of 'the pleasant land of Beulah' all this was in the unforeseeable future. More than once in her writings E. M. Delafield was to ponder on the blacking-out of confidence between growing girls and their mothers. The scene in the meadow might be called the crystallization of a moment before innocent trust evaporated.

Marrying well into middle age, Henry de la Pasture had got out of step with his own generation. Consequently, his niece Monica, daughter of his eldest brother, was only three years younger than his wife, Monica's aunt by marriage. Monica married Charles Charrington, a member of the brewing family, and her daughter, Dorothea, was born a month after her Uncle Henry's daughter Edmée. Resemblance between the families stopped there. Charles Charrington was himself a Protestant, but agreed that his daughter should be brought up as a Catholic. His point of view changed when Monica light-heartedly abandoned both husband and child.

To her devout family, Monica's disregard for the commitments of marriage and motherhood greatly increased any original disapproval of her 'mixed marriage'. Her daughter, Dorothea, who at the moment of writing is still alive in her nineties, was handed about like a parcel among the Charringtons and de la Pastures. She frequently came to rest in the nursery of Edmée and Yolande. The latter, always known as Yoé, was a plain awkward child. While Edmée, the pretty little eldest girl, would be called down to the drawing room to be shown off to visitors, Yoé and Dorothea would be left free to play romping games in the nursery. Not unnaturally, Dorothea remembered preferring Yoé to Edmée, her exact contemporary.

Besides recalling that she had loved Yoé more than Edmée, Dorothea remembered the kindness of her great-uncle Henry, and the charm his company had for the nursery children. This cousinly association was disrupted in 1903, when Charles Charrington divorced his wife and remarried. Dorothea, previously contented in the faith she shared with her cousins, was now ordered to join the Church of England. The following year, Monica Charrington married Sir George Bullough, first and last Baronet. By this remarriage, an additional sin in the eyes of the family, Monica produced a daughter who, in due course, became the second wife of the Earl of Durham. Second marriages, some from divorce, but mostly from the death of husband or wife, were far from uncommon in E. M. Delafield's family, and they provided useful material for more than one of her novels. In real life, only an exceptionally clear-headed genealogist could hope to find the thread through the tangled web of step-parents and their assorted progeny.

Edmée's early education was left in the hands of a sequence of French governesses. Later, these were fused into a composite portrait of 'Mademoiselle', who added a touch of Gallic exoticism to *The Diary of a Provincial Lady*. Their tuition was superseded when Edmée was sent to a convent boarding school, an experiment on her mother's part at surrendering her daughter to outside influences. The experiment was hardly a success from the mother's point of view. Mrs Henry de la Pasture evidently felt that she could only keep her hold over her daughter's development by nipping other influences in the bud. Consequently, Edmée found herself changing schools at short notice, and for no very clear reason.

The next chapter, in which Edmée looks back at her schooling, in a previously unpublished reminiscence, will explain, in her own words, why her mother continually removed her daughter from convents which must have been chosen by herself. Repeated announcements by Miss de la Pasture that she wished to enter religious life were, as will be seen, almost entirely discouraged by the conventual authorities.

This phase of Edmée's education filled the years between the ages of ten and eighteen. During this period her parents ceased to use East Butterleigh House as a country home. They chose, instead, The Falls, Llandogo, Monmouthshire, a house in a Wordsworthian situation, 'a few miles above Tintern Abbey'. The poet's evocation of the dramatic landscape found an echo in the imagination of the future novelist:

> The sounding cataract
> Haunted me like a passion: the tall rock,
> The mountain, and the deep and gloomy wood,
> Their colours and their forms, were then to me
> An appetite.

Cataract, mountain and gloomy wood continued to haunt E. M. Delafield, giving her a background for tragedy in two of her novels.

The Falls was renamed The Priory, and in reference books, Count Henry became stabilized as 'of Llandogo Priory'. It does seem, however, that in 1905, the family moved to a smaller house nearby. Part of the year must have been spent in a London house, of which Edmée had such glowing recollections that she dedicated a book to her sister Yoé on the theme of their shared young days in Chester Square.

It was in the gardens of Chester Square that Muriel Dashwood, sister of Edmée's future husband, saw the frail Mr de la Pasture supported between his daughters. Miss Dashwood was struck, at the time, by the smart appearance of the girl who was to marry her brother ten years later. In contrast, the gaucheness of the younger sister was emphasized by dowdy clothes which did nothing to enhance a face with an outsize nose. This walk took place in 1908. Not long afterwards, the family must have returned to Llandogo, for it was there, on 12 October, that Henry de la Pasture died suddenly, of a heart attack.

His death was an acute loss to his daughters. Although in her novels E. M. Delafield often described maddeningly sanctimonious fathers, these came from her creative fantasy rather than from her own experience. Their loss drew the sisters closer, in an alliance against their mother's possessiveness towards her pretty eldest, and lack of interest in the plain and awkward younger sister.

At his death, Count Henry was respectfully memorialized in the *Monmouthshire Beacon*. He would be greatly missed in Llandogo, said the obituary, because, although a Roman Catholic, he was liberal in his views. He was also recorded as having taken a great interest in every local good work, and as having been a generous contributor to many causes. Apparently, to the *Monmouthshire Beacon*, adherence to the Church of Rome was likely to be synonymous with a closed mind, no interest in good works, and an uncharitable parsimony.

When her father died, Edmée was eighteen years old, of an age to make her début in society, whether or not she was to be presented at Court. As Chester Square had happy memories for the sisters, it would not seem that they were exposed to the full rigours of the London Season. On the other hand, Edmée was familiar with the Season's machinery which she described in one of her most remarkable books. Injunctions from their mother to 'hold themselves up' and 'to be natural' must have been distinctly unnerving, even in a social round restricted by mourning for their father.

Although to experience a London Season was usual, it was not invariable in such circles as those frequented by the de la Pastures. Sonia Cubitt, daughter of Edward VII's mistress, Alice Keppel, has described being put to a severe preliminary test at the age of seventeen. Just out of the schoolroom, she was sent to luncheon at 10 Downing Street, where the hostess, Margot Asquith, placed the young girl between her husband, the Prime Minister, and Arthur Balfour, the Foreign Secretary. The potential débutante was sent home with a note signed 'Margot'. The note read, 'Dearest Alice, Do not attempt to bring Sonia out. Try something else.'

As it happened, Mrs Keppel's daughter turned out to be exotically attractive, but no such consolation was available to Mrs Henry de la Pasture. Contemplating her daughter Yoé, she may well have thought that to 'try something else' would be the least painful solution for all parties.

The girls did, however, have a refuge from their mother's somewhat overpowering personality, in the home of her sister Constance at Penstowe, near Bude. Francis Phillips, Constance Bonham's first husband, had died, and in 1904 she had married Major Algernon Thynne. Penstowe continued to be an island of repose and recuperation throughout the lives of Edmée and Yoé. Although losing her husband, Algernon Thynne, in the First World War, Aunt Constance survived into her ninety-first year, her house still a sanctuary. Her nieces never appealed to her in vain for shelter in moments of crisis.

As a playwright, Mrs Henry de la Pasture had her greatest success with a dramatization of her novel *Peter's Mother*. The play ran for six months at various West End theatres, and received the additional accolade of being performed at Sandringham in December 1906, by command of King Edward VII. At that date actresses, however virtuous their reputations, were not received at Court, the label 'rogues and vagabonds' still adhering to the profession. The rule did not, of course, apply to female writers of plays, particularly to someone as well connected as Mrs Henry de la Pasture. The Lord Chamberlain's Office has a record that Mr and Mrs Henry de la Pasture were summoned to a reception at Buckingham Palace on 1 March 1907, possibly as a result of royal enjoyment of *Peter's Mother*.

After such an occasion, *The Times* habitually published descriptions of dresses worn by the female guests, details their dressmakers were happy to supply. Mrs de la Pasture's gown, as recorded, combined sumptuousness with good taste. Ecru chiffon, covered by Brussels tulle, was embroidered with trails of wistaria in silver and crystal. Of a deeper shade, the train was showered with crystal and silver ornaments. The standard of magnificence set by her mother must certainly have made a mark on her daughter's consciousness. In her novels, E. M. Delafield never hesitated to describe the clothes worn by any character on any occasion, though after the age of Edwardian elaboration had passed, the gorgeousness was seldom up to Mrs de la Pasture's opulent level.

Henry de la Pasture's estate, declared at less than two thousand five hundred pounds, was left to his wife, and afterwards to his daughters. From his limited fortune, it would seem reasonable to deduce that his wife, besides her literary earnings, must have also possessed the other assets needed to dress her in ecru chiffon and embroidery of wistaria. The executors of the will were Charles Charrington, first husband of the runaway Monica de la Pasture, Lord Mowbray, husband of another niece, Elizabeth Constable, and Lord Clifford of Chudleigh. Charles Charrington was, of course, an Anglican, but the other two executors came from English families of Roman Catholic tradition, with whom the emigré de la Pastures had become linked by a succession of marriages.

Through Henry de la Pasture's sister, Elizabeth, there were connections by marriage with Constables, Mowbrays and Stourtons, whose vast family filled chilly houses and even chillier convents. Although the tradition of annual child-bearing wore down many of the wives, it is fair to say that there were exceptions. For example, the wife of the eighteenth Lord Stourton, in the course of twenty-three years, produced sixteen children, five sons and eleven daughters. Five of the daughters became nuns, and their prayers for their mother's well-being must have been an effective supplement to an excellent constitution, for Lady Stourton lived to the age of eighty-four. Contemplating the enormous number of children that her connections had produced, Edmée, as a novelist, had every excuse for believing that an illegitimate child of an erring wife could be passed off as a cousin.

Whether or not Mrs Henry de la Pasture thought of trying something other than a conventional début for Yoé, she was no laggard in building a new life for herself. Two years after her husband's death she married Sir Hugh Clifford, a cousin of Lord Clifford of Chudleigh, who had been an executor of her husband's will. Himself a widower, with a son and two daughters, Sir Hugh was an exact contempory of his second wife. He differed in other ways from the kindly but ineffectual Henry de la Pasture. He had joined the Malay States Civil Service, and the K.C.M.G. awarded to him in 1909 was a recognition of his work as an able administrator. Sir Hugh had, in addition, acquired a profound knowledge of Malayan languages and customs.

Ten years earlier, in April 1898, the editor of *The Academy* had sent *Studies in Brown Humanity* to Joseph Conrad for review. Conrad, struggling to establish himself as a writer, found that the author, Hugh Clifford, had written a book full of insight and unrivalled knowledge, but not one to be considered as literature. In December of the same year, 'The Bookworm', literary critic of the *Singapore Free Press*, published an article surveying Conrad's work to that date. *Almayer's Folly* and *The Nigger of the Narcissus* were chosen for commendation, but the anonymous critic picked many holes in the local background. Conrad could only defend himself by writing that his details of Malayan customs had been copied from impeccable sources. He only learned later that Hugh Clifford had been the author of the article.

This bout of literary tit-for-tat was the prelude to an admiring friendship between Clifford and Conrad. The latter wrote that had he one hundredth part of Clifford's knowledge, he could move mountains. Clifford, on the other hand, sent his book of stories, *In a Corner of Asia*, to Conrad for criticism. Conrad took the stories seriously and made suggestions as to how tension could be heightened by cutting out superfluous adjectives and adverbs. *Chance*, the first of Conrad's novels to have a popular success (in which the 'Chance' of the title depends on the coincidence of two characters being called Powell), was dedicated to 'Sir Hugh Clifford, K.C.M.G., whose steadfast friendship is responsible for the existence of these pages'.

The marriage which gave Edmée and Yoé a stepfather distinguished as a public servant and literary critic, took place in the crypt of Westminster Cathedral on 24 September 1910. At the time the daughters of the new Lady Clifford were staying with their Thynne aunt in Cornwall, only learning later of the wedding. Sir Hugh's career led him to take up appointments in East Africa as well as Malaya and Ceylon, but an increasing shadow was cast by what the *Dictionary of National Biography* tactfully described as 'cyclical insanity'. His wife's literary career did not cease immediately, although she did not again write a play to follow the success of *Peter's Mother*, whose run in the West End had probably owed something to the help of her friend W. S. Gilbert. The three last novels which appeared by Mrs Henry de la Pasture might be called a running down of production. There was, however, a daughter waiting in the wings.

The devotion between Edmée and Yoé had survived the ambiguity of their mother's attitude towards her children, and upheavals caused by sudden changes from convent to convent. Even more disturbing must have been the moment when Edmée became conscious, as she could hardly fail to do, of the disparity between her appearance and that of her sister. As Muriel Dashwood had noticed, Edmée had a turn for dressing in the fashion of the moment while Yoé, with an almost grotesque nose and an awkward carriage, got herself up to look like a crone in a fairy story.

To have a mother who was well known as a novelist, and who had links with the theatrical world, might suggest that Edmée would have led a less circumscribed life than did the girls who were her contemporaries. This was true as far as her own early attempts at writing were concerned, though, otherwise, it will be seen, she was kept on a tight rein. Having been told by her mother to write from her own experience, Edmée described the most dramatic episode of her childhood, a fall from a tree, in which her arm had been badly fractured. When she came to write this drama as fiction, Edmée's taste for tragedy, although condemned by her mother, got the better of her artistic conscience. The beautiful dark-eyed heroine, whose name was Violet, died from her broken arm. Even when she was an experienced novelist, Edmée never quite lost a predilection for solving the crisis of a story by physical catastrophe.

Literary and theatrical connections do not seem to have modified Mrs Henry de la Pasture's belief that young girls should be presented to the world untouched by any hint of intellectual independence. The recurrence in Edmée's books of the exhortation, 'Darling, who knows best, you or your Mother?' and the brusque dismissal of an offer of help by the snub, 'You can help me most by doing what you're told as soon as you're told,' sound as if they were familiar admonitions in the days of Chester Square.

The sisters remembered their days in Chester Square as an age of lost innocence, before the pressures of the grown-up world forced them to think of their futures. To put it bluntly, this meant proving to be sufficiently attractive to find a husband with means to support a wife and the additional qualification that he should belong to the same social class. It was Eaton Square, adjacent to Chester Square but built on a larger scale, which Edmée came to regard as the central repository of the tradition in which girls of her generation were brought up, a spiritual stunting to be compared in remorselessness to the foot-binding inflicted on Manchu female children.

If the wheels of the juggernaut of the London Season could crush young hopes and self-confidence it was, at least during the summer months, a machine that moved. Matters were different in country places such as Llandogo, 'a few miles above Tintern Abbey'. There the gentry houses, of varying degrees, were inhabited by families of unwed daughters, the supply of possible husbands drying up all too soon, as generation succeeded generation. When Edmée used a Monmouthshire background in her novels, she peopled the landscape with groups of spinsters, who, if they had ever been young, had long since consigned youth to oblivion. As will be seen in the next chapter, Edmée's mother discounted the only proposal her daughter seems to have received, creating in Edmée's mind the uncomfortable feeling that an admirer with no future was worse than none.

Sir Hugh and Lady Clifford sailed for Ceylon in January 1911. They left behind them Edmée and Yoé, doorstepped on to their aunt at Bude but with little occupation to fill their days. Edmée had, however, a plan which, in prospect, should not only have given her a full-time occupation, but also settled her fate for life. On 9 June 1911, she came of age, and no longer needed the sanction of her natural guardian for the course she proposed to follow. She was accepted by a French religious order, established in Belgium, and began a trial period as a postulant.

Twenty years later, Edmée, by now well known as the novelist E. M. Delafield, and admired for her gift for comedy, wrote an account of the next year of her life. Criticism of her mother's possessive attitude obviously made it impossible to publish this history of religious experience in her mother's lifetime, and it remained unpublished after the deaths of both daughter and mother. In the next chapter, Edmée's description of her failure to keep her vocation to the religious life is appended as she wrote it, except that the short sentences have been joined into paragraphs. The story, for so it may be called, is on two levels, the postulant's account of the life of the Order which she was attempting to enter, followed by her spiritual struggle which ended in an escape from its bounds. Intensely vivid to the mind's eye are the black figures of the postulants, sometimes prostrate in adoration or humiliation, sometimes pacing sombrely in their regulation exercise.

When, in her convent-school days, Edmée had announced that she wished to join a Community, the authorities had usually been discouraging. If they sensed that there was a core in Edmée's personality which would not melt down into the convent mould they will be seen to have judged rightly. Edmée's perception of her mother's possessiveness, only realized as she developed a life of her own, showed an attitude of mind that would never have abnegated rational thought to the Rule of the Community. The little girl who had listened to *The Pilgrim's Progress* in a Devonshire meadow had become something of a stranger to the mother whose voice had made the Land of Beulah sound so pleasant. In the next chapter Edmée, herself, describes the spiritual crisis from which she emerged with an increased independence of character.

II

'BRIDES OF HEAVEN'

The motives that led me, as soon as I was twenty-one, to enter a French Religious Order are worthy of but little discussion, and less respect. I belonged to a generation that was not taught to think clearly, and to a family that lived under the obsession of the word 'loyal'. It was not 'loyal' to think for oneself, to question anything said or done by one's parents, or to admit that one was not happy at home. It is necessary only to add that I was the victim of an emotionally loving, terribly possessive parent who had, in all probability, not the slightest idea of the terrific opposition that she was continually putting up against my natural development, in her unconscious determination that I should grow up to be nothing but an extension of her own personality.

One other factor counted for a good deal, in my 'religious vocation'. I had, in common with the great majority of my contemporaries, been brought up to believe that it was something between a minor tragedy and a major disgrace, for a girl to remain unsought in marriage after her twentieth birthday. Since the only proposal of marriage that had come my way was from a youth of the type described, correctly, by my mother as 'boys who don't *mean* anything', I was acutely conscious of being a failure. To renounce the world, in these circumstances, comes easily.

A less ignoble motive was that I really wanted work. It was before the days when girls – at any rate girls in my particular walk of life – were allowed to take 'jobs', and in any case I was untrained, and likely to remain so, having too much conscience, and too little initiative, to dream of breaking away from the dependence in which I had been so carefully reared. Finally, I was by birth a Catholic, and quite a number of convent-schools had been privileged to receive me as a pupil, between the ages of ten and eighteen. From each of these

14

establishments I was snatched away, usually at the shortest possible notice, for reasons that I was never told. (I have since come to the conclusion that most of them would have boiled down into one reason: namely, that my mother was unable to bear the thought of my coming under any influence excepting her own.)

It is to the credit of most of these religious establishments that in only one of them was I ever taken seriously as a prospective nun. There was no kind of convent-pressure brought to bear upon me, even after I was grown-up, and had announced my vocation, and was visiting regularly at the house of the Order that I wished to join. In fact I was well and deservedly snubbed by the Superior, to whom I naively said: 'I have decided that *this* is the Order to which I shall belong.' 'You do not yet know,' she trenchantly replied, 'whether the Order has any wish to receive you.' It was a French Order, with houses all over the world. In most of them, pupils of good family were received. It was an 'enclosed' Order – which means that the nuns might not go outside the walls of the convent except when actually travelling from one house to another. Contemplation and prayer, of course, were amongst the objects of the Order, as laid down by its foundress – a Frenchwoman. The mother-house had been established in France, but after the expulsion of the Religious Orders it was moved to a large country-estate in Belgium.

There, besides a big *pensionnat*, was the Noviciate, in charge of a French novice-mistress. The rest of the community lived quite apart from the Noviciate, and was only seen by them in the Chapel and on a few formal occasions. The community – *la grande communauté* – was under the rule of a French Reverend Mother. (She might equally well have been English, Irish, Spanish or Italian. The Reverend Mother of the house at Genoa was English, and that of one of the largest of the Spanish houses, Italian.) The mother-house was also the headquarters of the Mother-General and her Assistant. Much of their time was spent away, in visiting the various houses – one of which was in America.

Notre Mère Générale, by the way, was an Irish woman. She had known, and worked with, Notre Mère Fondatrice, which gave her a kind of historical sanctity in the eyes of the younger members of the community. In this connection I once made a most terrible mistake, of which the magnitude can only be fully understood by those who know the degree of veneration accorded by a devoted community to a loved and respected Superior. It is really only a little less than that which might be offered to a canonized Saint from Heaven, should one suddenly elect to walk the earth. Just before I went to start my religious life at the Belgian Noviciate, *Notre Mère Générale* came over to England. I was given the privilege of an interview.

I have no doubt whatever that she was kind, and that I was timid, but so little impression did any of it make upon me, that I afterwards remembered nothing whatsoever of the occasion. I only knew it *must* have taken place because, some months later, when I was a *postulante* at the mother-house, I was stopped in a passage, and very kindly spoken to by an elderly nun, who addressed me by my Christian name. Something in my reply must have perplexed her, for she said: 'You remember seeing me in London, don't you?' 'No, not at all,' said I truthfully. 'Do you know who I am?' I did not know that either, and said so. She went away, laughing heartily.

It was only from the horrified explanation of the *maîtresse des novices* that I learnt that I had admitted to *Notre Mère Générale* in person that I had completely forgotten ever having met her at all. To the honour of the *maîtresse des novices*, be it added that, deeply and genuinely distressed as she was by this extraordinary lapse, she did not rebuke me for it, because she thought that my honesty showed *de la simplicité* – a virtue which she rightly held in high esteem.

To go back a little way: when it was finally decided that I should be allowed to enter the Noviciate, I went to stay for a little while as a 'lady-boarder' at one of the English houses of the Order. This was by no wish of my own: I had begged to be allowed to enter at once. But since the wishes of a *postulante* or novice are the last thing in the world ever to be considered, nobody took any notice of this. On the contrary, I was sent to Belgium under the escort of an elderly French lady, who was not supposed to know why I was going there – a small piece of quite unnecessary mystery-making highly characteristic of convent-mentality. It was about the middle of *les grandes vacances* when I arrived, and for nearly a fortnight I was left wandering about the deserted school, wearing a black veil pinned to my hair, and my own blue serge coat and skirt, as a kind of compromise between the secular and the religious, but not otherwise admitted in any way into my new life.

There was one solitary American child, spending her holidays at school for some reason unknown to me, but as it would have been contrary to all regulations for us to be left tête-à-tête, an elderly nun always chaperoned us on our daily walk round the recreation ground. I had, once more, been forbidden to explain my position, which involved me in many difficulties with the little American – who probably guessed the truth perfectly well. The rest of my time was spent in the chapel, eating my solitary meals in the refectory after the American child had left it, and sitting in a small, cold bedroom, which I remember contained no looking-glass.

It rained nearly all the time, and the large, unwarmed house was bitterly cold, and I had nothing to do. The time seemed endless. Suddenly, it came to an end. One morning, without the slightest warning, I was suddenly fetched by the Assistant Novice-Mistress, whom I shall call Soeur Marthe. I was to come at once to the community side of the house, where the weekly Chapter was being held, and to receive the *bonnet de postulante* from the hands of the Superior.

There are three stages in the life of a professed religious of the Order I was entering. The first of these is her reception as a postulant. This admits her to the life of the Noviciate, but is a purely probationary period, lasting never less than three months, usually six, and sometimes a good deal longer, at the discretion of the novice-mistress. A postulant wears the regulation underclothing, a voluminous black stuff gown, reaching to the ground with a little black cape over the shoulders, fastening across the front so as to conceal the lines of the figure, and a hideous little white frilled bonnet over which is pinned a black cotton veil that falls down behind. The underwear consists of a long, coarse white shift, fastening high at the neck and at the wrists, a baggy pair of white cotton drawers coming nearly to the ankles, a thick flannel petticoat tied round the waist, and a still thicker black stuff petticoat over it. The advantage of the latter is that it serves as underskirt, when the postulant is sweeping, or otherwise actively employed, and pulls up her habit, tucking it into either side of her girdle – a stout black cord like an old-fashioned bell-rope. No stays are worn, and stockings – of grey or white cotton – are kept up by garters of black elastic. List shoes are worn indoors and cheap, heavy black walking-shoes for out of doors. Undergarments of this kind are worn by all members of the community alike, from the youngest postulant to the Superior General. Postulants, in reference to their black veils, were familiarly known as *corbeaux*. After being a *corbeau* one became, if admitted to the rank of novice, a *colombe*, i.e. a white veil.

The postulant takes no vows, but on becoming a novice, she takes them for the period of one year. She vows Chastity, Poverty and Obedience. The ceremony which accompanies this 'clothing' as it is called, is made as spectacular as possible. Usually two or three postulants, sometimes more, make this 'first profession' at the same moment. They are dressed as brides, clad in white satin, lace and jewels, and each wears a wreath of orange-blossom above a wedding veil. In the course of the ceremony, the brides of Heaven lie under a pall, to signify that they die to the world. A lock of hair is cut from the head of each, and they then go in procession from the chapel, and return clad in the habit of the Order, with a white veil instead of a black one, a soft wimple in place of the frilled bonnet, and with a great wooden rosary hanging from each girdle.

Perpetual vows are not taken until after two years have elapsed. (I think it is two, but it may be longer than that.) But a postulant is, or at any rate feels that she is, a long way from her *prise d'habit*, and it is of the life of a postulant that I am now writing. Actually, it is practically identical in detail – after the first two or three weeks – with that of the first- and second-year novices, and *corbeaux* and *colombes* live side by side in the noviciate, under the rule of the novice-mistress and her assistant. (In using the term 'novices' I shall include 'postulants'.) Let me say at once that both the novice-mistress, whom we may call Mère Immaculée, and Soeur Marthe, were exceptional women – Seour Marthe particularly. Mère Immaculée was then, I imagine, about sixty-five. She had been novice-mistress for thirty years, and there was nothing that she did not know about Catholic young girls and their religious vocations. In appearance, she was rather like a shorter, stouter Mussolini, but with a more humorous expression. She had an iron will, a fund of common-sense, and an infallible *flair* for detecting any form of humbug or affectation. She was practical, rather hard, and of limited imagination, and implacable honesty.

Originally, I am sure that she had been a woman of very strong racial prejudices. She came of a noble French family, had never been outside France in her life, and knew very few words of any language but her own. One felt, instinctively, that the English, the Irish and the Americans – all of whom she regarded as belonging to one and the same race, more or less – seemed to her barbarians, whom only the Catholic Church and her own training would render moderately pleasing to God. But she was absolutely just, and never consciously showed this prejudice – nor another, equally strong, in favour of the nobly-born. There were no Germans in the Noviciate when I was there – but if there had been, Mère Immaculée would have shown no prejudice whatever. One of the most curious things about her was her faculty for deliberately lashing herself up, when she felt that the good of her novices required it, into a violent temper. That she *had* a naturally violent temper, I have no doubt, but she also had enormous self-control, and the training of years behind her. I never saw her 'lose her temper' as the saying is – but I often heard her working herself up, by means of a long harangue to the assembled noviciate, from a quiet, explanatory rebuke, into a loud and wrathful torrent of furious abuse. At the end of her peroration she would bang on the table with her fist, hurl into our midst: *'Je suis fort mécontente!'* in a stentorian shout, and stump violently out of the room, very often banging the door behind her.

One of her duties was to read every letter that came into, or went out of the Noviciate. It might have been supposed that this would present difficulties to a Frenchwoman who knew none of the languages, save one, in which these letters might be written. (There were about 40 of us in the Noviciate – French, British, Spanish, Italian, American, Danish and Basque.) Mère Immaculée made extremely light of it. I never knew whether anybody translated the letters for her, but I can vouch for it that in my own case, not a word escaped her. She twice rebuked me for using a mildly slang expression in a letter to my sister, and she also objected to any term of endearment beyond a conventional one at the beginning. On one occasion she was unable to make out one word in my mother's writing, and she called me into her room and made me translate it to her. She was nothing if not thorough.

Most of the instructions that she gave us were sound and practical, from the point of view of fitting us for convent life. Her views on matters of hygiene were, however, such as *could* only have emanated from a Frenchwoman of her generation, and a nun to boot. A bath, she asserted, was an absolutely unnecessary luxury. Some countries – (we all knew which countries she meant) – had conceived of the strange idea that bodily cleanliness was a virtue. Nothing of the kind. Our Lord had never mentioned such a thing. The Saints had not practised it – on the contrary. The taking of a bath, unless ordered expressly by a doctor, was contrary alike to modesty and to the vow of poverty. It was possible to be *quite clean enough* without ever taking a bath at all. And she would end with a grim pleasantry perhaps best given in her native French: '*N'ayez pas peur! Quand vous sentez mauvais, on vous le dira!*'

I am sorry to say that in association with my neighbours, I often had occasion to wish that *on* might indeed do as she suggested. Clean linen was infrequent, baths were non-existent, and the heavy serge habits were only cleaned twice a year. In hot summer weather, the results may be imagined. I suspect that Soeur Marthe, whose mother had been a Scotswoman, held a different view from that of Mère Immaculée on the subject of personal cleanliness, and perhaps on other subjects as well. If so, she never betrayed it. Soeur Marthe was a warmer, more spontaneous person than Mère Immaculée and, unlike most Spaniards, she had a great sense of humour. She was artistic and deeply musical. (Mère Immaculée was neither.) She gave us a good many instructions, taught Church history, doctrine and the like, but was not officially in charge of our souls. That is to say we might not, in case of spiritual import, apply to her for advice, but only to Mère Immaculée.

Not that the discussion of individual spiritual difficulties was encouraged. Mère Immaculée made the shortest possible work of those who sought to talk to her about themselves. '*Allons, allons, pas d'histoires! Tout, ça, c'est faire s'occuper de vous, n'est-ce-pas?*' In practically every case, this must have been a perfectly accurate diagnosis. It was inevitable that it should be so, for the first, last and hardest lesson to be learnt by those who sought to enter the religious life was the absolute destruction of the 'self'. All of us were young – only one novice was over thirty, and she was regarded as antediluvian – and all of us, presumably, were conscious of having made a sacrifice in renouncing home, the world, earthly affections and so on. Some of us had met with opposition from our families, which gave a sense of martyrdom, others had no doubt been wept over as victims, and thus made to feel interesting. Every one of us, I feel sure, had had the gratification of talking over her vocation in detail, even if only with her confessor, before entering.

Once inside the Noviciate, all that was altered. Talks about oneself, and one's vocation, were of the rarest, and were conducted by Mère Immaculée with wholesome briskness, and a total absence of sentimentality. At all other times, personalities in conversation were not only forbidden, but made impossible. Silence, of course, was the rule throughout the day, except at recreation – 40 minutes in the middle of the day, and half-an-hour at night. The conversation was then entirely directed by Mère Immaculée, and was always on strictly general lines. Even a too-frequent use of such expressions as *'je pense'* – *'il me semble'* was at once rebuked. Nor might anybody say *'mon mouchoir'* or *'ma cellule'*. *'Notre mouchoir'* and *'notre cellule'* – even *'notre déjeuner'* was *de rigueur*, since nothing was owned by the individual, only by the community.

French was always spoken, except on very special holidays, when *'le permission des langues'* might be asked. To most of us, this presented no difficulties, since most of us had been brought up at convent-schools. As a rule, the Spanish novices were reasonably fluent in at least one other language besides their own, and the Italians all knew French, and English, and very often Spanish as well. Our two Americans, and one English novice from Yorkshire were the least at home, in speaking French. Were we happy? I am sure that we were, although most of us suffered at intervals from terrible home-sickness, when we wept silently – and were never consoled, or noticed in any way – one of the most effective cures in the world for a fit of crying.

But we were kept incessantly occupied, and we had none of us been in the convent long enough to have suffered in health from the shortage of sleep and the enormous dietary errors committed at our expense, and of which I will tell later. So far as I know, each one of us was genuinely eager to assimilate the routine of her new life, and speaking for myself, the change from discontented inactivity to ordered occupation, was an absolute revelation of unsuspected enjoyment. I may as well say here that, besides the daily activities of sweeping, dusting, bedmaking, and so on, and the many hours spent in the Chapel, each of us had been put, from the start, to the individual work for which – after examination by a committee of professed nuns – she was considered best equipped. For instance, I had at once been given one or two classes of children to teach, my subjects being English, French, and elementary music. When my pupils came out top in examination, I was carefully *not* congratulated, and should probably never have known of their success at all if the children themselves had not told me. But one was learning all the time to do one's best and not to expect any recognition and that, on the whole, was I think quite wholesome and desirable.

I remember, in this connection, our senior novice – an Italian of three-or-four-and-thirty, who had taken Red Cross classes in Rome and was a recognized *infirmière*. She had been appointed to assist the convent infirmarian, a South American nun well on in her fifties. Soeur Lucia once told me that the work was a great trial to her, because she was obliged by obedience to dispense drugs and other treatment that outraged every modern law of hygiene. I can well believe it. The convent attitude towards health was explained to us fully and uncompromisingly by Mère Immaculée more than once. 'The health of the individual is of no importance whatsoever,' said she blithely. 'You have made the sacrifice of that, just as much as of everything else. If you are in danger of becoming a burden to the Community, that is the responsibility of your Superior, not yours. All that you have to do, is to go on until you drop. And believe me, you will not drop easily. Never yet, in all my years in the religious life, have I known anybody die in the Noviciate. If you are tired, or have a headache, offer it up to Our Lady, and stop thinking about it.' She did not say 'Do not talk about it' because that was implicit in the Rule, which forbade personalities. If any of us required opening medicine, we asked permission to apply to the infirmarian. This could only be done in a set form of words, and the infirmarian's sole reply was to pour out a very strong mixture, in which the main ingredient was liquorice. The only other ailment that we were instructed to report was a sore throat. I believe there had once been an outbreak of diphtheria, at the Mother-house.

Another of Mère Immaculée's pronouncements concerned the performance of surgical operations. 'If, in later life, such a thing should be advised by a doctor, your Superiors will decide whether your life is of sufficient value to the Community to justify the expense. If it is not, you will either get well without the operation or die. In either case, you will be doing the will of God and nothing else matters.' She also added, with unintentional cynicism: 'Sometimes, a nun's own family may offer to pay for her to have an operation. In that case they may do so. As a rule, however, once they have consented to the sacrifice of letting her enter the convent, they are prepared to leave her in the hands of her Superior.' In actual fact, although hygiene was negligible, cases of real illness met with much more care than might have been deduced from the above. But I imagine that Mère Immaculée's object was to destroy the mental attitude of self-pity in her novices, and to prevent them from magnifying small physical miseries.

The worst of these was the lack of sufficient sleep. A five o'clock bell snatched us from the heavy sleep of early youth, and brought each one of us instantly to her feet. The last office was said in the Chapel between 8.30 and 9.30 and all lights were out by, approximately, 9.50. I suppose that for some of us it was enough, but for others it certainly was not. The Spanish postulant whose place was next to mine in the chapel was only sixteen, and every night, in spite of strenuous efforts, she slept as she knelt. When we had to stand up for the Psalms, I used to push her to her feet, and hold her up by one elbow. One night, we fell ignominiously to the ground together, drunk with sleep. Mère Immaculée, who knew everything, knew the reason for our collapse perfectly well, but made no reference to it whatever, and a faint hope that I entertained of being sent to bed early on the night following, remained unfulfilled.

Nothing else was as bad as this agonizing struggle with sleep, repeated nightly, but meals, to me, were also a great difficulty, although in a lesser degree. Because we were an 'active' Order – one, that is to say, that combined the work of teaching with prayer and contemplation – we neither abstained nor fasted except on those days when it was ordained by the Church. (Even then, the Novices were never allowed to fast. On the contrary.) One of the most astonishing dictums of Mère Immaculée was the following: '*On ne mange pas parce qu'on a faim. Un animal mange parce qu'il a faim. L'homme mange pour se donner la force de travailler.*' This was, I think, especially intended for those of us who found the Belgian standard of meals exacting, and who – like myself and many others – were naturally small eaters.

For us, the real difficulty was to finish the excessive amount of heavy food, in the very short time allowed for its consumption. To leave, or refuse, any part of it, would have been contrary to obedience and to poverty alike. To take longer over eating it than the regulation twenty minutes, was contrary to the Rule. It must also be remembered that many of us were accustomed to plenty of exercise, taken in the open air. In the Noviciate, our only out-door exercise was a slow pacing up and down the gardens for about half-an-hour daily – once in winter and twice in summer. And even this, if a breath of wind blew, or a spot of rain fell, was at once abandoned by the orders of

Mère Immaculée – true Frenchwoman that she was – for an equally slow pacing up and down a long corridor that was too narrow for more than three of us to move abreast. It was not a regime that conduced to appetite.

In the early days of my postulant-ship, I was invariably obliged to ask a concession in regard to the length of time I spent over the two meals of the day – dinner and supper. (Breakfast was only a bowl of *café au lait* and two pieces of dry bread.) When the presiding nun had given the signal for Grace, and Grace had been said, we all had to leave the refectory walking out two by two. As soon as the Noviciate, at the other end of the house, was reached, and Mère Immaculée had given the signal, for recreation to begin, I had to ask her: '*Ma mère, puis je aller finir au réfectoire?*' On receiving her permission I went down again and finished my unwanted portion of thick soup, roast meat or boiled fish, and stewed fruit. Sometimes green vegetables replaced the stewed fruit, or eggs the fish. I can give no better example of the scale on which these portions were served, than by saying that when eggs were the *plats du jour*, there were never less than two on each plate, and sometimes four.

The food, as far as I remember, was good, and certainly well-cooked, and I do not think there was any unreasonable monotony. But the rule enforcing a given quantity – and such a quantity – on all alike, and especially the compulsion on us to eat it within a given time – twenty minutes – must have been disastrous to appetite and digestion alike. The evening meal was on the same lines as the midday one, except that the soup was omitted. A large piece of bread accompanied both dinner and supper, and we drank cold water. Being determined to conform to the Rule as soon as possible, I quickly learnt to bolt my food within the prescribed twenty minutes, and also to eat whatever was put before me. Eggs, which had always disagreed with me from babyhood, I found almost impossible – but not quite. A few hours after eating them I was invariably sick, but Soeur Marthe – having once assured me cheerfully that '*vomir de temps en temps soulage l'éstomac, et vous fera du bien*' – ignored this unpleasant idiosyncrasy altogether, and never made any exception in favour of my leaving the eggs.

Although we did not fast, we were – after the first six or eight weeks – allowed to undertake certain bodily austerities after permission to do so had been obtained from Mère Immaculée. (Some of these were also imposed by her as penance for specific faults against the Rule, as I shall tell later.) There were three principal ways of thus mortifying the flesh. One was the use of the *discipline* – a small wire scourge, to be used by the penitent on her uncovered back and shoulders, whilst kneeling upright. If properly handled it drew blood. Another was the wearing of '*le bracelet*' – an expanding circle of barbed-wire points, to be worn under the sleeve, above the elbow. The pressure, after a little while, became agonizing. It should be explained that the number of strokes given with the *discipline* and the length of time during which the *bracelet* might be worn, were regulated by Mère Immaculée. The third mortification was to remain kneeling for a given length of time – *les bras en croix* – that is to say with both arms extended straight from the shoulders. Postulants were only permitted a very sparing use of these aids to sanctity.

Once a week a Chapter was held by Mère Immaculée in the Noviciate. Each of us then knelt on the ground before her and publicly admitted, in a set form of words, to any breach of the Rules of which she had been guilty. In no sense of the word was it a confession, such as the sacramental confession made to the chaplain. Only offences against the convent regulations were mentioned. They were received by Mère Immaculée with a brief and vigorous rebuke, to which she usually added a mention of such shortcomings as one might have omitted. She then pronouned sentence: '*Vous ferez le Chemin de la Croix une fois.*' '*Vous porterez le bracelet pour un quart d'heure.*' A favourite penance was to make the penitent go around the room, kneeling at the foot of each sister, and there kissing the floor in token of humility. Another was to order her to prostrate herself, flat on her face, at the entrance to the Chapel or the refectory, where the entering sisters were obliged to step over her. The idea of 'humiliation' thus exemplified was not really a sound one. It was impossible not to realize that one's fellow-novices, who might themselves be in the dust the very next day, were compassionate rather than contemptuous, and I am sure that most of us felt the dustiness of the attitude to be far more of a trial than its lowliness. It was one of the very few directions in which I ever thought that Mère Immaculée's common sense and knowledge of human psychology were at fault. As for her sense of hygiene, it was non-existent. When, on receiving a rebuke, one had to kneel and kiss the floor, she always insisted upon a *real* contact between one's lips and the actual boards. With this exception, and granting in the first place the Catholic and conventual outlook, most of her methods were sound and practical, from the point of view of making us into useful members of the community later on.

The foremost of her tasks, and of ours, was the complete destruction of *individuality*. We had received new names, we had cut ourselves off from the past, none of us ever spoke of our homes, our relations, or ourselves. We were forbidden to ask questions of even the most remotely personal nature. The letters that we might write or receive from even our nearest relations were strictly censored. (For instance, we might not give any account of our days, except in the most general terms. Nor might we use any expression of endearment beyond the conventional one at the beginning of a letter.) Even our handwritings had to be made anew, so that all dangerous evidence of 'character' might be eliminated, and the conventional French sloping, pointed hand substituted. Mère Immaculée's idea was that an envelope addressed by any religious should be wholly indistinguishable from an envelope addressed by another religious belonging to the same Order. With this end in view, we did fortnightly 'copies'. I can still hear the despairing moan that escaped from the Spanish nun who was teaching us, as she spied – from an incredible distance – my 'copy'. '*Je vois une écriture anglaise – quelle horreur!*' One's national feelings were considered no more than were one's personal feelings.

At the daily recreation, conversation had always to be general. It was impressed upon us that we must *never* seek the society of any one companion. If we were indoors, we sat on little wooden stools, ranged all round the walls, and darned stockings. Each novice sat down on whichever stool happened to be nearest when Mère Immaculée gave the signal – for I need hardly say that we neither sat, stood, nor walked upon our own initiative, but always awaited the order of the Novice-Mistress. She had the eye of a lynx for any dawning shade of mutual liking between two of her flock, and never allowed it to survive her vigorous and public rebuke. If Mère Immaculée, at the weekly Chapter, said: '*Soeur X et Soeur Z se recherchent*' – and added a few scathing comments on this irreligious, disobedient, and childish silliness, one might be very certain that Soeur X and Soeur Z would exchange neither look nor word for months to come. We knew that any signs of personal preference were the worst of the sins against our training.

It must be remembered that each one of us was passionately anxious to do her duty, as interpreted by the Rule and Mère Immaculée, and to be faithful to her vocation. Only one novice – an Italian – left the Noviciate, in my time, before taking her first vows. So complete was the detachment in which we lived that, although Soeur Maria must have been the centre of a certain psychic disturbance, and – as I learnt afterwards – had actually been fetched away, after many conferences with the authorities, by members of her family I do not think that any of us, her daily and hourly companions, had the least suspicion that anything was happening. Mère Immaculée simply told us, one day, that Soeur Maria 'for reasons of health' had left us. We might remember her in our prayers, but were not to speak about her, or discuss her departure. I never heard the subject mentioned again.

Is it difficult to leave the convent, after entering, and before taking the final vows? I am in a position to answer this often-asked question, from my own personal experience. I had been a postulant for nearly eight months. My first vows had been spoken of, and although the date had not been definitely settled for my *prise d'habit*, it seemed probable that I, and one or two others, would make their professions very shortly. I suppose that subconsciously I must have known a growing doubt as to my fitness for the life that I was undertaking. It is only necessary to say here that the real inward crisis came about very suddenly, when I learnt that my only and much-loved sister had decided to adopt the same life – in another Order. What I had felt to be endurable for myself, I could not endure for her. And the thought of the utter and complete earthly separation that must necessarily take place between us, was more than I could bear.

A very tiny incident brought the climax. It was the Sunday before Lent: the last day until Easter on which we might write home, since no letters were allowed throughout Lent. I had written to explain this to my sister. I found my letter, torn in several pieces, lying on my desk. Mère Immaculée's explanation was that I still showed an altogether inordinate affection for my relations 'in the world' and that, in order to impress this upon me, she had destroyed my letter. Nor would she give me leave to write another one. I was still very young for my age, and I had never been taught to think clearly, or even honestly. It did not occur to me that Mère Immaculée might be mistaken in her interpretation of the Will of God. I only felt that, if these were God's requirements of those upon whom He had bestowed the grace of a religious vocation, it was impossible for me to conform to them. Therefore, I had no religious vocation.

I told this to the chaplain in Confession first, and then, by his orders, to Mère Immaculée. I cannot deny that at first she was very angry, and told me that I was giving way to a temptation of the devil. For several days, she refused to speak to me. I have always thought that she talked it over with Soeur Marthe, the Assistant Novice-Mistress, and that it was Soeur Marthe – always understanding and warm-hearted – who persuaded her to believe that I was at least sincere. For several very difficult weeks, I stayed on in the Noviciate, carrying out my duties as usual. The strain was so great that, in less than two months, I lost nearly three stones in weight, and came away looking like a living skeleton. For I did come away. It was made hard, but not impossible.

The worst ordeal to which I had to submit was an interview with a French Jesuit priest. He was a very clever and eloquent man, of great personality. At first he persuaded me gently, even offering to arrange for my admission to another Order, if I was unhappy in this one. Then he became angry – it was a calculated, deliberate anger, of course – and threatened me with the wrath of God, and the terrors of Hell. Finally, he denounced me as a craven, who, putting her hand to the plough had looked back, and for whom there would be no mercy, either in this world or the next. He even told me that, if I insisted on returning to the world, God's curse would be upon me, and upon all those with whom I might associate. It seems incredible but I believed every word of it. At the end of the interview I was utterly broken – but I still knew that I could not remain in the convent.

I also saw the Reverend Mother General, and she was very kind and utterly remote, and nothing that she said seemed to me to have the slightest bearing upon my particular case. She had outlived, or sublimated, all earthly affections, and spoke as if they *could* not rank as a living factor in the religious life. Unlike the Italian novice, I had no relations available to come and fetch me away. I had to fight my own battle. The result was a compromise. I was to go to another house of the Order, not as a novice, but as a secular boarder, and recover my health, and think things over. This other house was in Rome: the stronghold of the Catholic faith. When I left the Mother-house, Mère Immaculée and Soeur Marthe both said goodbye to me kindly and affectionately, and promised me their prayers. They felt sure, they said, that one day I should come back. I never did. That was twenty years ago. I dream still, from time to time, of being a *postulante* in the Noviciate in Belgium, and finding myself unable to come away.

III

EDMÉE BECOMES ELIZABETH

After twenty years, when she came to write 'Brides of Heaven', Edmée was prepared to give respectful admiration to the nuns she had called Mère Immaculée and Soeur Marthe. She was looking at the past across a gulf filled with experiences beyond the comprehension of those still enclosed in the Order she had left. Except for one punishment, which aroused pity rather than revulsion, Edmée considered that Mère Immaculée possessed a deep psychological insight into the characters of the novices she was required to train. To an outsider, it would also seem that Mère Immaculée made another misjudgment, in her underestimation of the strength of Edmée's own character.

The crisis described in the last chapter, when a letter to Yoé was destroyed, might possibly have been intended as a test of the postulant's submission to the Rule of the Order, but Edmée's insistence that she had lost her vocation seems to have come as a genuine surprise to the Mistress of the Novices. Edmée must, also, have found her increased value to the Order a baffling complication. After months of being treated as barely worthy to be a postulant, it became clear that not only did her superiors wish to save her soul from an obvious temptation of the Devil. They were also anxious to retain a potentially useful member of the Community, who had already shown some talent for teaching. It is likely that they may have had an additional apprehension in that the pens of spoiled nuns are apt to be dipped in vinegar, if not in vitriol. After what might be called a spiritual debriefing, Edmée did indeed turn her months in the convent into material for several novels, but half a century was to pass before the factual account of her entrance and exit into religion was to be published.

During the time that her eldest daughter was passing through an experience that was to alter her attitude towards the religion in which she had been brought up, Lady Clifford had been mostly abroad as the wife of a Colonial Official. She followed Sir Hugh when he was appointed Governor of the Gold Coast, and it was there, in 1912, that she fell ill with yellow fever. Returning to England, she was carried off the steamer on a stretcher, but, essentially tough, she recovered after a convalesence in Switzerland, where she was attended by her daughter Yoé. Assuming that Edmée's life as a postulant had ended in 1912, it seems that the threat that religion would separate the sisters had passed.

Lady Clifford was not one to allow an attack of yellow fever to hinder her creativity. She wrote what was to be her last novel, *Michael Ferrys*, only a year after she had been a stretcher case. Although she lacked the insight into character that was to be the gift of her daughter, *Michael Ferrys* has a biting edge to its narrative. The family mostly concerned live either in self-regarding comfort or self-induced austerity. The author never allows religious orthodoxy to interfere with her perception of the absurdity of the behaviour sometimes indulged in by the ostensibly pious.

Dedicating her fifth novel, *Tension*, to her mother, Elizabeth, as by now she called herself, showed she had learnt that no author should recklessly discard material. ('Save this,' as the narrator in Alison Lurie's novel *Real People* frequently notes.) The dedication reads, 'To supplement the offering of a very early and unfinished effort of which the dedication ran: "To my matternal Parent".'

With the example of her 'matternal Parent' before her, it is not surprising that Elizabeth should have begun to write at an early age. It was, however, to be four years before she was to pick up the torch fallen from the hand of her mother. These were years which caused an immense upheaval in the lives of Elizabeth's fellow countrywomen. Elizabeth herself emerged from the years of trial as a professional writer, instead of a girl struggling in the glue of an insipid social life.

When the First World War broke out in August 1914, the British Red Cross Society was already well established in Exeter, with Miss Georgiana Buller at its head, a post she had held since 1910. Georgiana Buller was then in her late twenties, the unmarried daughter of General Sir Redvers Buller VC of Downes, near Exeter. In military history General Buller's name is associated with the early disasters of the South African War, but it is fair to say that he left a happier memory with his troops than with the War Office. His daughter found, not infrequently, that men who had served in the ranks under General Buller remembered him with warmth as a leader with a genuine concern for their welfare.

Even though she came from a well known Devonshire family, Miss Buller's appointment at such an early age must have been a daring step for the period. Although she had a countenance alive with intelligence, her skin was swarthily unfashionable in an age that admired pink cheeks and golden hair. She was known to have refused at least one offer of marriage, but her appearance did not immediately suggest that she was likely to be pursued by the male staff of any organization which she commanded, and perhaps this may have influenced those who appointed her.

Some account of Miss Buller's subsequent career is relevant to Elizabeth's progress as a novelist, though the material she gathered was to be mixed with imagination. At the declaration of war, Georgiana Buller had already risen to be Deputy County Director of the Devonshire Red Cross. She immediately established the Exeter Voluntary Aid Hospital, taken over by the War Office in 1916. Appointed Administrator, the only woman to hold such a post, of a Central Military Hospital of 1500 beds, and forty-eight affiliated auxiliary hospitals, Miss Buller held the position until demobilized in 1920. Deservedly, she was created a Dame of the Order of the British Empire.

It was the Exeter Voluntary Aid Hospital that accepted Miss de la Pasture as a VAD worker in 1914, and there she remained until 1917. In her religious life the strain of obeying the Rule had been somewhat softened by constant occupation, and a feeling of usefulness. Work at the hospital offered usefulness, without the oppression attendant on the noviciate, and the pay, £1 weekly, represented financial liberty to a girl who had never earned before. It was here, in her off-duty hours, that Elizabeth learned the discipline of writing at moments snatched from other commitments, a lesson that remained with her throughout her literary life. Built up, brick by brick, the novel grew, until Elizabeth felt that she needed to get the reaction of an audience, and she was lucky enough to find in Yoé and two friends a group of listeners both intelligent and enthusiastic.

To these three Elizabeth dedicated the book in its final form, with a special mention of the youngest. This friend, Mabel Lloyd, did, indeed, do more than listen and praise. She took the necessary steps to launch the new venture, and acutely presented the book to the firm of Heinemann. Its author had given it the unpromising name of *Equipment*, and chosen as pseudonym E. M. Van der Veldt, in order to avoid confusion with the well known Mrs Henry de la Pasture. F. Tennyson Jesse, a reader for Heinemann, took an immediate fancy to the book and recommended it for publication. She did, however, deplore the title as suggesting a treatise on war material, and Elizabeth's chosen pen-name as having an alien, even enemy, sound. The difficulties were overcome by F. Tennyson Jesse putting forward the title *Zella Sees Herself*, while Yoé evolved the nom-de-plume E. M. Delafield, so bestowing a name on her sister which was to make her famous.

William Heinemann had a knack of spotting potential winners to add to his stable. For example he had snapped up *On the Face of the Waters* by Flora Annie Steel, when her previous publisher had turned down the book as antagonistic to the accepted view of the Indian Mutiny. Heinemann was completely vindicated. *On the Face of the Waters* was not only a best-seller, but also remained in print for the next thirty years. With the same keen nose for a future success, he wrote to Miss de la Pasture, as he later knew her to be. He would, he said, like to publish *Zella Sees Herself* 'after the War, paper being scarce'. Having reached such a promising stage, Elizabeth felt that post-war publication was too distant a period for which to wait. She called on Mr Heinemann, who reacted favourably, agreeing to publish *Zella Sees Herself* in March 1917.

It is a poor heart that feels no elation on first coming into print. Elizabeth's jubilation took the form of cramming her six presentation copies into the basket attached to the handlebars of her bicycle. With this happy load, she pedalled through the streets of Exeter, hoping that everyone she happened to know would cross her path. When the book went into a second impression, Elizabeth made what she called a timid inquiry as to the possibility of a royalty payment. Learning that it would be convenient for his latest author to receive a cheque, Mr Heinemann sent her a payment of over fifty pounds. Having expected about fifteen, Elizabeth was filled with astounded delight. She had glided down the slipway and into the open sea of novel writing. It was from this time that the name of Edmée ceased to be used except by her immediate family. New friends were to know her as Elizabeth, and Edmée settled into the past as an evolutionary phase, now outgrown.

The novel carried round so triumphantly in Elizabeth's bicycle basket is the story of a *poseuse*. Completely self-conscious, Zella approaches every situation solely intent on making the impression which is expected of her. During her education at a convent in Rome, the heroine of *Zella Sees Herself* becomes converted to Roman Catholicism, more as a gesture than from religious conviction. Her engagement to marry is made, and broken off, in much the same spirit, but the reader is left in some doubt if Zella has learnt from her mistakes. Such experiences, Roman convent, conversion, broken engagement, were to recur in different forms in later writings by E. M. Delafield. It seemed as if she needed to work over these themes more than once before she could fully expand her gifts.

Zella Sees Herself is a novel of some complexity, with traces of the influence of the 'matternal Parent' at war with the daughter's determination to achieve an individual style. Later E. M. Delafield was to develop a more incisive manner, but in her first novel there is one descriptive trait to which she was faithful throughout her writing career. No female character sits up in bed, dresses for the day, or changes her clothes for a party, without the reader learning the delicious details of what she takes off or puts on, sometimes starting from the bare skin.

Naturally, in novels based on the late Victorian or Edwardian period, stays laced up the back played their part. ('I may be a lone, lorn grass widow, but I will *not* sleep in my stays,' Kipling's Mrs Hauksbee remarked.) On this foundation of whalebone, petticoats were laid, gowns being the final top dressing. E. M. Delafield did not neglect to describe shoes, and she paid even more attention to hats. Hats are not even excluded from the last of her novels, *Late and Soon* (1943), when hatlessness in church had been explicitly sanctioned by the Archbishop of Canterbury.

Interest in hats may have been hereditary, Mrs Henry de la Pasture's being of formidable size and contour. This necessitated the type of hat box which had half-globes of wire gauze attached to each surface, sides, bottom and lid. The ingenious arrangement allowed six hats to be anchored by pins through their crowns, the brims thus reposing flat. The hat boxes must long since have disintegrated, but the wire gauze contraption was discovered, by a later generation, to make an excellent strainer at the kitchen sink.

To support the galleons of velvet and plume that were fashionable when Elizabeth first grew up, a fine head of hair was a necessity. Those with scanty locks would be obliged to buy a matching tail to bulk out their own deficiency, which might, paradoxically, have been shorn from the head of a novice renouncing the vanities of the world in her final vows. Ardent brushing created the shape that the mode of the moment dictated, and on to this superstructure a hat was skewered by dangerously sharp pins, an operation that was compared to the making of an omelette, only to be accomplished at the last moment.

When Elizabeth began her war work, she moved out of the world abundant in feathered hats, and, more significantly, she began to make contacts outside her own class. Even her time as a postulant had been spent among women who *la Mère Fondatrice* would have described as *bien*. Breaking into new circles resulted in one of the best of E. M. Delafield's early novels, *The War Workers*, whose particular date of publication was owed to William Heinemann's instinct for catching the popular mood. Urged by him Elizabeth put aside her second novel, and wrote of her experiences as a war worker while they were immediately topical.

The War Workers opens with a prudent disclaimer that the Supply Depôt, in which most of the female characters are employed, bears any relation to a real institution. Such a denial is, of course, frequently the sign of a guilty conscience on the part of an author. Charmian Vivian, in control of the Supply Depôt, may or may not have been an intentional portrait of Georgiana Buller, but she is a tyrant, beating hell out of her mesmerized subordinates. Other dominating women occur in later novels by E. M. Delafield, but Miss Vivian remains well in the front rank, in her determination that no shred of power shall be delegated. The Buller family of Downes remained suspicious of the intentions of the author, so much so that when Miss de la Pasture had become Mrs Paul Dashwood, and a country neighbour, there was a certain apprehension about sitting next to her at luncheon. If, as an organizer in her own young days, Dame Georgiana herself had been unduly forceful, she mellowed into a sympathetic friend to the children of her contemporaries.

The pivot of *The War Workers* is, however, the hostel to which the underlings of Miss Vivian retreat, exhausted, at the end of the day. Levels of refinement vary among them, but each woman is aware of subtle differences in speech and behaviour. Cold, dirt, and bad food have, after three years of war, reduced nerves to an acute edginess, which results in an excellently described row over hurt feelings. E. M. Delafield's disclaimer of using her actual experience might have seemed slightly dubious to the workers from the Supply Depôt if they happened to read the account of crouching over a smouldering fire in the common sitting room, or queuing to fill hot-water bottles from a kettle over a decrepit gas-ring.

Miss Vivian only meets her match when a clergyman's daughter, Grace Jones, arrives as an assistant. More on a level, socially, than the rest of the Depôt staff, she is tough enough to resist Miss Vivian's steamroller methods. Grace Jones can admire the Administrator's dedication, and appreciate the results when a trainload of troops, recipients of food and cigarettes, call for 'Three cheers for Miss Vivian', but deplores the overriding arrogance. The last word, after a crisis, comes from Charmian's mother, Lady Vivian: 'I should have whipped her when she was small.'

Elizabeth admitted that she had got into trouble over *The War Workers*, and, even more candidly, that she deserved to do so. On the other hand, the reviews were an advance on those for *Zella Sees Herself* to which both the *Times Literary Supplement* and *Punch* had given heart-warming encouragement. When *The War Workers* appeared, in the spring of 1918, the reviewer in the *Literary Supplement* coyly speculated as to the sex of E. M. Delafield, judging the author to be female on account of the accurate use of the word 'camisole' to describe a precise garment. Additionally, the reviewer thought that 'inarticulate VADs from the length and breadth of England' would be thronging round E. M. Delafield to press 'her gory hands in gratitude for the portrait of Miss Vivian'. From *Punch* came a whoop of joy. Having originally praised *Zella Sees Herself*, the reviewer put forward the hope 'that the next victim will provide an analysis as entertaining as her two predecessors.'

Immediately on finishing *The War Workers*, Elizabeth returned to *The Pelicans*, her second novel, set aside on the advice of her publisher. Begun in Exeter in June 1916 and finished a year later, *The Pelicans* finally appeared in September 1918. By then the hope that the war would eventually end must have been getting stronger, though more weeks were to pass before the dam of despair broke and engulfed the German Army. The age of casualties in Elizabeth's family gives an idea of the greed of Moloch. In 1916, Hugh Clifford, son of Elizabeth's stepfather, was killed in his twentieth year. Twelve months later, Algernon Thynne, husband of her mother's sister Constance, was killed as he approached his fiftieth birthday. Among the brothers of Elizabeth's future husband the losses were even greater.

Although *The Pelicans* was begun in Exeter, Elizabeth herself did not spend the last year of the war in Georgiana Buller's organization. In her own words, she accepted an appointment in the Ministry of National Service, whose South West Regional Headquarters was at Bristol. It was at Bristol that she remained until demobilized, by which time she had become a novelist with three well reviewed books to her credit, and, to at least one reviewer, she had a reputation for enjoyable astringency.

If the Armistice of 1918 brought Elizabeth's war work to an end, she had all the more time for literary production. When *The Pelicans* appeared she must have been at least half-way through her next novel, which was also to be concerned with religious hopes and fears. *The Pelicans* is particularly remarkable for an agonizing account of a conversion to the Roman Catholic Church, an entry into religion, and a death in the convent. Her experience as a postulant was one that Elizabeth examined on a number of occasions. Even when she might be thought to have written it out of her system, she continued to walk round the subject, and to look at it from different angles.

The symbolism of the pelican as the Church, a mother bird who feeds her children with drops of blood from her own breast, brings about the most tragic moment of the novel. Rosamund, whose sister Frances has entered an enclosed order, is not allowed to attend her sister's deathbed, the Rule being more important than the indulgence of family affection. (It should be pointed out that, from an ornithological point of view, the legend of the pelican is a misunderstanding, which grew from the bird's habit of macerating fish in its long beak, and dropping it into the gaping mouths of its young.)

If the iron Rule of the convent demonstrates one kind of pelican principle, the determined do-gooder, Mrs Tregaskis, called by herself Bertie, is a bird of a different feather. She has adopted Rosamund and Frances in early life, but in spite of her benevolence, she grates on their nerves, as she does on those of most people with whom she comes in contact. Her insistence on forcing Minnie, a cliché-talking sycophant, on to her family as governess not only fails to provide the children with an education, but exasperates her husband to such a degree that murder would not surprise the reader.

These first three novels had been published by William Heinemann, who must have been gratified by praise from reviewers, and who can hardly fail to have congratulated himself on having picked out E. M. Delafield's potential. Her success, however, had caught the attention of a literary agency who wished to sneak her away from Heinemann in favour of the firm of Hodder and Stoughton. Mrs Henry de la Pasture had long been a member of the Society of Authors, to whom Elizabeth now applied, wishing to clarify her position should she want to change her publisher. It appeared to the Society that a poaching policy towards Heinemann's authors was in operation.

Although her next novel, *Consequences*, was published by Hodder and Stoughton, Elizabeth took to heart the advice of the Society of Authors and, in future, saw to it that she had a contract, which with Heinemann she had not had. William Heinemann was reported to be furious at this defection, which was understandable, but he can only have had himself to blame for not placing Elizabeth under contract. Whatever the negotiations which led to this change of publisher, Elizabeth did not remain in the hands of the agency suspected of author-poaching. In A. D. Peters she acquired an agent with whom her relations were professionally satisfactory and, privately, of the friendliest.

Consequences, published in June 1919, and dated as written in London 1917–Bristol 1918, was admitted by the author to be partly autobiographical. The story runs from the mid 1890s to 1911, with the background of a large London house not unlike the Eaton Square mansion that was to play an oppressive part in *Thank Heaven. Fasting*. *Consequences* is, however, much more loosely constructed than the later novel. From being a petted drawing-room child, a pretty doll to be displayed to callers, Alex grows up to develop strong lesbian feelings, unrecognized above all by herself. She does accept a proposal of marriage, but breaks off the engagement. The solution seems to her to be the religious life, not admitting to herself that it is the magnetism of Mother Gertrude, rather than the love of God, that attracts her.

Alex's emotional life is concentrated on this preceptress, and when she realizes that Mother Gertrude will be transferred to another House of the Order overseas, the life-long separation in prospect is too great a wrench. Alex feels that she has lost her vocation, but, unlike Elizabeth in the same situation, she is fully professed, and has spent years as a member of the Community. Alex returns to the world as a female

Rip van Winkle, or William Allingham's Little Bridget, who, after seven years, found that 'her friends were all gone'. There is no place left in her family for the woman who had, long ago, been petted by the grown-ups. Alex's solution is to seek oblivion in a pond on Hampstead Heath. Incidentally, *Consequences* gives an example of the change in fashion since 1911 concerning London residences. Downshire Hill, with its charming houses of manageable size, was regarded as so far outside the social pale that a coachman would profess ignorance of such an address, and a cab driver demand to see his fare before climbing so disreputable an alp.

Both the *Times Literary Supplement* and *Punch* continued to take an interest in Elizabeth's development as a novelist. The former thought that the dice had been too heavily weighted against Alex, but admitted that she was an all too familiar type, whose friends eventually give her up in despair. *Punch* suggested that the book might be considered anti-conventual, even compared to *Zella Sees Herself*, but considered that a new aspect of an original and stimulating writer had been displayed.

Consequences took its title from the paper-and-pencil game of that name. Papers are passed round a circle, each player making an entry and folding the paper so as to give no clue to his or her neighbour. Someone (male) meets Someone (female) Somewhere. Remarks are exchanged, the Consequence written down, and What the World Said may be added. Shortly before the reviews of her novel appeared, Elizabeth met Paul Dashwood, probably at Waterloo Station. The Consequence was that they were married on 17 July 1919, which was the day of the bridegroom's thirty-seventh birthday, the bride having celebrated her twenty-ninth ten days earlier. What the World Said can be sometimes deduced from the later writings of E. M. Delafield, now Mrs Paul Dashwood.

IV

'WRITING IN SINGAPORE'

Elizabeth's own account of her marriage into a circle of squires and baronets appeared as a short story in *The Girl Guides Book*, which was published in the late 1920s or early 1930s. The title, 'A Perfectly True Story', might, with more truth, have been modified to 'a perfectly half-true story', describing as it does the arrival of a young girl from a snug London life to stay with a family whose home is an appropriately large house in the South Midlands, not far from Oxford. Met at the station by a daughter of her hostess in a pony cart, she suffers a shock at the sight of the girl's billy-cock hat and indeterminate tweeds, being herself wrapped in the skins of grey squirrels. The other women of the family wear men's cloth caps to outface the elements.

The little Londoner's talk of the theatres and concerts of the metropolis is countered by assurances that these cultural delights are available in Oxford for those who otherwise like to live among horses and dogs. Shown to be incompetent at field sports, the visitor claims that she can drive a pony cart, only to be bolted with, an accident which happened to Elizabeth in far less romantic circumstances. Rescued by the eldest son of the house, the heroine has obviously no choice but to marry him and reconcile herself to the rigours of country life, mitigated, it is to be hoped, by concerts in Oxford.

Kirtlington Park, the house described in 'A Perfectly True Story', stands about seven miles north of Oxford. Built by a Sir James Dashwood who died in 1779, it remains a fine example of the golden age of Georgian architecture. The interior is equally imposing, though the chief recollection of the last generation of Dashwoods to inhabit their ancestral home was the childhood pleasure of sliding down the perilous marble curve of the grand staircase. The parents of these little romps, Sir George and Lady Mary Dashwood, although falling below the Mowbray standard of procreation, came near to it with eleven children who grew to full age.

That part of Oxfordshire abounded in large families. Lord and Lady Jersey had five Villiers children spending the winters at Middleton, while at Bletchington Lord and Lady Valentia came near to filling their house with six Annesley daughters and two sons. Not only did all these children meet at Christmas dances and theatricals, but they joined in games of hockey and riding parties. Some mothers considered that hockey, as played by rules invented according to the whims of the players, was too fierce for their cherished offspring. The riding parties also caused parental disquiet, particularly over the number of falls that Paul Dashwood and his sisters managed to take in the course of a single morning's ride.

Elizabeth's meeting with a future husband who came from such a predominately sporting background lacked the fairy-tale climax of 'A Perfectly True Story', but was not without a romantic element. In April 1919 Sir Hugh and Lady Clifford returned from the Gold Coast. Travelling with them was Major Paul Dashwood OBE, who, before the 1914 War, had been a civil engineer. Lady Clifford, always partial to attentive young men, recruited Major Dashwood to help disembark her mountains of trunks and hat boxes. During the voyage he had learnt that Lady Clifford had two daughters, the elder pretty and of a literary turn, the younger sister plainer and less interesting. There was a meeting at the London Terminus when Elizabeth came to welcome her mother from the boat train, and one of Paul's brothers came to greet him. Subsequently, Paul went to call on Lady Clifford, praying, he later told his daughter Rosamund, that he would meet the pretty, literary daughter.

Matters moved fast. Paul was due to take up an appointment in Singapore, and the Cliffords' return to Nigeria would leave Elizabeth once again to fend for herself, with the added imminence of her twenty-ninth birthday, and no serious suitor in sight. Paul's parents had given up the struggle to live in Kirtlington, and it was to a house of more convenient size that Elizabeth was asked to stay. Paul's sister Muriel, a forthright character popular with Paul's children, remembered Elizabeth's anxiety that, after so brief an acquaintance, Paul might decide not to propose. He did, however, propose, and was accepted.

'"How, exactly, would you have your bridesmaids dressed, and what colour would you choose for your going-away frock?" said Frederica thoughtfully. "Let's all say in turns."' This rather agonized

41

passage from *Thank Heaven Fasting* was written twelve years after Elizabeth's own wedding. She had not, however, forgotten the predilection of young girls for this particular bridal phantasy. Frederica's absorption in the trappings of a wedding is almost macabre, because not only does she lack the ability to attract men, but has reached the stage of active dislike for them. Of the two other girls in this imaginative session, one, her sister, breaks off an engagement owing to Frederica's bullying and the other, a friend, has to accept a paralysingly dull bridegroom.

If Elizabeth and Yoé ever indulged in any such speculations, they were put into practice, as has been said, on 17 July 1919, at St James's, Spanish Place. *The Times* had a detailed account, with the explanation that the wedding was celebrated at short notice owing to the imminent departure of Sir Hugh and Lady Clifford for Nigeria. It is rare for bridesmaids' dresses to seem anything but fussy in cold print. Elizabeth's choice of sweet pea shades of blue and mauve, topped by hats of net from which dangled streamers of blue sweet peas, sounds to have been without the *panache* of the dress in which the mother of Elizabeth and Yoé had gone to Buckingham Palace. As Yoé, naturally the chief bridesmaid, and Muriel Dashwood, sister of the bridegroom, were neither of elegant appearance nor graceful carriage, the wedding cortège started under a handicap.

Possibly Mary Clifford, daughter of Sir Hugh and therefore ranking as a stepsister, and Phillis Rushbroke, a childhood friend, to whom, as 'Phillida', two of Elizabeth's novels were to be dedicated, restored the balance of looks. The bride herself wore cream satin, with a veil held in place by a diamond bandeau. Traditionally, something should be borrowed for a bride to wear. If the bandeau was a present, rather than a loan, it would have been a useful addition to an assortment of jewellery which Elizabeth later had the habit of depositing in a Plymouth pawn shop.

Muriel Dashwood was in the position of being able to compare Lady Clifford's second husband with her first, having seen the ageing Count Henry supported by his daughters in Chester Square. Miss Dashwood was uninfluenced by Sir Hugh's undoubtedly distinguished career. He was, she told Jeoffry Spence, 'a dreadful little man and quite mad'. Unhappily, the last part of her judgement turned out to be only too true.

Paul Dashwood's best man was the Honourable Caryl Annesley,

who was to succeed his father as twelfth Viscount Valentia. He belonged to the days in Oxfordshire when Dashwoods and Annesleys between them came near to fielding two cricket elevens. These teams had been decimated not only by the wartime loss of the elder Annesley brother but by the death in action of three Dashwood sons. (A fourth was to die later in what Kipling has called 'a skirmish on a frontier station'.) One of the surviving brothers came to the wedding, together with Lady Mary Dashwood, who had given her new daughter-in-law lace with which to decorate the bodice of her wedding dress. This was a welcoming gesture towards a bride who had not only an exotic French ancestry, but was also a Roman Catholic and a writer of books. Elizabeth was, however, indisputably a lady.

In at least two of her novels, Elizabeth gives a convincing portrait of a cad and a bounder, against whom girls are to be warned in vain. No such accusations could be made against Paul Dashwood, although in the bride's family there was a suggestion that he was considered to be rather a 'clodhopper', belonging to a somewhat Philistine race. He may have fallen below the intellectual standards of Cliffords and de la Pastures, but his work as an engineer in West Africa, for which he had been awarded the Order of the British Empire, was known to have been successfully carried out in difficult, even dangerous, circumstances.

It was in June 1919, a month before her wedding, that Elizabeth made the dedication of her novel *Tension* to her 'matternal Parent', a final offering before they separated for two years. Lady Clifford returned to West Africa, and Elizabeth followed her new husband to Singapore. Whether the author's mother appreciated the portrait of the dominating Lady Rossiter, the most clearly realized character in *Tension*, is a matter for speculation. As a professional writer herself, it would be unlikely that she did not make a connection between the sequence of aggressive women in her daughter's novels and Elizabeth's view of her own upbringing.

The setting for *Tension* is a commercial college on the Devonshire coast, more or less supported by Lady Rossiter's husband, Sir Julian, whose wife's meddling in the name of kindness has reduced him to cynical impotence. It is Lady Rossiter's determination that she can make no mistakes in her benevolence that produces the 'tension' of the book's title. The only people who can stop her in her tracks are two detestable children, with whose father she is in unacknowledged love. Mark Easter, the children's father, is in what might be called sexual baulk, being the husband of a wife confined in a home as a nymphomaniac, alcoholic, morphine addict. Lady Rossiter, determined that nothing shall interfere with her platonic passion, manoeuvres the unhappy Easter so that he cannot accept the love of Miss Marchrose, for whom, indeed, her own husband has an unacknowledged feeling of attraction. This is a victory for Lady Rossiter, but she suffers continual minor defeats from students, who are unappreciative of her attempts to bring beauty into their lives. Saccharine self-restraint almost gives way when her lady's maid refuses the loan of a volume of Walter Pater, being already supplied with a copy of *East Lynne*.

The Paul Dashwoods remained for two years in the Malay States, but a social life based on daily visits to the Club was far from congenial to Elizabeth. There is, however, a rather charming photograph of herself and Paul seated on the sand, with palm trees behind them. Even the unbecoming bathing dresses of the period, usually of dark blue serge, cannot detract from their obvious enjoyment of the occasion, and the pleasure with which they smile into each other's eyes. The domestic struggles with which Elizabeth was to deal so poignantly in her future writing had not yet begun to cast a shadow.

Although there is plenty of evidence that Elizabeth was happy with Paul in these Malayan days, the voyage out, the crowding experiences of a home in a strange continent, and life as a married woman, had no influence on the subject she chose for her next novel. Only years later did she write a sketch, collected in *As Others Hear Us*, which may have hinted at the reaction she met with among her husband's associates in Malaya. Elizabeth had, of course, an attractive appearance, so there was nothing of a physical self-portrait in the conversation between two old friends, meeting with the awkwardness engendered by a long separation:

'Remember that woman in Singapore who had written a book?'
'By Jove, yes. Plainest woman I ever saw in my life. Couldn't ride for toffee.'
'Ah, I dare say.'
'Feller I know married a woman who wrote books once.'
'Did he really? By Jove, poor devil!'

Whether a report of a single incident, or a synthesis of remarks heard down the years on the subject of literary women, the dialogue's beauty lies in the sudden meshing of the minds of the two old friends. Ignorant of each other's triumphs and disasters, agreement is complete on the unwisdom of marrying a writing wife.

Even if aware of the prevalent low opinion of women who wrote books, Elizabeth did not falter in her stride. She finished *The Heel of Achilles* in June 1920, and, in a dedication to Yoé, rejoiced, in verse, at their twinship of spirit, and in their childhood's games of imagination:

> . . .
> You were my faithful ADC
> When I was a Captain bold,
> But Watson I to your Sherlock Holmes
> In the Baker Street days of old.

Elizabeth went on to hail the excitement of the lives they were both leading in different hemispheres:

> And now you work at a real career,
> And I'm writing in Singapore.

The 'real career' was an attempt by Yoé to qualify as a doctor, a project frowned on by Lady Clifford. Knowing her younger daughter to be exceptionally ham-fisted, there was some reason in the mother's disapproval.

Her war work had given Elizabeth a window into the language and attitudes of classes other than her own, but *The Heel of Achilles* is the first novel in which she tackles the question of a girl from lower middle-class circles marrying into the world of the gentry. Lydia Raymond, the rather unpleasant heroine, rises by force of calculation, coupled with a skilled discarding of the ladder by which she mounts. At the top of her particular ladder, Lydia marries Clement Damarel, a well connected young clergyman, who takes her 'downalong' to Devonshire, a rustic expression Lydia is surprised to find used by the Damarel family.

Damarel has helped Lydia out of a nasty predicament when, as secretary to a Jewish millionaire, Lydia finds that she has been used to cover up his wife's adultery. Lydia does indeed need to be rescued from involvement in this scandal, but usually she is a situation snatcher, adroit at turning circumstance into self-glorification. As an orphan, and later as a widow, she derives satisfaction from being able to claim the centre of the stage, even though her unflagging egoism had destroyed her husband's feeling for her. Lydia even steals the limelight at her sister-in-law's wedding by giving birth to her daughter in the midst of the celebrations.

It is this daughter, Jane, who represents Lydia's Achilles Heel, by rebelling against her mother's deep, but over-possessive love. Driven to accept Jane's determination to marry a Canadian airman (the time is 1914), Lydia makes the gesture of abdicating her domination. The situation does, however, remain in Lydia's control. As Jane leaves for her honeymoon, it is round the mother who is losing her daughter that the company converges. In *Tension* the intolerable Lady Rossiter finally alienates those around her by unshakeable insensitivity. Lydia uses her considerable mental powers to impose her personality, and is only defeated by her daughter, the first person she has truly loved. Elizabeth, in after years, listed *The Heel of Achilles* among the books she would rather not have written, but as a fairy story in which Cinderella does all the scheming for herself it has a sparkle sometimes lacking in *Tension*.

The Heel of Achilles must also have overlapped in its writing with the commencement of work on *Humbug*. The seventh of E. M. Delafield's novels, it has 'June 9th, 1920. Singapore–February 17th, 1921. Kuala Lumpur' on its last page. The change of address signified a professional move by Paul Dashwood, to a job connected with building the causeway from Johore to Singapore Island, a construction of ill-fated significance in 1941.

Eight months for a novel of nearly three hundred pages is rather a quick rate of production, but Elizabeth also had the distraction of giving birth to her first child when she was two months gone with her book. Lionel Paul Dashwood was born on 13 August 1920. Something of his charm is to be found in the Provincial Lady's son Robin, whose character Elizabeth agreed was founded on that of Lionel. Born when the First World War was barely over, Lionel was to be snatched, tragically, from his family while training for National Service at the beginning of the Second.

As epigraphs for *Humbug*, Elizabeth chose two passages from Samuel Butler and one from Tolstoi. Both the quotations from Butler deplore the failure of communication between people, children as well as grown-ups. Condemning the aggressively parental approach of the Church Catechism, Butler suggests that it should be rewritten in consultation with children. The sentence which Elizabeth quoted from Tolstoi is short, but all-embracing. 'Education, as a deliberate moulding of people into set forms, is sterile, illegitimate and impossible.' Mère Immaculée had had, Elizabeth remembered, an infallible instinct for detecting humbug, but the Mistress of the Novices would hardly have agreed with Tolstoi on the impossibility of education.

With these signposts to point her way, Elizabeth wrote of the grown-up characters in *Humbug* as representing types 'that I fear to be far from extinct – of amateur educationalists'. Remote from England, and indeed from Europe, she looked back with indignation, rather than nostalgia, at the confusion in which girls of her generation had been brought up. Their emotional lives, she felt, had been distorted by constant pressure on their affections, amounting to moral blackmail.

Lily Stellenthorpe, the heroine of *Humbug*, suffers from the pain of being spoilt by her parents, while Vonnie, her mentally handicapped sister, is put to one side. There is, of course, an echo of the nursery days of Edmée and Yoé in this situation. In the novel Vonnie's dimness of mind is slurred over by sweetly phrased neglect. The sisters are continually urged to be 'good, happy, little children', an admonition leading to Vonnie's resolute silence about her chronic earaches. When Lily has a screaming fit at what she, rightly, sees as unfair favouritism of herself over Vonnie, she is told that God will be angry with her for naughtiness and ingratitude.

Convinced by the reiteration of her parents that God will be angry and mete out punishment to naughty children, Lily tries to bribe him with promises of good behaviour if he will spare Vonnie the agony of an earache. Her prayers are unanswered. Against the rules of the nursery, and Vonnie's wish to avoid a fuss, Lily fetches their nurse, compounding her disobedience by the lie that Vonnie had sent her. 'God could hardly do more than he had already done, even to a liar. . . .'

Although the earache is treated, it soon dawns on Lily that if Vonnie were to die she would be happy in Heaven, and forever free of her sad life on earth. Vonnie does indeed die, but during her last illness the parents are blind to Lily's agony, bidding her to play in the sunshine 'like a happy little child'. After her death, Vonnie, no longer an embarrassment, has an apotheosis in a quantity of photographs. Lily, whenever an east wind blows, feels 'sheer, jubilant triumph', because Vonnie has escaped beyond its power to give her earache.

After the poignancy of the first two chapters, which support Samuel Butler's view that family life is a prison, the story of *Humbug* proceeds with less emotional turmoil. There are, however, two portraits etched almost with ferocity, Lily's father, Philip Stellenthorpe, and her husband, Nicholas Aubray. Lily's father plays on his daughter's nerves by offering no explanation to his rules beyond saying, 'Father says it will be best that way.' Heaven, or rather E. M. Delafield, does eventually punish Philip by sending him a son who is cheerfully impervious to his father's hen-like fussing.

The constrictions of Lily's upbringing have left her in a state of misty innocence, and no enlightenment comes from a few months at a convent. From there she is returned home, ill from under-feeding, and suffering from a costiveness that modesty among the nuns has left undiagnosed. The next school she attends, with the unfortunate name of Bridgecrap, merely intensifies her feeling that she is not like Real People, and no one tells her that this state of mind is prevalent in adolescence. She is even more confused by a visit to her aunt Clotilde in Italy. Aunt Clo derides her brother Philip's attempts to guide his family with the gossamer threads of hurt feelings, advocating freedom from moral restraint as admirable in itself.

It is in Italy that Lily meets Nicholas Aubray, somewhat older than herself, and with a promising career not exactly specified. Lily agrees to marry Aubray, without much idea of what is involved. Mrs Hardinge, a cousin more conventional than Aunt Clotilde, feels it is her duty to give the motherless Lily a 'little talk' on the eve of her wedding. The embarrassment of both parties is intense.

> Mrs Hardinge gazed at [Lily] with an apprehensive look.
> 'You've lived in the country all your life, after all. You – you know – Well, dear,' said Mrs Hardinge in a sudden burst of courage, 'after all – you've seen the animals.'
> The expression was perhaps infelicitous.
> Lily, terrified and over-tired, began uncontrollably to cry.

Nicholas Aubray, the husband approached in this bewildered spirit, is a really splendid bore, equal to any created by Elizabeth von Arnim or Ivy Compton-Burnett. He is a 'shouting bore', as Byron described Maria Edgeworth's father. Even when making love, 'he often exclaimed joyously and loudly that it was a topping world.'

Lily finds that she has exchanged a father who always called her 'my little pet' for a husband whose usual endearment is 'little pal'. After Nicholas's rather unexpected sortie into adultery with another 'little pal', Lily accepts his plea for forgiveness. When her son, the fruit of the reconciliation, is born Lily makes the resolution that she will strive to eliminate the humbug which has dogged her own upbringing from that of her child.

From her writings it does not seem that E. M. Delafield had more interest in glimpses of the future than could be satisfied by an occasional visit to a fortune-teller. Writers are, however, notoriously possessed with a kind of literary second sight. Having to concentrate on the actions of a character of their creation, there is an instinct that tells them how such a person would behave in circumstances beyond the scope of an immediate situation. There are two instances of this prevision in *Humbug*. If Lily's protectiveness towards Vonnie is a reflection of the relationship between the author and her own sister, the agonizing earaches from which Vonnie suffers were to be a not infrequent horror in the life of Elizabeth's own daughter Rosamund. Similarly, the eccentric Aunt Clotilde tells a story that she had been betrayed by the only man who had supremely mattered to her. This poltroon had basely fled with his ungenerous wife, but the situation has an eerie resemblance to a non-marriage in which, fourteen years later, Yoé de la Pasture was to involve herself.

When she had finished *Humbug*, now the mother of a son, as was her heroine, Elizabeth dedicated the book in a few lines of verse,

> To Paul.
> Husband and Comrade.
> For the friendship of our days,
> For your very pleasant ways,
> For the many times we've laughed,
> For your kindness to my craft,
> Let me dedicate to you
> The book of mine I hold most true.

Whether or not Paul Dashwood relished the dedication of a book in which the newly married heroine finds her husband unsympathetic on all but the most mundane levels, a man only to be kept in tolerable humour by the support of continuous flattery, it is hard to say. Elizabeth was responsible for a number of portraits of husbands whose wives respond as they know is expected of them. Indeed, she might be said to have become an expert in writing of the ingenuity of wives in giving an impression that causes of complaint will be swiftly eradicated. The study of Nicholas Aubray is by no means that of the most disagreeable among Elizabeth's irascible husbands, but he stands rock-solid in his capacity to bore.

Although Malaya made remarkably little impact on Elizabeth as a writer, she early realized that there was an aspect of Colonial life to which she was not prepared to submit. At Johore she found herself among wives, faded by the climate, and with little occupation beyond the limited gaieties of the Club. While Viceroy of India, Lord Dufferin had remarked on the tragedy inflicted on Indian civilians: 'the voices of their children are not heard in their homes.'

This tragedy Elizabeth saw on all sides in Malaya, where the belief was still strong that British children could only be saved from physical and moral deterioration by being shipped home to their native islands. Elizabeth decided that her family's future should not be so compromised, and she took firm steps to prevent a separation from her child. Whether or not she would have left without her husband, had he decided to continue working in Malaya, is problematical, but, as it was, Paul followed her as the tail of a kite dances after the kite itself. With the bold assurance that she could keep the family afloat by her writing, a project only to be achieved in England, Elizabeth sailed from Malaya in the spring of 1922. Paul and the baby Lionel went with her, and so, presumably, did the manuscript of her next novel, *The Optimist*, begun in the previous August and finished in March 1922.

The Dashwood family sailed on board the SS *Mentor* of the Blue Funnel Line. This company continued to serve the Far East into the 1960s, when a passenger had the habit of remarking, 'It's funny about the Blue Funnel.' An agreeable surprise, that might be called funny, happened to Mrs Dashwood ten years later, bringing the voyage from Malaya again before her. Returning in the SS *Berengaria* from a profitable lecture tour in the United States, she was recognized by her table steward. He remembered her from the SS *Mentor*, when she and Paul had sat at the Captain's table. Nostalgia led the steward to give

Elizabeth a priority of service at meals which impressed her table companions far more than any *réclame* her lecture tour might have given her.

V

DOWNALONG TO DEVONSHIRE

The Optimist, the first novel which Elizabeth published after her return to England, was dedicated to 'C. A. Dawson-Scott in affectionate admiration of her work'. The dedication was also a token of gratitude to a writer who had given *Zella Sees Herself* a gratifying review in *The Bookman*, and had so become the first literary figure to spot the potentialities of E. M. Delafield. Elizabeth's dedications were frequently warm and informal. This one reflected her advancement as a writer, from the days when Mrs Dawson-Scott had invited her to tea as a tribute to *Zella Sees Herself*. On that occasion there had been an immediate click of sympathy between a girl starting her career, and a writer who had worked in many fields of literature.

Catherine Amy Dawson-Scott had begun her own career with a book on women's rights, published at the age of twenty-one and called, unambiguously, *Sappho*. When Elizabeth first came to tea in 1917, Mrs Dawson-Scott was in her fifties, married, and the mother of three children. Her daughter Marjorie, a girl of seventeen, was also delighted with Elizabeth. The friendship became closer when Marjorie Dawson-Scott married Arthur Watts, the artist, brilliantly successful as an illustrator of *The Diary of a Provincial Lady*.

Having founded the Women's Defence League, with the object of training women to replace men called to the colours, Mrs Dawson-Scott went on, in 1917, to found the To-morrow Club. Her most permanent memorial is, however, the PEN Club, which flourishes, world-wide, to this day. John Galsworthy became the first President of PEN, a brilliant choice of someone prepared to work, practically to the end of his life, in the cause of promoting international communication between writers. Galsworthy also campaigned to recruit for PEN among his distinguished friends, effectively, for example, in the case of Professor Gilbert Murray.

My dear J.G., [Murray wrote, in reply to a letter asking for his support] I am most surprised that I am not a member of the PEN club. It looks like a ray of common sense amid the clouds of international amity in which I normally welter. However, we must close it up. . . .

As a recruiting sergeant Galsworthy was more successful than H. G. Wells, who travelled to Russia in the hope of persuading Gorky and other writers, to become members of the PEN Club. This expedition, which Malcolm Muggeridge has described 'as surely the most Quixote-like enterprise ever undertaken by man', ended in failure, but otherwise the PEN Club spread its bounds ever wider across the globe.

The Optimist, whose dedication expressed Elizabeth's admiration for Mrs Dawson-Scott's achievement, is in some ways the oddest of her books. It is largely dominated by Canon Morchard, the Optimist of the title, who, at first, shows signs of becoming a rival in tyranny to Samuel Butler's Mr Pontifex. Elizabeth, an admirer of Butler, may have chosen, perhaps subconsciously, to work on the same theme. After a period of struggle to force his sons and daughters into the mould that fits his ideals, the Canon, to the surprise of the reader, develops what might be called symptoms of saintliness. He even bears with fortitude repeated rejections by publishers of his life's work, a study of Leonidas of Alexandria.

Undaunted, Canon Morchard begins to make notes for a Commentary on St Paul's Epistle to the Philippians. Those well read, as Elizabeth herself was, in the works of Charlotte M. Yonge must have welcomed this private joke. The Reverend Edward Underwood, father of thirteen children in *The Pillars of the House*, is engaged on just such a Commentary when he succumbs to tuberculosis. There is the slightest touch of Harold Skimpole, both in Mr Underwood and in Canon Morchard, but it is unlikely that either Miss Yonge or Miss Delafield had the Dickensian humbug consciously in mind.

Despite her convent education, Elizabeth, in her writing, always handled the Church of England and its ministers with a confidence as to their functions which her acquaintance among the clergy in Charlotte M. Yonge's novels must have increased. She was not deterred by a reviewer of *The Optimist* in the *Church Times*, who complained of Canon Morchard as an 'utterly impossible clergyman', from deciding to transfer her allegiance to the Anglican Communion. Paul is known to have left the question of the children's religious upbringing for their mother to decide. His tolerant attitude may have been more of an influence than Elizabeth realized, in her decision not to bring up her children in the church in which she had been bred. Although her early novels had had religious questions influencing the story, it was to be seven or eight years before she achieved a masterpiece on the theme of warring beliefs.

It was Elizabeth's sister-in-law, Muriel Dashwood, who took her for an interview with the Bishop of Oxford so that change of faith might receive, as it were, episcopal sanction. Anxious to behave correctly, Elizabeth asked if she should kiss the Bishop's ring, but was assured this was not an Anglican requirement. Her future writings might, sometimes, be placed on the Index of the Church she had left, but as a writer she was liberated from its artistic constraints.

The brave plan to support her family by her writing seems to have been joined, in Elizabeth's imagination, with the wish to go 'down-along' to Devonshire. It was in Devonshire that, to quote the ineffable Philip Stellenthorpe from *Humbug*, she had been 'a happy, little child'. The deep lanes, with their springtime cascades of primroses, gave her annually a moment of pleasure to blot out 'winter's rains and ruins'. At Christmas she regularly saved the boxes in which crackers had come, and, in due course, packed them full of primroses for her friends. She enjoyed the grotesque juxtaposition of the pictures of families in paper caps which decorated the lids and the warm, mossy smell of the flowers within.

After a spell at a house called Westcott, whose Victorian Gothic windows added a touch of bizarre charm, the Dashwoods, on 1 September 1923, took the lease of Croyle House near the village of Kentisbeare. It was here that Rosamund, their only other child, was born in January 1924. Although Elizabeth's stock in trade as a writer was apt to be dark with domestic crises, Croyle itself remained a happy home for the rest of her life. At the time of the move no one would have guessed that she would have barely twenty years in which to enjoy the flow of family activity.

During the temporary tenancy of Westcott, Elizabeth finished *A Reversion to Type*, a novel dated May 1922–February 1923. Jim, the bad hat of a county family with the awkward name of Aviolet, is shipped to Ceylon, with the idea that his prospective death from alcoholism will take place at a distance. On the voyage out he meets and marries Rose, a beautiful girl, but, from his family's point of view, of appalling vulgarity of birth and behaviour. Jim manages to drink himself to death with remarkable celerity, and Rose has no option but to return to the Aviolets, her small son, Cecil, being the heir presumptive to the family estates.

The Aviolets live in a routine where the most normal movements of daily life are discussed in depth before being put into action. The picture of the slow turning of the wheels of country house life is more convincing than the dealings in the pawnbroker's shop of Rose's uncle (an uncle in every sense of the word). Elizabeth, it is true, was no stranger to the sign of the three brass balls, being in the habit of pawning her jewellery when hard pressed for ready cash, but she was only familiar with the customer's side of the counter. Rose, beautiful and earthy, suffers from the knowledge that her son is a dangerous fantasist, and that her in-laws attribute this to the bad drop of pawn-broking blood. Only after Cecil has just escaped a prison sentence, for stealing silver cups and having them fulsomely engraved to himself, does his mother slough off her guilt and recognize that the bad blood is an Aviolet inheritance. She is able to make this clear in a passionate tirade to her dead husband's brother, Ford Aviolet, who had consistently thwarted Rose's sensible plans for her son's regeneration.

Croyle, new home of the Dashwoods, stood on the Bradfield Estate, not far from Bradfield Hall. This impressive Elizabethan pile was, at that time, owned by the Honourable Mrs Adams, who had remarried after the death of her first husband, the son of the first Baron Waleran. Her own son, William, was to succeed his grandfather as second Baron in 1925. Lottie Adams was the sister of Lord Glentanar, and an heiress of money spun by the Coats mills. She had also inherited a confidence in her own impeccable rightness from an abrasive Scotch mother, who, based on a vast house in Hill Street, Mayfair, dominated her family by direct control. Mrs Adams's strident social tactics were a contrast to the behaviour of her brother Lord Glentanar, an unassuming character, devoted to a beautiful Norwegian wife, and to that of her sister, Maud, Duchess of Wellington, whose charm and kindness illuminated a multitude of good causes. The Dashwoods' move to Croyle coincided, roughly, with Paul's appointment as agent for the Bradfield estate. For five years the ferment of Elizabeth's resentment of Lottie Adams's behaviour bubbled below the surface, until it mushroomed into a dazzling comic creation.

Before Elizabeth achieved this release of her feelings (and the Provincial Lady came to birth to begin her guerilla warfare with Lady Boxe) she hatched a number of novels, including some of her most accomplished. When she filled in her *Who's Who* entry for 1934, Elizabeth listed as Recreations not only Reading Other People's Books, but also Criminology. This latter interest was to a certain extent professional, as a novelist, but was also linked with her work as a Justice of the Peace, which she became soon after her arrival in Devonshire. She never scamped her duties on the Bench, and left some perceptive notes on the lessons she had learned from its proceedings.

Owing to her childhood visits to Devonshire, the Clerk of the Court in which she sat had known her, she says, 'since babyhood'. Knowing of her association with the Women's Institute, then a relatively new organization, it is not unlikely that the Clerk of the Court recruited Mrs Dashwood as a suitable person to be sworn in to the Commission of the Peace. She was the first woman to sit on the Bench at Cullompton, and the Clerk instructed her that it was her duty to hear every case that came before the Bench when she was sitting. After she had become respected by her fellow magistrates, the Clerk also revealed that originally they had opposed sitting in judgment with a woman among them. One elderly member had gone so far as to insist that he would resign should a female be sworn in. He was educated and intelligent, but kept his word and resigned, leaving the rest of the bench to cope with the innovation as best they might.

After less than two years Mrs Dashwood JP found herself accepted by her colleagues, who had ceased to warn her, as they had originally, when 'an unpleasant case', usually of sexual or criminal assault, had to be heard. Elizabeth felt strongly that not only was it her duty, as the Clerk had told her, not to avoid 'unpleasantness', but, whatever the culpability, it was surely wrong that a female, witness or accused, should give evidence to a room full only of men. Her appointment caused her to be interviewed by the *Western Morning News*, when she was asked what she felt about a recent execution in Glasgow. On this macabre occasion a junior magistrate, female, had been obliged to attend. Elizabeth replied that she trusted never to face such an ordeal herself, but she saw that it might well be an inescapable duty. In the duties which she did have to face, she found it was essential to send mothers of children, offenders or witnesses out of Court. The children spoke more freely without parental solicitude or prompting. Samuel Butler would have approved her attitude.

A Messalina of the Suburbs, the only novel of Elizabeth's to deal
with an actual murder, was finished at Dawlish in 1923. The dedication to 'M.P.P.(Margaret)' is dated August 1923, so the move to
Croyle, Elizabeth being five months' pregnant with Rosamund, must
have followed immediately. The dedicatee was Doctor Margaret Posthuma, a psychiatrist, with whom Elizabeth enjoyed discussing all
ideas that sprang from the perversity of the human mind. Doctor
Posthuma was eventually responsible for bringing Elizabeth together
with Cicely McCall, whose liveliness endeared her to the whole family
and who became a cherished visitor to Croyle.

The plot of *A Messalina of the Suburbs* would have been familiar to
every reader of newspapers, being undisguisably based on a famous
murder case. The book's dénouement, the death by hanging of the
heroine, had, in real life, been a matter of fierce debate among those
for or against capital punishment. To recapitulate the foundation of
the novel, Mr Thompson had been murdered by his wife Ethel's
lover, a merchant seaman of the name of Bywaters. In the subsequent
trial, which rocked the country, Mrs Thompson was tried as an ac-
complice of Bywaters, although when her lover attacked her husband
she was certainly shocked and astonished. Her protests at the moment
of the murder did not outweigh the letters she had written to Bywaters, describing the failure of attempts she had made to poison
her husband. The jury did not believe that the letters were fantasies
designed to keep Bywaters's interest in their affair from fading.
Mrs Thompson and Bywaters were hanged in 1923, both declaring to
the last that she was innocent of the crime.

Elizabeth was certainly not alone in finding the psychological
aspects of the tragedy to be fascinating, but she was first in the field
to use the tragedy as the foundation of a novel. Ten years later F.
Tennyson Jesse, Elizabeth's earliest promoter at Heinemann, availed
herself of the same tale of pity and terror with an increasing success.
A Pin to See a Peepshow not only did well in dramatic form, but, nearly
half a century later, became an admired television serial.

Although Elizabeth is never very clear as to which areas of London
she considered to be suburban, her ingenuity makes *A Messalina of
the Suburbs* a remarkable study of lower middle-class life at its most
sordid. Elsie, the Messalina/Mrs Thompson, is seduced by the father
of the family in which she works (to use today's idiom) as an au pair.
The squalor of the seduction scene is illuminated by flashes of Gothic

phosphorescence, and is as sexually explicit as the laws and reticences of the period would allow. Elsie's career then follows the pattern of a disagreeable marriage, and a lover over whom her hold is precarious. Unlike the climax of F. Tennyson Jesse's novel, Elizabeth did not, as it were, escort a woman convicted of murder to the scaffold. Elsie is last seen realizing that she is about to enter a tunnel at the end of which there is nothing but an inescapable drop.

VI

THE WAY THINGS WERE, IN A
WRITER'S LIFE

Elizabeth's daughter was born on 15 January 1924, and given the name Rosamund, presumably from her mother's affection for Maria Edgeworth's child of that name, who had a tougher time in fiction than her namesake in life. Elizabeth had not faltered in her writing career after the birth of Lionel, nor did she pause in her literary progress at the arrival of her second child. Before the month was out she began *Mrs Harter*, which was to be finished in the following August. The enigmatic Mrs Harter has lived in Singapore, a rare instance of Elizabeth drawing on her Far Eastern experience.

There is a slight reminiscence of the early novels of John Galsworthy in this study of the impact made by an alien personality on a closed country community. Mrs Harter attracts Captain Patch, an exceptionally decent chap, a complete contrast to her luridly unpleasant husband. The story is seen through the eyes of Sir Miles Flower, a rather crippled baronet. His wife Claire has dramatized herself into the sacrifice of marrying him, but, unfortunately, the sacrifice has been lost in the dramatization. The Flowers are the leading figures in a neighbourhood which watches the development of the romance between Bill Patch and Diamond Harter with fascinated disapproval.

Claire Flower's position as châtelaine of the Manor House is challenged to a certain extent by the Rector's wife, Lady Annabel Bending, previously married to a Colonial Governor, and retaining some of the dignity of her former position. It is thought that, had the Rector employed a curate, Lady Annabel would have referred to him as 'the A.D.C.'. Although this portrait of a Governor's Lady may have been the result of Elizabeth's observation when stationed in Malaya, it might also have owed something to her own mother. Lady Clifford had, after all, turned an involuntary ADC into a son-in-law.

Sir Miles is sustained in the irritations of his daily life and crippled state by a passion, reciprocated but undeclared, for Mary Ambrey, a widowed cousin. Together they can admire the struggles of Mrs Fazackerly, a penniless neighbour, widow of a brutal husband and daughter of an aged father who takes sadistic pleasure in catching his daughter out in untruths over household expenditure. Mrs Fazackerly is, however, a more stimulating caller at the Manor than the Kendal family, a retired General, his wife and four spinster daughters. Already in their thirties, the Miss Kendals are in complete subjection to 'Puppa' and 'Mumma' as they call their parents, the attempted French pronunciation being a relic of the days when 'Papa' and 'Mama' in plain English was considered, in some circles, to be a common way of speaking.

Miles Flower and Mary Ambrey watch the growth of the romance between Diamond Harter and Bill Patch, until a crisis is reached with the arrival of Mr Harter. Elizabeth had a fondness for solving the problems of the characters about whom she wrote by a fatal accident. It is one such disaster that sends Mrs Harter away from the circle where she has been both a stone in the social shoe and the grain of sand round which a black pearl of gossip has formed. Mrs Harter is a survivor, far more suited to a tougher straightforward world than to the web of reservations and subtle hints which direct the life of an English village.

During the early stages of working on *Mrs Harter*, Elizabeth was photographed with both her children, probably, to judge by Rosamund's size, in April 1924. With plump bare feet sticking out from under a white frilled frock, Rosamund looks to have been a flourishing baby. Lionel is square-set and round-faced. Later, he had a habit of lowering his head and looking at the camera from under a lock of hair, but at four years old he was cheerfully uncomplicated in appearance. The mother of Lionel and Rosamund has a somewhat harrassed air, suggesting a lack of confidence in her own skill as a baby handler.

Fourteen years after this photograph was taken, Elizabeth, in an interview, discussed the question of whether mothers of young children were justified in following a profession. Her opinion fortifies the view that she may not have been entirely at ease with a baby on her knee. She advocated that the care and training of children should be in the hands of properly qualified minders, paid for by the working mother. Rather disingenuously, she supported her argument by quoting the Russian system of crèches where mothers at work, theoretically all mothers, deposited their children at the age of one month. As will be seen, Elizabeth had not found the Soviet system of child care ideal.

Even allowing for possible distortions by the interviewer, Elizabeth's views on marriage – 'not before twenty-five for a woman' – would have sounded somewhat bleak to the girl she had been. She would seem to have forgotten her own depression at being unsought in marriage at the age of twenty, when the prospect of making a wiser choice at twenty-five might have appeared chimerical.

The mother and children photograph must have been taken at a moment when Elizabeth was becoming ever more deeply involved in the life of the village of Kentisbeare. At the initial meeting of the Women's Institute, on 14 April 1924, Mrs Dashwood was unanimously elected President. She retained the position to the end of her life, giving her time and talent unstintingly not only to Kentisbeare but to the movement throughout the country. Many countrywomen at that date led isolated lives, drawing water from wells, living after dark by the light of oil lamps, and with outdoor earth closets as the only sanitation. The unending burden of domestic work, unalleviated by mains water or electric grid, allowed little time for learning skills that might make life easier, and even less for social pleasures.

Elizabeth saw the value of the widening prospects that Women's Institutes brought to the countryside. Although her pen was not infrequently dipped in acid, she seldom allowed herself more than a passing joke at the expense of a particular Institute. Indeed the most trying episode through which the Provincial Lady passes is in suffering the hospitality of an ancient, aristocratic President, and the appalling cold contracted from a night in an arctic stately home. A more usual embarrassment, familiar to all who address village audiences, is to find, seated in the front row, an expert on whatever subject the Provincial Lady has chosen to speak.

With *Mrs Harter*, her eleventh novel, Elizabeth had made considerable progress in paring away the prolixity of her earlier style. She was consequently in line with a number of novels written between 1921 and 1931 whose sentences would have appeared uncomfortably bare to a previous generation. Elizabeth had a sharp eye for literary mannerisms, and in a series of parodies which she called *The Sincerest Form* . . . she raked like a machine gunner across the field of upstanding novelists, including H. G. Wells, Arnold Bennett, Eleanor Smith, G.B. Stern, Evelyn Waugh and Rosamund Lehmann.

A Note in Music, the novel which had followed the success of Rosamund Lehmann's *Dusty Answer*, obviously appealed to Elizabeth as the story of the familiar predicament, a woman whose sensitive nature is lacerated by the grimness of everyday life. The heroine of *A Note in Music* has to endure the spiritual isolation of life in a Northern city. In this particular parody sympathy was added to the flattery of imitation. To quote from *Still Dustier*:

> How could one stop one's husband from talking about county families? The habit was growing on him. As for her, she knew she was the only woman left, even in the provinces, who wore elastic-sided shoes with black lisle thread stockings.

E. M. Delafield never inflicted quite such a cruel fate on the Provincial Lady but there were occasions when the unsuitability of the latter's clothes added awkwardness to meetings with county families.

What Marcel Proust called 'the tune of the song, which in each author is different', makes itself strongly heard in Elizabeth's next novel, *The Chip and the Block* (1925), a favourite of Rosamund Dashwood among her mother's books. The Block himself, Charles Ellery, might almost be called a secular Canon Morchard. As a reviewer in *Punch* pointed out, Ellery also has traits of Harold Skimpole in his egocentric disregard for the needs and sufferings of others. The development by which Charles Ellery ceases to be a plague to his family, when he marries a second wife who can control him, is highly enjoyable for the reader. The *Times Literary Supplement* praised 'the episode of Mrs Foss' as being 'discreetly handled'. In the idiom of the time this would have conveyed to an alert reader that sexual seduction (by Mrs Foss of young Paul Ellery) had actually taken place.

Mr Ellery comes across even more clearly in 'The Tortoise', a short story in a later collection, *The Entertainment* (1927). On holiday beside the Bristol Channel, Mr Ellery, who takes pride in being a Leveller, has an enjoyably democratic exchange with an ancient fisherman. Depression sets in when Charles Ellery learns that the old fisherman is as deaf as a bulkhead but has perfected answers to the remarks of visitors, which he knows to be of unvarying and identical banality. Always at the head of the tourist's inquiries is the prospect of rain, to be judged by the visibility of Lundy Island.

The harrowing situation of an ex-soldier suffering from shell-shock and depression forms part of the plot of *The Optimist*, but the hero concerned has not only private means but a marketable literary talent. Things are very different for Major Jack Galbraith, who, after a shaky start, turns into the hero of *Jill* (1926). He and Doreen, a wife married in haste during the First World War, live on their not particularly brilliant wits. An upper-class background and Jack's gallant war record are their only, and ever-depreciating, assets. As their *train de vie* requires them to dine and dance expensively, their financial position is chronically desperate.

Some hopes are pinned on a scheme by which oil shale might be extracted from off-shore Cornwall, but Maxted, the promoter of the scheme, is, in the language of the period, such an obvious 'wrong 'un' that nothing comes from this prevision of the oil rigs of today. An attempt to interest Oliver Galbraith, Jack's prosperous stock-broker cousin, does, however, lead to both Jack and Oliver meeting Jill. Daughter of Pansy Morrell, who lives precariously on money wrung from a series of lovers, Jill has retained what might be called a worldly-wise innocence.

Philanthropically, Cathie Galbraith, wife of Oliver, rescues Jill from the squalor of the hotel, where Jack and Doreen live on reduced rates for adding class to the clientèle. Her hostess is, however, sent into a state of shock by the revelation that Jill prefers to wear grubby underclothes rather than pollute the bathroom by washing them. Cathie's final attempt to turn Jill into a good little secretary has a less than philanthropic aspect. Cathie is too blinded by the contemplation of her own perfections to recognize that her husband is reacting against the blandness of his life, but subconsciously she is aware that Oliver has a *tendresse* for Jill, the obliging Bohemian. The scenes between the two women, originally comic, become ever more sinister.

Jack Galbraith has the good fortune to be rescued from a zombie round of unenjoyed dissipation by Jill, who also thwarts an attempt at suicide. Having fallen in love with Jack, the young girl is able to marry him when his wife, Doreen, manages to hook a rich admirer. While not actually criminals, Jack and Doreen live each day under the steady dunning of the hotel manager, besides being obliged to cadge continually for meals and cigarettes. E. M. Delafield was to reconstruct this rickety ménage in a later novel, with distinctly less pity for the young couple's predicament. She also used much the same background for the title story in the collection, already mentioned, called *The Entertainment*.

The point of the story is the appalling boringness of the entertainment offered, when two city gents take two chorus girls out to luncheon. The girls' frocks are described with considerable relish, and when 'The Entertainment' first appeared in a magazine the artist faithfully illustrated the exaggerated styles, but unfortunately was not able to do so in colour. While the two men argue about useful business contracts, and whether Dark Dynevor is a likely winner in his next race, the girls struggle to behave with sophistication, when obliged to deal with a liqueur, chosen in ignorance, and to them unpalatable.

Besides 'The Tortoise', already mentioned, *The Entertainment* included 'Reflex Action', a slightly confused story concerning a *nouveau riche* heiress, and a lady's maid who knows, socially, what is what far better than does her employer. As a private family joke, it is mentioned that 'the Earl and Countess of Duns Tew' are to be visited. Duns Tew was the Oxfordshire village in which Captain Robert Dashwood, brother of Paul, had settled his family. It is not recorded if this fictional ennoblement was accepted with pleasure by Elizabeth's in-laws. This collection also included 'Family Group', the first of E. M. Delafield's short stories to deal in depth with the horror of a seaside holiday when small children are confined in unfriendly lodgings. The story has an additional twist. The clerical husband of the worn-out mother says, reverently, that God may send them the blessing of more little ones.

After four or five years at Croyle, a snapshot has survived to show the appearance of the Dashwood family at about the time that Elizabeth wrote *The Way Things Are*, published in 1927. Rosamund, born at Croyle, stands in the middle of the group, smiling cheerfully, her round face framed by a shock of fair hair. Her brother, Lionel, has his head lowered and looks to be absorbed in a detached train of thought. Paul Dashwood also appears to be taking a minimal interest in being photographed. He gazes at his pipe, and it is easy to feel that a balloon inscribed 'It depends', later an habitual response of the husband of the Provincial Lady, may rise, at any moment, from a head on which the hair is perceptibly growing thinner.

Elizabeth, the wife and mother, smiles towards the camera, but her head is bent forward so that her bobbed hair shadows her face. She had naturally a tall, slim figure, but she had also a tendency to stoop.

An awkward stance was apt to be developed by girls who had grown taller than many of the men with whom they had to dance. When Lady Clifford hissed 'Be natural' at her daughters, their shyness made stooping an only too easy reaction.

In her previous novels, Elizabeth had ridden her creative fantasy on a loose rein, adding romantic embellishments to such parts of a story that came directly from her own experience. With *The Way Things Are* she not only imposed a stiffer literary discipline, but she kept the romantic part of the plot under sterner control. The result was the most remarkable book of the first half of her writing career, and the foundation on which she was to build two later, separate, successes.

The setting of Laura's life in *The Way Things Are* is the one that Elizabeth herself was inhabiting at Croyle, a setting that was carried over in her play *To See Ourselves*, and, of course, into *The Diary of a Provincial Lady*. Always a sad heroine, Laura's life is not, domestically, merely a matter of pinpricks. It could better be compared to the Chinese Death by a Thousand Cuts. Her efforts to interest herself in the mostly unsuccessful farming experiments of Alfred, her husband, grate on her own nerves and arouse little response from Alfred. Her devotion to her attractive, but excitable, younger son, at the expense of his stodgy elder brother, causes her guilty pangs, but these are not strong enough to make her amend her habit of favouritism. Worry that the servants will give notice, and prove to be irreplaceable, is intensified by the knowledge that she lacks the skill to cook for her family. Laura's literary work, in some respects like her creator's, is more than a hobby, but only keeps her bank account balanced on a tightrope.

When Laura actually acquires an admirer, who is as wet as his name – Duke Ayland – sounds, he adds another problem to those that already beset her. The unconsummated affair is conducted against a background of children smitten by whooping cough, bath water seldom raised above the tepid in temperature, and the permanent smoking of the oil lamps by which her home is lit. Having announced that she wishes to go to Plymouth with the object of inspecting the new university buildings, she is guiltily conscious that this is a cover-up for an assignation with Duke Ayland. Her plans are torpedoed by the non-arrival of a new cook. Failing to escape for a day from the cage of her home, it is little consolation for Laura to be assured by her household that, anyway, it was early closing day in Plymouth.

The Way Things Are, in spite of comic flashes, is an essentially grey book. Neighbours are either patronizing from a position of greater affluence, or of a paralysing boringness. The one dashing girl in Laura's circle is condemned for her heavy make-up and overbearing manners. A man-eater who chews her victims and spits them out, Bébé, called Bay-Bay in derision by her detractors, is eventually defeated in her pursuit of a well-known author. Bébé disappears to America, but no such loophole offers itself to Laura.

Finally, the latter accepts that it is her own limitations that oblige her to remain enclosed in the limitations of her surroundings. The double bed which she shares with Alfred is an uneasy resting place, rather than a foundation for connubial bliss. Indeed, the only hint of a love life between husband and wife is given when Laura discovers Johnnie, her favourite child, deep in one of the works on contraception by Doctor Marie Stopes. He has unearthed the book from among his mother's underclothes, and shows even more ominous signs for his future by having also decked himself with his mother's jewellery.

Although *The Way Things Are* may be grey in essence, as the *Times Literary Supplement* pointed out, it is also extremely funny. At one moment Duke, Laura's admirer, makes a remark that in her eyes shows him to have made a false, even unflattering, estimate of her character. Her reply requires a vast effort at self-control: '"Nothing in the least like that," Laura assured him, trying to keep a sense of profound indignation from quivering in her voice.'

Johnnie supplies some intensely embarrassing moments of comic relief when he insists on singing a song to one of his mother's neighbours. Smug and dowdy, this woman's self-confidence is based on the knowledge of her ability to cook, and on the songs about birds and flowers by which her children impress the company. Johnnie's choice of song, 'Oh, what a short little shirt you've got, You'd better pull down the blind,' creates shock waves which drown his mother in confusion. Johnnie may, she feels, live down this ribald outburst, but Laura herself is likely to be forever tarred with the brush of vulgarity.

Probably the most extreme compliment to *The Way Things Are* was paid by Rachel Ferguson, author of a skit, *The Provincial Lady Goes Too Far*. She tempered her admiration by complaints that when E. M. Delafield went to the United States or Russia, she lost the control of her imagination, and consequently her work became undistinguished, even pedestrian. About *The Way Things Are*, however, Rachel Ferguson's praise was unstinted. In *Passionate Kensington*, published in 1939, she declared that this was E. M. Delafield's completely perfect novel. She had read the story of the struggles of the unfortunate Laura at least fifty times, and proposed to do so fifty times more. For a novel which had been published ten years earlier, and been followed by a number of remarkable studies, Rachel Ferguson's acclaim was a tribute no novelist would despise.

VII

IN THE ORBIT OF LADY RHONDDA

At a time when she must have been three years old, Rosamund Dashwood remembers a scene in her nursery with all the clarity of an infant's first impressions. Her Nanny was making the effort of teaching her to count in English, while a *mademoiselle*, Marguerite, was struggling to convey the same numeration in French. The counterpoint of one-two-three, *un-deux-trois*, was a symptom of her mother's hope of making Rosamund as fluent in two languages as she was herself. This ambition, Elizabeth's daughter declares, was to remain unfulfilled.

The Nanny seems to have been rather a shadowy figure, but Rosamund retained an unloving memory of Marguerite. To the keen nose of a young child, this *mademoiselle* smelt horribly powdery, and her black-clad person was made additionally unattractive by a tendency to shriek. Elizabeth, on the other hand, developed Marguerite into a consistently comic member of the Provincial Lady's household. Elizabeth's command of French made it possible for her to bestow embarrassing remarks on Mademoiselle to underline an awkward situation. The Provincial Lady considers, '"Ah, mon doux St Joseph!"' to be a profane comment on a domestic crisis, though probably those without the illumination of a convent upbringing might have missed the reference to St Joseph's chastity.

Rosamund's day would end in the drawing room, with her mother reading aloud, *Vice Versa* a favourite book, or playing a game of Ludo. The room itself was described, in an interview with *The Queen*, as low-ceilinged, with lavender-painted walls and Parma violet curtains. This description actually belongs to the 1930s, when Elizabeth's great success may have allowed for the room to have been redecorated. Its upholstery certainly sounds to have been more elegant than the drawing room of Elizabeth's imagination in *The Way Things Are*.

Like Jane Austen, Elizabeth had no writing room of her own. She worked at a table near the drawing-room window, which was in itself an interruption, the dogs of the household being invariably on the wrong side of the glass door. A Justice of the Peace has to deal with nothing except problems, and these were constantly coming before Elizabeth. The Women's Institute also raised problems for Mrs Dashwood, its President, to settle. In 1924 she gave a talk on 'Nominations', in which she explained to the newly hatched Kentisbeare Institute how officers should be elected. The following year she offered the garden at Croyle for a fête, agreeing to be in charge of the tug-of-war, not a position that immediately suggests itself as appropriate for someone of such a slim figure.

By the mid-1930s Elizabeth's work was appearing in a variety of periodicals, and her career in radio was expanding. Sometimes, in the latter medium, her work was found to be uneven, but she was valued for her ability to see everyday life in terms of comic desperation. Her journalistic output was, indeed, amazing, considering that she was rarely without a novel in hand. Some writers emerge from a working session blinking like moles coming to the surface. Elizabeth's friends insist that she never was to be found in this condition. She was a stranger to the sensation of returning to ordinary life from a creative trance. Writing was the strongest thread in the cable of her existence, but it remained, always, an integral, never a separated strand.

Her unremitting devotion to her work came to the notice of Elizabeth's American publisher, Cass Canfield, when he was delayed in fetching her for a dinner engagement. He arrived late, to find Elizabeth scribbling in a note book with the concentration of one who had disciplined herself to snatch any moment in which to write. Canfield thought the habit had grown from Paul Dashwood's disapproval of his wife's independent career, which had prevented her from setting up in a work room of her own. Apart from the churlishness of such an attitude, for his wife's earnings bolstered the family finances, it is open to question as to whether Cass Canfield's opinion was well founded.

Another point of view has been put forward by Hamish Hamilton, himself devoted to Elizabeth and cherished by her as a dear and sympathetic friend. Jamie Hamilton went to the first night of *To See Ourselves*, the only play of Elizabeth's which was produced at a West End theatre. He recalled, long afterwards, that Paul accepted the caricature, easily recognizable, of himself in excellent part. He does not seem to have resented appearing before the public as a pedestrian figure of fun. Nor did he dismiss her books as likely to be beyond his comprehension or possibility of enjoyment. As will be seen, he was eager to read the first novel of Elizabeth's to be published by Macmillan.

When Elizabeth dedicated *The Suburban Young Man* (1928) 'To All Those Nice People who have so often asked me "To Write a Story about Nice People"', she may be suspected of pulling the leg of the Nice People. As *Time and Tide* pointed out, the people may be nice, but the author has firmly placed the main characters in a nasty emotional hole. Although this is the second book which concerns Elizabeth's idea of the suburbs, the reader is left uncertain as to whether Putney, Streatham or Wembley is intended.

Peter, the Suburban Young Man, has fallen in love with the well born Antoinette, who, rather surprisingly for that date, has found a job as a typist. Peter's Scotch wife, Hope, the mother of his twin sons, remains in admirable control of the situation. She waits calmly until Peter and Antoinette prefer not to face the class awkwardness that their marriage would inevitably cause. Antoinette, the great-niece of one earl, has the opportunity to marry another, while Hope accepts without rancour the return of Peter. This triangle has been composed of Nice People, but other characters do not qualify. Antoinette's mother, for example, after a lifetime of amorous fancies, warns her daughter that even the most painful infatuation will pass: '". . . all of a sudden it's over. There's no one there – or rather," said Lady Rochester with rueful candour, "There usually is someone there – someone else – ".'

After three books published by Heinemann, Elizabeth moved, for one novel only, to Hodder and Stoughton. Her next twelve books, an awesome number to have achieved in only eight years, appeared under the imprint of Hutchinson. She then moved to the firm of Macmillan, where she was to stay for the rest of her life. *What is Love?* (1928), the first book for her new publisher, was more loosely put together than *The Way Things Are*. It was, however, acclaimed in the *Daily Telegraph* as a study of the pangs and ecstasies of first love to be compared with Elizabeth von Arnim's *Fräulein Schmidt and Mr Anstruther*. Other reviewers were made uneasy by the harshly drawn portraits of Vicky, a modern young woman, and Simon, a philanderer.

The most disreputable character in the book is not, as it happens, young. Ellie, the heroine, has been abandoned at an early age by a mother whose amatory career resembles that of Lady Rochester in *The Suburban Young Man*. Both these middle-aged sirens may have been suggested to Elizabeth by the character of her father's niece Monica, whose behaviour had cast a shadow of scandal over her profoundly respectable Catholic family. On the other hand, Ellie, almost spastic in her clumsiness, may owe something to the awkward way in which Yoé struggled with life.

Unlike Yoé, Ellie is beautiful, with a perfection that enchants Simon, the sophisticated young man. He raises Ellie into a state of bliss by proposing marriage, but his love wears thin at the spectacle of Ellie's physical incompetence. Having just refrained from seducing her, he finds himself increasingly exasperated at Ellie's inability to arrange a vase of flowers, or choose the shoes to match her dress. Leaving Ellie lamenting, Simon pairs off with Vicky, Eton-cropped and the wearer of an eyeglass (both period touches). Cold-blooded Vicky may be, but she has the sense to see that only disaster would result from the linking of Simon and Ellie.

When *What is Love?* was first published, in November 1928, Paul Dashwood wrote a rather testy letter to Macmillan. Would they send him the complimentary copies of *What is Love?* which he assumed they were holding on account of his wife's absence in the United States? As E. M. Delafield's husband, he was anxious to read the book, so would they stop keeping the copies due to the author and send them forthwith? Elizabeth's visit to America was presumably for promotional purposes, but, of course, not yet in the character of the Provincial Lady.

Although local good works, the needs of her family and the demands of her bank manager were hurdles in the obstacle race of Elizabeth's writing career, by 1929 she had accumulated enough sketches for Macmillan to bring out a collection. The title, *Women Are Like That*, was rather dispiriting, but the dedication to Yoé was a light-hearted recollection of their youth in Chester Square: 'When I go through Chester Square nowadays it is for the decorous purpose of attending a Committee Meeting. I am, in fact, pretending to be a grown-up, but the Square Garden of you and I knows better.'

Although the bond between the sisters was stretched by their separate lives, Elizabeth had obviously brooded on the theme of sisterly possessiveness. 'Oil Painting circa 1890' is as grim a story as she ever wrote. Frederica, completely dominated by her sister, is unable to break out of the grisly tyranny of love. There are traces of Lady Clifford's bullying of her daughters in the command to 'be natural' which is levelled at the sisters, but the story itself is a trial outline of the most poignant sequence in *Thank Heaven Fasting*, even to the use of the name Frederica.

'The Sprat' is also a story destined to be expanded in *Challege to Clarissa*. An impresario, Arthur Lawrence, gives a deliciously expensive luncheon to a musical spinster who has recently inherited a fortune. He thus ensures that the concert of his protégé, Radow, a pianist of genius, will have the necessary backing. Both Lawrence and Radow make wonderfully comic reappearances in the later novel. Lawrence shows that he is equally capable of subduing the appallingly tough Clarissa as he is of delicately casting the sprat that will catch the mackerel, in this case the musical spinster, Miss Duquenois.

On the subject of what she called amateur educationalists, Elizabeth had expressed her resentment in *Humbug*, 'the book of mine I hold most true.' When she came to arrange the education of her own daughter, she was anxious to avoid the moral pressures which had made her own convent years unhappy, and she was equally apprehensive of the tendency among Dashwood women to grow taller and broader as they approached maturity. Elegantly slender herself, she felt that hearty games might fix Rosamund's childish chubbiness into a permanent solidity. It also seemed unnatural to her that, to her children, French should be a lesson rather than part of a bi-lingual culture.

With these conflicting ideals, Elizabeth did not, it seems, send Rosamund to as many different schools as she had herself passed through, but Rosamund remembers four establishments of varying educational efficiency. By the end of 1929 she had been released from the disliked thrall of Marguerite, and she was dispatched to a boarding school where she was made aware that she was the daughter of a distinguished mother. Rosamund relished being trotted out as an exhibit to prospective parents, the clever little daughter of E. M. Delafield, only five years old but in the class with children of six and seven. More serious teaching took place at Mickleham, to which Rosamund was transferred at the age of ten. Elizabeth approved of this school to the extent of making a public recommendation.

With the idea of improving Rosamund's French, she was next dispatched to Switzerland where, she records, she immensely enjoyed the skiing, but her command of the French language remained static. Finally, she was deposited at Queen Margaret's, Scarborough, a school of high reputation but hardly handy for visits from parents who lived in South Devon. It was here that she remained until 1941, when she joined the Women's Auxiliary Air Force, and, as her mother wrote to Marjorie Watts, home life had come to an end.

It was probably through Mrs Dawson-Scott, a writer with many literary connections, that Elizabeth originally met Margaret, Viscountess Rhondda, founder and editor of *Time and Tide*. Their association, personal and professional, was of the happiest, but there were those who found Lady Rhondda a capricious employer. John Betjeman wrote, in verse, of the pain caused when Lady Rhondda had dismissed him from his position as Literary Editor of her magazine. He called the poem 'Caprice', the name of the restaurant in which the blow was delivered, and an expression of his feelings towards his employer. These emotions had come back to the future Poet Laureate when, three years later, he found himself sitting two tables away from the one at which Lady Rhondda had given him the sack. Time had not softened the blow, and Betjeman remembered going out into the street, wondering 'Which loss was the greater, The cash or the pride'.

No difficulties of the kind that had so distressed the poet and admirer of *The Unlucky Family* arose between Margaret Rhondda and Elizabeth, a valued member of the board of *Time and Tide*. Elizabeth was seven years the younger, but found that she and her friend shared views in discussing the constricted lives of young girls in Belgravia during the Edwardian decade. Their lives had been dominated by the hope of marriage and its reverse, the fear of a fading existence as an old maid. Margaret Haig Thomas herself had married at the age of twenty-five, but not with any success. Her business life, with political and literary interests, may be supposed to have filled the place of the family she had wished for but never had.

These interests were Lady Rhondda's protection from the tedium of the sporting world in which her husband moved. Becoming strongly attached to the feminist cause, she even went so far as to attack a letter-box with a chemical bomb. This violent act took place in Monmouthshire, her husband's neighbourhood, and resulted in a brief spell in prison in Usk. After five days she forced her own release by means of a hunger strike.

Realizing the potentialities of his heiress, her father turned Margaret into a business colleague. By the time he was created Viscount Rhondda, with remainder to his daughter, they had travelled the world on business together. Three years earlier, in 1915, they had, indeed, been lucky to survive the torpedoing of the SS *Lusitania* off the south-west coast of Ireland. Margaret was unconscious when she was taken from the water, having floated for three hours in a life jacket. With age Lady Rhondda increased in size to a point when more than five days' hunger strike would have been needed to fit her into even an outsize life jacket. The contrast could hardly have been greater with the slim and elegant Elizabeth.

With the coming of peace, Margaret Rhondda went on to found *Time and Tide* in 1920, as a strongly Liberal periodical with a policy of supporting feminist causes. As Anthony Lejeune points out in the *Dictionary of National Biography*, the tide of time deflected the magazine from both these aims. Not only was there a distinct veering towards the Right in the paper's political stance, but Woman became seldom mentioned as a cause to be promoted.

During the 1930s there was a constitutional argument as to whether women, holding peerages which would have allowed men to sit in the House of Lords, should be entitled to do so. Nancy Mitford represents the ferocious Uncle Matthew, Lord Alconleigh, as objecting on the grounds that these liberated peeresses might insist on using the peers' lavatory. Some peers may have shared this apprehension, but it is known that among the Lords there was considerable nervousness as to what sort of a shindy Lady Rhondda might raise were she allowed to take her seat among the Viscounts.

VIII

ENTER, A PROVINCIAL LADY

When Lady Rhondda had a sudden need for a space-filler in *Time and Tide* she felt she could do no better than appeal to Elizabeth, respected as a novelist, and valued for the versatility of her contributions to the magazine. Elizabeth has recorded that she attached a note to her first instalment recommending the waste-paper basket should the editor find it unsuitable. The inspiration for a new line of business had come to her when she was planting the winter bulbs. Reflecting that every woman she knew had been so engaged in November, for years stretching back into the mists of antiquity, she was certain of a response from every other Provincial Lady.

> November 7th [1929]
> Plant the indoor bulbs. Just as I am in the middle of them, Lady Boxe calls. I say, untruthfully, how nice to see her, and beg her to sit down while I just finish the bulbs. . . . Do I know [Lady B.] asks how very late it is for indoor bulbs?

With these opening sentences, Elizabeth not only establishes the sense of immediacy, that something is happening NOW, but also brings to the fore Lady Boxe, the most completely realized character throughout the *Diary*. Lady Boxe, domineering in the manner of a modern Lady Catherine de Burgh, continues to plague the Provincial Lady for the ensuing twelve months.

A few months before the *Diary* opens, the Labour Party had achieved an absolute Parliamentary majority, and Ramsay MacDonald had become Prime Minister. Even more recently, on 29 October, the American Stock Market had collapsed, but from the point of view of Robert, husband of the Provincial Lady, the former event remained more ominous than the latter. Until the Pound shot downhill in September 1931, global finance took second place to what Robert regarded as the near criminal activities of the Labour Government.

Robert, like Paul Dashwood, is agent for an estate, in his case the estate owned by Lady Boxe. Consequently, Robert's wife is obliged to behave towards her husband's employer with a civility she is far from feeling. When Lady B. excuses herself from staying to tea 'as she has to call on such a number of Tenants . . . I seriously think of replying that [Robert] is out receiving the Oath of Allegiance from the vassals on the estate, but decide that this would be undignified.'

Elizabeth admitted herself that the Provincial Lady's children, Robin and Vicky, approximated roughly to her own, but she is generally agreed to have exaggerated the domestic problems with which the diarist battles. That cooks and parlour maids were sometimes poised to give notice is not surprising, considering the sulky range with its ancient pedigree, and the eternally smoking oil lamps which needed to be cleaned daily.

Many of Elizabeth's portraits of husbands bear a close resemblance to Hilaire Belloc's description of an English Squire: 'The man was independent, dull, offensive, poor and masterful . . .'. Robert is not given such a roughing-up, but he is not, admittedly, an intellectually stimulating companion. His response to questions as to what his wife should wear, what he thinks of a new acquaintance, and to the news that a guest is expected, ranges from silence to active disapprobation, as on the occasion when he comes upon his wife experimenting with a new and expensive lipstick. He can only be checked with difficulty from ringing for the cook to complain of lumpy porridge, a course that would be a prelude to the handing in of the cook's notice.

Lady Boxe's hectoring invitations keep her agent's wife in a state of nearly open mutiny. Although the social crimes of Lady Boxe are a source of general disapproval among her neighbours, their discussion is the cement that binds a far from homogeneous community together. Bidden to a dinner party to meet distinguished literary friends, the Provincial Lady issues the warning that should Robert and herself be introduced as 'Our Agent and our Agent's wife', the latter will at once leave the house. She is not driven to such extremes, but on another occasion Lady Boxe refers to her Agent's wife as a Perfect Mother, causing her to be shunned by the assembled company.

Before the literary dinner party the depressed condition of her evening dresses obliges the Provincial Lady to fall back on the help of Mademoiselle, normally employed to look after Vicky, aged six. Mademoiselle makes daring excisions from a dress only too familiar to the neighbourhood, with the idea of making it unrecognizable. To her employer's bleated, '"Pas trop decolleté,"' the French lady replies cheerfully, '"Je comprends, Madame ne desire pas se voir nue au salon."'

To cut pieces out of garments that had lost claim to be fashionable was no solution to the problem of those who, in 1929, wished to bring their wardrobes up to date at the smallest possible expense. For ten years the skirts of evening dresses had been rising ever higher only, as 1930 approached, to begin to descend gently at the back. This fashion, almost more trying to inelegant legs than short all round, was quickly succeeded by hemlines which fell to the wearer's ankles. A crisis of coûture ensued, only to be matched twenty years later by the advent of Christian Dior's New Look.

Having prepared for the dinner party by having her shingled head specially trimmed, to match Mademoiselle's surgery on her dress, the Provincial Lady can only look with loathing on Lady B.'s skirt which touches the floor. Lady B. increases the enormity of her behaviour by announcing that, 'Nowadays, there isn't a Shingled Head to be seen *anywhere* in London, Paris or New York. Nonsense.'

Although Elizabeth allowed Laura, heroine of *The Way Things Are*, to have a small literary reputation, to the Provincial Lady no such label is attached. She therefore meets the neighbours on an equal footing when the best-sellers of the moment are discussed. The company agree that *The Good Companions* is a very *long* book, and that *High Wind in Jamaica* is quite a short book. Lady Boxe's guests then split as to whether any children would just not have noticed that one of their number is permanently missing, having fallen to his death from a window. The Provincial Lady is uncomfortably reminded of this argument as to children's insensibility when her own, on being informed of the illness of Mademoiselle, show a brassy indifference. Vicky merely says, 'Oh,' while her brother Robin, of whom his mother has hoped better things, says, 'Is she?' and asks for a banana.

This exchange with the children takes place when an epidemic of measles has passed through the family, sending them to convalescence at Bude, where Elizabeth herself was to recuperate throughout her life. She had already drawn on her imagination to fill the *Diary* by inducting, as it were, Our Vicar and Our Vicar's Wife, the latter possessing the only too familiar inability to leave when paying a call. Laid low by measles, with the deadline ever inches away, Elizabeth let herself expand on the character of Old Mrs Blenkinsop and her mother-pecked daughter Barbara.

Mrs Blenkinsop has a characteristic which Elizabeth allotted to the more disagreeable females about whom she wrote, a frequently expressed opinion as to their own perfection. This, in the case of Mrs Blenkinsop, is concealed behind a smoke-screen of unconvincing humility, while explaining that she keeps up the morale of her friends by her sunny approach to their problems: 'People say, she adds deprecatingly, that just her Smile does them good. She does not know, she says, what they mean. (Neither do I.)'

It seems to be agreed among visitors to Croyle that Elizabeth was apt to exaggerate her domestic troubles when she sat down to write, and that, though she was herself a small eater, the meals were good and plentiful. There were, however, two crises, which have come down on the authority of the Rugg family, employed at Croyle in a variety of capacities. Frank Rugg once drove to collect a cook and house-parlourmaid from the station, and had to take them back again next day. Apparently the approach to Croyle, over a bumpy field track, gave them a feeling of intolerable isolation. In a reverse situation a rather plump cook once arrived and almost immediately gave birth to a baby.

Another episode in the Rugg saga was an accident in a pony trap, when the pony came home without the trap or Mrs Dashwood. When rescued from the overturned cart by Mr Rugg, she was said to have been making notes of the experience, and the incident was of use as the climax of 'A Perfectly True Story'. The Provincial Lady does not have much truck with horses, transport being by an antique motor-car, which not infrequently behaves with mule-like obstinacy. Arthur Watts's own favourite among his illustrations to *The Diary of A Provincial Lady* was said to have been that of a united family car push.

One of the financial linchpins of the Provincial Lady's frequently tottering budget is the amount for which she is able to pledge a diamond ring, bequeathed by a great-aunt. (She would almost certainly have cancelled the bequest had she known that the ring would spend more time in the hands of a Plymouth pawnbroker than decorating the hand of her niece.) There is, however, a happy occasion when the latter is able to redeem her diamonds. The pawnbroker had reached the stage of facetious intimacy which causes him to inquire, '"And what name shall we say this time?"' Now he glances at the calendar and congratulates the Provincial Lady on being just within the time limit for redemption. Robert has received an unexpected legacy, and for the moment the cloud of debt rolls back towards the horizon.

Matters improve to such an extent that Robert's wife is able to tell Lady Boxe that she is just off to the South of France for a holiday. This definite score on the part of 'our Agent's wife' is countered by Lady B.'s typically downsetting remark that, for the South of France, it is the wrong time of year. Why not make it Scotland? The Provincial Lady is left to concoct a melodramatic fantasy in which Lady B.'s blue Bentley is splintered to atoms in a collision with a motor-bus. The fantasy allows the chauffeur to escape unscathed, but Lady B.'s fate is left uncertain.

Although she describes herself as nearly drowned in an over-ambitious swim to a distant rock, the holiday passes like a happy dream. A slight yearning for an improbable romantic encounter leads the Provincial Lady to meditate that ordinary travel is distinctly different from fictional railway journeys, when handsome, sympathetic strangers are invariably encountered. All the Provincial Lady gets is a painfully wakeful night, owing to a persistent argument in the corridor on the theme, endlessly repeated, 'Mais voyons – N'est-ce-pas qu'un chien n'est pas une personne.'

The dogs in Elizabeth's life were more like personages than merely *personnes*. Seldom was a group photographed at Croyle without a cluster of dogs in the foreground, and frequently the sitters have their arms full of puppies and kittens. The Provincial Lady, however, has only one stray kitten in her household, who quickly becomes the mother of her own kittens and has to be kept as far as possible from Robert's line of vision. Her sex originally misdiagnosed, the kitten's name has to be changed from Napoleon to Helen Wills when she is seen playing with a tennis ball. An expert on the history of lady champions of lawn tennis will at once be able to date the period as post-Suzanne Lenglen, but pre-Alice Marble.

As the *Diary* began to make its appearance, Elizabeth had two other preoccupations, the publication of *Turn Back the Leaves*, due in the early months of 1930, and, even more exciting to her as a new venture, the production at the Ambassador's Theatre of her play *To See Ourselves*. The first volume of the *Diary*, in the meantime, comes to a close with a small and early ball given by Lady Boxe. To her extreme distaste the Provincial Lady finds herself clutching her host-ess's hand while a shuffling circle repeats 'For Ole Lang Sine', the only line known to the company.

IX

TURN BACK THE LEAVES

This novel, which runs from 1890, the year of Elizabeth's birth, to 1929, was published in February 1930. It was dedicated in the warmest terms to 'A. D. Peters, kindest, most efficient and most patient of literary agents'. Considering the high speed of E. M. Delafield's literary production, it would seem that celerity, rather than patience, would be the quality most needed by anyone handling her affairs. The dedication of *Turn Back the Leaves* was followed by an Author's Foreword, which ran:

> The author wishes to state that this book is in no way intended as propaganda, either for or against the Roman Catholic faith. It purports only to hold up a mirror to the psychological and religious environment of a little-known section of English society as it existed for many years, and still exists to-day. No character in the book has been taken from any living counterpart.

It happens that, in a copy of the first reprint (March 1930), a rather unformed hand has underlined 'propaganda' and 'against', adding 'oh yeah!!' in the margin for additional emphasis. Elizabeth might have had some difficulty in handling this sceptical reader.

Turn Back the Leaves begins with a doomed love affair and ends, forty years later, with the old Catholic family it has devastated decaying in their near-derelict, Queen Anne house. Edmunda, the young and beautiful wife of a middle-aged Baronet, Sir Joseph Floyd, falls in love with Lord Charles Craddock, a diplomatist. Although Craddock is in love with Edmunda, he is a womanizer who lacks understanding of the force of her passion and the grip of the Roman Catholic Church on her conscience. Sir Joseph had wished to become a monk, but has been persuaded by his confessor that his paramount duty is to carry on the line of the Catholic Floyds at Yardley.

To Edmunda, a girl from an impoverished Irish family, to find a Catholic husband seemed almost a miracle, the match having been arranged by Sir Joseph's spiritual adviser. Unhappily, she is repulsed by the physical realities of marriage, and the children, which were its purpose, remain unconceived. Edmunda's seduction by Charles Craddock has some points in common with those accomplished by Elizabeth's less aristocratic cads, but he does, at least, face the disaster he has brought about. It is painful to read the harrowing passage in which Sir Joseph comes to realize that the much-wanted child which Edmunda is carrying cannot be his. Finally, the domestic chaplain discovers Lady Floyd in tears, in a broken-down summer house at Yardley, and the scandal breaks.

Priestly counsels eventually convince Sir Joseph that God requires him not only to forgive his wife but to take her back. This he does, her infant daughter, Stella, being maintained elsewhere by Craddock. Sir Joseph, partly out of revenge, conquers his own distaste for sexual relations when Edmunda, broken-spirited, returns to Yardley. Her beauty fades rapidly as she bears three more daughters, dying in childbed at the birth of the longed-for heir. Neither husband nor wife have disturbed the silence which the drama of the past has imposed on them, but Sir Joseph finds himself increasingly in trouble from the conflict between indulgence of his physical nature and the teaching of his Church on purity. The strain eventually affects his mental balance, but meanwhile he marries again, on the advice of his confessor. His second wife, Theresa Delancy, a distant cousin, has supported Edmunda through the scandal of the birth of Stella, and now takes on Edmunda's children, Helen, Veronica, Cassie and Joey, as if they had been her own.

Eight years later, Theresa, the second Lady Floyd, suffers a continual reproach from her conscience that Stella, her godchild, is growing up without the blessing of a Catholic education. It is at this point that Theresa begins to emerge as the real heroine of *Turn Back the Leaves*. Plain and dowdy, thrifty from the force of circumstances, and of limited imagination, she acts up to her own standard when contemplating the spiritual perils of Stella's future. The child has grown up in some luxury, but the nurse and governess supplied by her father are, inevitably, at odds with each other. Stella has learnt to propitiate whichever she happens to be with, and at ten years old the habit of double-dealing has become ingrained.

1. Elizabeth's father, Count Henry de
la Pasture, c. 1895

2. Elizabeth's mother, Mrs Henry de
la Pasture, from *The Bookman*, 1906

3. The Priory, Llandogo, Monmouthshire. Elizabeth's father died here in 1908

4. *Left to right:* Yolande, Elizabeth's sister; their cousin, Dorothea Charrington; Elizabeth. East Butterleigh, Devon, 1898

5. 'Miss E. M. Delafield'. Probably taken when she was in the Red Cross at Exeter in 1917, and reproduced in *The Bookman* in May 1921

6. *Above:* Elizabeth and Paul
Dashwood, Far East, 1919–20
7. *Below:* Elizabeth with Lionel
and Rosamund, Croyle,
Kentisbeare, summer 1924

8. Croyle House, Kentisbeare, from the south-east, *c.* 1930

9. *Left to right:* Rosamund, Cicely McCall, Lionel.
Foreground: Yo-Yo, the keeshound. Croyle, *c.* 1938

10. Elizabeth and Paul at Lady Clifford's house, Villa Rosa, Torquay, during the 1930s

11. Lady Rhondda, founder and editor of *Time and Tide*, 1953

UNDERGO PERMANENT WAVE.

12. *Above:* Drawing by Arthur Watts of the Provincial Lady. From *Time and Tide*, 1932

13. *Below:* Elizabeth with Yo-Yo, puppy and kittens (Anthony and Cleopatrick), *c.* 1939

14. E. M. Delafield by Howard Coster, taken in the 1930s

Theresa Floyd is not stupid, but she follows, unflinchingly, the teachings of her Church. These give her the conviction that she has the Church's sanction in her endeavour to rescue Stella from the damnation of a Protestant upbringing, no matter what the cost may be to herself and her family. 'With a superb courage of which she was wholly unconscious,' she appeals to Sir Joseph for help in fulfilling her duty towards her godchild. The priest, who had been chaplain at Yardley during the crisis of Edmunda's first pregnancy, assists Theresa in her determination to bring Stella back to what had been her mother's home. He does, however, warn Lady Floyd that she is asking much of Sir Joseph, and in time the priest proves to be right. The daily sight of Stella, who has a look of her mother, is a perpetual reminder to Sir Joseph of his first wife's betrayal, and certainly a factor in the increasing misery of his fanaticism.

Stella, made adaptable by the insecurity of her life, settles easily into the routine of Yardley, daily Mass, Benediction, and Feast Day services. Sir Joseph's attitude to his own children is so austerely remote that his aversion to the sight of Stella is barely noticeable. Years at a convent school have had a levelling effect on the four girls. It is only when Stella makes her début at a garden party, a unique event at Yardley, that it becomes apparent that there is a difference between her and the younger girls. Lady Floyd, while treating Stella as a daughter, has decreed that she should be known as a 'cousin', and given Stella her own surname of Delancy, remarking that, among the enormous families of her kindred, one child more or less would cause no surprise.

If the portrait of Theresa Floyd stands on its own throughout the novel, the picture of beautiful, tumble-down Yardley is almost equally important. The broken fences and starveling cattle in the park have their own message of decay, repeated inside the house where the valuable, the beautiful and the shoddy mingle unsorted. Lack of money has contracted daily life to a few rooms, and to the chapel, a converted orangery, where the Blessed Sacrament is reserved. Except for a month or so of summer, the cold of Yardley never relaxes its grip, unabated by a number of oil lamps, which add a burden to the inadequate domestic staff without influencing the freezing temperature.

Upstairs, the children have a refuge with Agnes Martinelli, a former nursery maid, whose superstitions add a spice to the gaunt religion of

Sir Joseph. Downstairs, a doddery Irish butler serves unappetizing dishes from a kitchen where an incompetent cook presides. Meals of stomach-turning horror frequently occur in Elizabeth's writings, but the boiled cod with egg sauce, followed by lumpy custard, a Lenten dinner at Yardley, strikes a particularly low gastronomic level.

An almost equally unappetizing dinner appears on the table of the Protestant Bourdillons: watery soup and underdone cutlets are followed by a gelatinous pudding. Stephen Bourdillon is an architect whose practice is based on his personal charm, which gives him an understandable excuse seldom to dine at home. His daughter Chloë, a girl of indeterminate age, happens to have patronized Stella before the child's removal to Yardley, and her father's acquaintance with Lord Charles Craddock adds a romantic touch to her slightly gloating interest in Stella's illegitimacy.

The garden party for Stella brings Stephen Bourdillon and his daughter to Yardley, he being on a professional visit to the Neville family – new, Protestant, neighbours of the Floyds. Tom and Peter Neville first appear as ordinary young men come to play tennis, but only too soon they turn out to justify Sir Joseph's disapproval of making friends with non-Catholics. They also give some reality to the continual chatter of Stella, Helen, Veronica and Cassie, which circles round 'the two main preoccupations of their lives: the Catholic Church, and their own chances of each obtaining a husband.'

Down the years, Sir Joseph has become ever more detached from family life, his alienation being increased by his habit of seeing profanity or obscenity in the most innocent remarks. He is especially mistrustful of his son Joey, whose adolescent curiosity in sexual matters has been reported from school. Sir Joseph welcomes the invitation from the Bourdillons to Stella to visit them in London. Even Lady Floyd is disquieted to perceive that Stella's presence is all the more odious to her husband in that his religious duty obliges him to suppress his feelings. Theresa, herself unaccustomed to people of professionally charming manners, has accepted Bourdillon as agreeable and a gentleman. She can hardly be blamed for failing to recognize him as an emissary from Satan, who will be instrumental in snatching back Stella into the jaws of the heathen world from which Theresa has so painfully rescued her.

Theresa's own faith is monumental in its grand simplicity, based on the certainty that, for a good Catholic, the will of God will work

out salvation in a race when all can win the prize. Agnes's approach
is more picturesque. She does not hesitate to make her own rules as
to what behaviour will be applauded or condemned by Heaven. When
Cassie wishes for a powder-puff to enhance her first appearance in an
evening dress, Agnes vetoes the suggestion: '"You may be sure Our
Blessed Lady never used a powder-puff."'

The evening in Lent when Cassie celebrates her seventeenth birthday by putting on a low-necked dress ends in a shattering encounter
with her father. Cassie opens the door to Sir Joseph on his return
from seeking spiritual direction at a Trappist monastery. He at once
erupts into fury on the sight of Cassie in an evening dress and with
her hair swept up in curls.

Even more disturbing than his anger at this immoral spectacle is
Sir Joseph's confusion as to who the vision might be. Later Lady
Floyd begs Cassie to pray for her father, so unhappy in spite of his
austerities. Tired and faint from fasting, he had, momentarily, had
the shock of seeing the ghost of Edmunda in her youthful beauty.

Cassie and her sisters have been in the habit of making mild fun of
Agnes's dictum that to bring a Protestant into the Church would
insure salvation, even after sudden death without the Last Sacraments.
Logically, this would mean that to take a Protestant for a husband
might, in time, guarantee the salvation of a wife. In any case, there
would already have been promises to allow the wife free practice of
her religion, and that any children should be raised as Catholics. Earlier in the nineteenth century it was often accepted that, in a 'mixed'
marriage, sons and daughters should follow respectively the faith of
their father or mother. Even in the family of the Duke of Norfolk,
leading Catholic layman, this practice prevailed. After a number of
conversions among aristocratic families, however, such flexibility was
banned. At the time of which Elizabeth was writing, couples who
had not received the sacrament of Holy Matrimony on account of
one party refusing to make the required promises, although legally
married, were regarded by the Church as living in sin. On this rock
romances were not infrequently wrecked.

This problem becomes acute when Peter Neville, son of the Protestant neighbours, becomes engaged to Veronica Floyd. Veronica has
declared her intention of becoming a nun, but she is assured that she
is far more suited to being a wife and mother than a Bride of Heaven.
The storm breaks when the Neville family realize the force of the

promises that will be required, and suggest that Veronica would not find much difference if she joins the Church of England. '"The difference," said Sir Joseph, "is that between eternal salvation and eternal damnation."' Veronica, after unavailing appeals to a variety of religious advisors, takes the risk, and elopes with Peter to marriage by a registrar.

Sir Joseph banishes Veronica from her home, her name to be unmentioned except in prayers, privately, that she may be reconciled to the Church. Having sailed with her husband to India in a state of mortal sin, this is immediately unlikely. Sir Joseph's fanaticism causes him to see even his children as souls in the abstract. It makes an opaque background for the shining faith of his wife, who accepts the troubles that come upon her as part of God's purpose, only visible to mortals as unfitted pieces of a Divine jig-saw puzzle.

To the slight disapproval of his family, Tom Neville, brother of Peter, is studying medicine, with the idea of specializing in the innovatory practice of psychiatry. Changing from his original object of studying at Zurich and choosing, instead, to go to Vienna, Tom appears to have switched from Jung to Freud. He proposes to Stella, now more or less liberated from Yardley, and she promises to marry him when he returns in two years' time, the engagement remaining a secret. Tom is much in love with Stella, but, though he understands the conventionality of her character, he fails to grasp the strain of duplicity developed from the insecurity of her childhood. Tom is able to estimate, only too soon, that Sir Joseph is on the edge of religious mania, but does not assess the opportunism which will cause Stella to jilt him.

Consequently, when Stephen Bourdillon introduces Stella to her father, Charles Craddock's, new, rich wife, she appears as an unattached young lady. Stella finds Craddock as charming as her mother must have done long ago. Overcoming her first distaste at being a social puppet, she allows Lady Charles to adopt her as a protégée, and finds herself more truly at ease than she has ever been in the Old Catholic world of Yardley. Although she assures Lady Floyd that she can remain true to her faith in the world of high society, the only need Stella has of its prohibitions is to break her engagement to Tom Neville, equally unwilling, as was his brother, to make the required promises for a Catholic wedding. Having discarded her first love, Stella accepts the proposal from an older man, with a brilliant political future, but a divorce in his past.

These events take place in the summer of 1914, so the outbreak of war is an excuse to hasten Stella's wedding, for which no church of any denomination can easily be found. Horrified appeals from Yardley quickly fade from her consciousness, seeming to belong to a vanished girlhood. At Yardley itself the rigours are increased by the lack of fuel and food. Cassie, the focal point of the last part of the novel, manages to escape to do war work in Bristol, much as Elizabeth had done. It is from Bristol that Cassie sees off her brother Joey to the Front, and hears that, in his view, their father is practically out of his mind. Even when Joey is reported missing, feared killed, Sir Joseph refuses to accept the possibility, believing that God has willed that his son will carry on the Floyd line at Yardley. It is now that Tom Neville, more percipient professionally than in affairs of the heart, tells Cassie that her father, indubitably, has religious mania. Cassie, who loves Tom with the lack of assertion characteristic of her gentle nature, can only agree.

The ultimate cataclysm at Yardley takes place after Veronica, left a war widow with two children, has arrived for a secret picnic in the Pavilion. It was here, long ago, that Edmunda Floyd was brought to confess her adultery to the domestic chaplain. If her ghost haunts the tumble-down summer house, she might be comforted by the laughter of her children and grandchildren. On the way back to the house, Lady Floyd promotes the recital of three Hail Marys to guide their footsteps in the darkness, and there is every need of spiritual comfort, for when they reach the house they are faced with the most painful scene that even Yardley has experienced.

While they have been secretly entertaining the daughter he has disowned, the cruellest of blows has struck Sir Joseph. News has come that Joey, the heir of his line, has been killed in action, with no priest near to give him the last sacraments. The shock breaks the frail chain which has held Sir Joseph's sanity. Fiercely he pushes his wife to one side, and looses a stream of malediction. He rails at his own denial of his vocation, at the lusts of the flesh which drove him to father children on a wicked woman, and at the curse which has given him no son by his marriage to Theresa. Recovering from his physical repulse, his wife, with the nobility which has always sustained her, leads Sir Joseph away, leaving the terrified household to face this last disintegration of the order of their lives.

It is from Agnes Martinelli that Helen and Cassie finally learn the story that lies behind their father's ravings. The girls, familiar with the moods of the nurse of their infancy, recognize that Agnes has something she feels to be delicate on her mind, but something that she can be persuaded to reveal. Asked who is Stella's real father, Agnes placidly replies, '"Lord Charles Craddock, dear – a Protestant and a very wicked man."' From there it is only a step for the girls to discover that Stella is the daughter of their own mother, Agnes excusing her share in the disclosure by insisting that it is right they should know Sir Joseph was a saint.

Sir Joseph's condition moves gradually towards paralysis, with periodical attacks of mania when he pours out confessions of frightful sexual excessess which he believes himself to have committed. His wife rides out these storms from the greatness of her heart, and the steadiness of her own faith. At the War's end Cassie returns to Yardley, with the hope that she will be able to leave again and find peacetime work. She nurses in her heart the advice of Tom Neville that she should not indulge in a myth of self-sacrifice, though he has been blind that it is in his power to rescue her. Her hopes are sunk when Helen emerges from her usual state of farouche misery to announce that she has found her vocation. She proposes to enter the noviciate of the Poor Clares, offering her life in this, the hardest, Order, as an expiation for her mother's adultery and her sister's apostasy.

If Helen has sacrificed herself in expiation, she has also sacrificed Cassie, who is obliged to remain at home, facing a life almost as enclosed and little less rigorous than Helen's among the Poor Clares. Theresa Floyd is last seen on her way to the chapel, for a brief visit to the Blessed Sacrament, before relieving Agnes in the constant care that Sir Joseph now needs: 'Moving stiffly and with difficulty, she passed up the stairs, and along the top corridor – avoiding unconsciously the worn places in the matting – and pushed open the shabby red baize door that led to the chapel.'

It would be hard to think of a novel in which religious questions are handled with more understanding of different points of view than Elizabeth achieved in *Turn Back the Leaves*. In her earlier novels Roman Catholicism had been an element in a number of the plots, but had been handled much more awkwardly. Among Elizabeth's shorter pieces there are somewhat romanticized pictures of an Irish girl in a Roman convent, and an Irish nun making her meditation. The author is said to have little experience of Ireland, but she had a tendency to see the country through a haze created by the supposed charm of its inhabitants. *Turn Back the Leaves* has none of these faults. Elizabeth may not have grown up in a prototype of Yardley, but she conveys its chilly atmosphere with such skill that it is hard for the reader not to feet a lowering of the body temperature.

The collapse of Sir Joseph into a state when his overwrought conscience fed him with terrible illusions had a parallel in Elizabeth's own family circle, although religion was not the catalyst in the case of her stepfather, Sir Hugh Clifford. When Sir Hugh gave his wife's daughter away at her wedding, his career in the Colonial Service was far from over. It was ten years later, in 1929, that he resigned, giving 'the serious illness of Lady Clifford' as a reason. For the two years before his resignation, he had been Governor of the Straits Settlements, High Commissioner for the Malay States, and British Agent for Borneo. Those who came in contact with him in these capacities were well aware that his mental balance was precarious. It has already been mentioned that he was suffering from what the *Dictionary of National Biography* calls 'cyclical insanity'. The tragedy becomes even greater when it is remembered that he was regarded by his fellow Colonial servants as an able administrator, and by Joseph Conrad as a friend with a deeper knowledge of the Far East than Conrad could claim for himself.

During the last phase of Sir Hugh's service overseas he had occasion to entertain a global tourist on whom the impression made by his host's mental state caused Sir Hugh, in a manner of speaking, to be immortalized. Noël Coward, for this was the world tourist, made use of his experiences in a number of plays and sketches, one of which, 'Mad Dogs and Englishmen go out in the Mid-day Sun', may be said to have passed into the language. During the Second World War, Coward happened to be dining with the playwright Terence Rattigan, and Jeoffry Spence, a young man who, although already an admirer of E. M. Delafield, hardly expected to find a link between Noël Coward and her stepfather. Coward told his companions that he had been entertained by an extraordinary man, practically a maniac, Sir Hugh Clifford, and that this experience had transmuted itself into 'Mad Dogs and Englishmen go out in the Mid-day Sun', the biggest hit in the show *Words and Music*. The appearance of a Colonial Governor and his staff belting out the song among the palm trees always drew ecstatic applause from an excited audience.

Turn Back the Leaves was greeted by reviewers with almost unanimous praise, Elizabeth's renown having been increased by *The Diary of A Provincial Lady*, running concurrently in *Time and Tide*. Almost the only disapproving voice came from Elizabeth's local paper, the *Tiverton Gazette*. While acknowledging that Miss Delafield had, as usual, written a clever and realistic novel, the reviewer found that the book did not make pleasant reading, and even took refuge in the novel reviewer's dug-out of despair by inquiring if the story was worth telling.

This was practically the only discordant voice. Both *The Times* and the *Times Literary Supplement* were in agreement over the lucidity of character created in Sir Joseph and his children. The *TLS* added, 'but Theresa is magnificent.' *Time and Tide* and *Punch* concurred in this opinion. The former thought Theresa particularly well done, and the latter that she was 'the triumph of the book'. From these examples it will be seen that *Turn Back the Leaves* was given consideration as an important novel by a writer who had developed in authority and power of characterization. This was a promising start to a year in which Elizabeth drank deeper of success than ever before, including a draught from the heady waters of the theatre.

X

AT THE AMBASSADOR'S THEATRE

Within a week of beginning her *Diary*, the Provincial Lady makes a note that she has received the Book-of-the-Month, chosen by the Book Society. She finds it to be 'the history of a place I am not interested in by an author I do not like.' Her irritation is increased when, seeking a replacement from the Recommended List, she is warned, in a special bulletin, that it would be 'the mistake of a lifetime' to reject the Choice. Depression sets in at the idea that she is merely one of a flock of readers whose reaction is easily predictable to the composer of a Book Society Bulletin.

The writer Hugh Kingsmill once expressed, to fellow writer Anthony Powell, his dislike for the articles that the critic and novelist Charles Morgan was then contributing to a Sunday newspaper. Powell asked him what he would say if, on the following Sunday, Morgan's article was devoted to praise of a Kingsmill book. '"In that case," said Kingsmill, "I should consider the whole question of Morgan's status as critic reopened on an entirely new basis, bearing in mind the fresh evidence to be considered."'

Coals of fire might be said to have been heaped on Elizabeth's head when, in December 1930, *The Diary of a Provincial Lady* appeared in book form, and was promptly chosen by the Book Society as the Book-of-the-Month. Whether or not she felt that she had to make the same readjustment as Kingsmill, she did leave a comment which may be quoted:

It never rains but it pours, and I always feel that it was rather a pity that Fate chose to arrange for the production of my play [*To See Ourselves*] at the Ambassador's Theatre within a week of the Provincial Lady's appearance as the Book-of-the-Month. As a near relative said, watching my excited and bewildered reaction to so much unwonted success: 'You remind me of the French simile: Un âne entre deux bottes de foin.'

This may have been Yoé's judgment on the double accolade, but sounds more like a remark of Elizabeth's 'matternal Parent'.

With this donkey's choice before her, it is likely that the bundle of hay Elizabeth would have chosen might have been the intoxicating sight and sound of the curtain raising on characters she had created, speaking words which she had written. *To See Ourselves* was an immediate success, broadcast on more that one subsequent occasion and included in Gollancz's *Famous Plays of 1931*. This was an annual publication, and, to show the competition which Elizabeth faced as a playwright, it is interesting to examine the two most famous plays in the collection.

The Barretts of Wimpole Street, by Robert Besier, is the one that is probably best remembered, and most often revived by professionals and amateurs, though the number of Barrett sons presents a handicap in its casting. In the original production there was an audience attraction in the appearance of Elizabeth Barrett's spaniel, Flush, played by Tuppenny of Ware. Besides the ready-made story of Elizabeth Barrett's elopement with Robert Browning, there is a strongly dramatic situation in her revolt against Mr Barrett's psychological bullying of his family. The climax is pointed up by Mr Barrett's incestuous feeling towards his daughter.

The other extremely popular production was *Autumn Crocus* by C. L. Anthony (Dodie Smith, in her subsequent career as a playwright). Austria, not yet generally notorious as Hitler's homeland, had become fashionable for holidays among those who prided themselves on their discernment. The *Lederhosen* and brightly embroidered braces of Tyrol had an appeal probably started five years earlier, when the first act of Margaret Kennedy's *Constant Nymph* had opened on an Austrian Alp, so touchingly that the audience dissolved into tears and remained sobbing until the final curtain. *Autumn Crocus* is less of an immediate tear-jerker, but the school-teacher heroine, already losing her youth (played by Fay Compton), also loses Franz Lederer, a Tyrolean inn-keeper in bright braces. There are several opportunities for a good cry, hardly lightened by the young couple, originally played by Jessica Tandy and Jack Hawkins, who insist in flaunting their unmarried relationship to the discomposure of other visitors.

To See Ourselves could hardly be more of a contrast to the above examples of sexual turmoil and frustrated holiday romance. Addicts of *The Diary of a Provincial Lady* who had been hoping to watch Lady Boxe or Our Vicar's Wife in the flesh must have been disappointed, but the refinements of domestic observation would not have been lost on them. Today the play's realism, which satisfied the audience in 1930, has retired into fantasy, the action played out against a lost social landscape. In this world people appear to make themselves impossibly uncomfortable in upholding standards already eroded by strong tides of change.

Although redeemed by occasional kindliness, Freddie, the husband of the heroine of *To See Ourselves*, comes close to the squire described by Hilaire Belloc. The curtain rises on the drawing room in which Freddie (Nicholas Hannen) and Caroline (Marda Vanne) are engaged in a duet, if it can so be called, when Freddie is absorbed in the *Morning Post* and is unresponsive to his wife's speculation as to whether she should change her hair style, or if she is starting a cold. The rapid onset of the cold itself is to play a vital part in the drama.

Freddie approves of the *Morning Post*, whose consistent policy is to show the Government led by Ramsay MacDonald in the worst possible light, though his attention is thereby inevitably drawn to news items designed to exasperate him. Trouble is also expected at the small paper mill which Freddie owns, and Caroline, whose depression mostly comes from lack of excitement in her life, is stimulated by the thought of industrial unrest. Dressed for dinner in a frock which does nothing for her fading prettiness, Caroline holds the stage with an appeal to the work force she imagines to be on strike at her husband's factory. Thinking herself to be alone and speaking in the manner of Richard II, 'I will be your leader . . .,' she finds that the young man who is trying to marry her sister, Jill, has suddenly entered the drawing room.

Between Caroline and Owen, the suitor of her sister, a flirtation develops, partly inflamed and partly handicapped by the influenza which overcomes Caroline at the end of the second act. Her efforts to induce Freddie to grasp that his wife is passing through an emotional crisis are continually frustrated. When asked how he would behave if Caroline fell in love with another man, Freddie replies that there are none available, except the Vicar who is over seventy.

This anti-climax comes from Freddie's complaisance at having settled a strike which had never been a real threat, and his attitude further upsets Caroline. As she gets ready for bed, Freddie wanders in and out from his dressing room, discarding his clothes in an unglamourous male strip-tease. His wife, meanwhile, anoints the pillows of their double bed with Vapex. Complaining of the perpetual disappearance of his toothpaste, Freddie has arrived at having replaced his stiff evening shirt with pyjamas, when he is astounded to find his wife in a state of hysterical collapse. His search for toothpaste has now to be extended to include the thermometer.

Growing up in literary circles, and with a fluent command of French, it is unlikely that Elizabeth had not read *Anna Karenina*, published in a French translation as early as 1877. Elizabeth's revelations of domestic disorder sometimes seem to have an echo in the opening page of Tolstoi's novel, when the head cook is inexplicably absent, the under cook and the coachman have given notice, and the English governess is seeking another post. Princess Obolonsky, the mistress of the house, is momentarily distracted from her distress at her husband's affair with their former French governess by the need to engage a temporary cook and to ensure that fresh milk for the children will be collected. Elizabeth's housewives do not, at least, have to cope with marital infidelity but on the other hand Prince Obolonsky is in such deep disgrace that he would not dare to ring for a servant, the threat which continually hangs over the head of the wife of Freddie.

It is not suggested that Elizabeth saw *To See Ourselves* in terms of a Russian tragedy. She called the play a domestic comedy, but the comedy is, in practice, limited to the behaviour of Freddie. His greatest pleasure is in calculating the time that it will take Jill, his sister-in-law, and Owen, her admirer, to drive from Devonshire to London, paying particular attention to possible hold-ups on the way. Before she sets off on this designated route, Jill faintly impresses Freddie with the idea that he and Caroline have sunk into a rut whose boredom has nearly driven his wife demented. Jill suggests that an expedition to Granada, and the vision of the Alhambra by moonlight, might raise the couple out of their present tedious routine. Geography means little to Freddie, but he does suggest a Continental holiday, perhaps with the opportunity to visit the scene extolled by Jill. 'Wasn't it,' Freddie says, bringing down the last act curtain, 'the Eiffel Tower by moonlight?'

The fame of the Provincial Lady was now so widespread that the critic of *The Times* (most probably Charles Morgan, so unloved by Kingsmill) could refer to Freddie's likeness to 'Robert' with confidence that his readers would grasp the allusion to another unresponsive husband. This critic also applauded the incongruous effect of Caroline's tragic face being covered with a mask of cold cream when she is about to burst into tears. On the whole, it seems that the personality of Freddie, as portrayed by Nicholas Hannen, carried the play, though Marda Vanne as Caroline was warmly praised. The rather priggish part of Jill was taken by Helen Spencer, whose performance as another younger sister, Paulina in *The Constant Nymph*, had been considered as the best in that play by its author, Margaret Kennedy.

Punch approached the play as a feminist tract, and demanded a counterblast from Mr Somerset Maugham. The reviewer was also somewhat uneasy at E. M. Delafield's declaration that 'every Englishman is an average Englishman', but concluded that a well picked foursome gave themselves and the audience a very jolly theatrical game. The *Manchester Guardian* grumbled slightly, but thought that the success of the play would be due to women's delight in the spectacle of Freddie being made such a dunderhead. Whatever women may have thought, it is reassuring to know, on the authority of Jamie Hamilton, that Paul Dashwood treated the show with impersonal good humour.

A year later Elizabeth gave an interview to the *Western Morning News* as advance publicity for the production of *To See Ourselves* at the Theatre Royal, Plymouth. She said that the theme of the play had developed from the contemplation of the dull lives endured by many women, buried in the country under a wet blanket of domestic cares and unresponsive husbands. She added that she had been lucky, both in the company at the Ambassador's Theatre in London and in the touring company that was coming to Plymouth. She would have been justified in adding, though unlikely to do so, that it was the skill with which she observed the world around her that had laid the foundation for this dazzling theatrical success.

XI

THE LITERARY CIRCUIT

Six months after *The Diary of a Provincial Lady* had had its spectacular triumph, and while the second round of the diarist's adventures were appearing serially, Elizabeth published her nineteenth novel. Having put so many of her deeper feelings into *Turn Back the Leaves*, it is hardly surprising that Elizabeth should have written *Challenge to Clarissa* in a lighter mood. Were it not for the almost vicious portrait of Clarissa Fitzmaurice, the book might be called knockabout. This rich harridan, having bought a reluctant ne'er-do-well, Reggie Fitzmaurice, as a husband, bullies the life out of his daughter, Sophie, and her son by her first marriage, Lucien Marley.

Clarissa's brassy confidence in the power of her money is a contrast to the ramshackle family of international aristocrats headed by the Princesse de Candi-Laquerrière, whose daughter, Aldegonde, had made the original mistake of marrying Fitzmaurice. The Princesse insists on refusal, when she hears that Clarissa is prepared to settle £5,000 on Aldegonde if the latter agrees to be divorced, adding a message that, in a year or two, Clarissa may need the money to pay someone to take Fitzmaurice away. Actually, Clarissa's only true emotion is her love for Fitzmaurice, one of the most outrageous of Delafield cads. Although this leads to her apparent defeat, the reader is left with an uncomfortable feeling that the only cure for Clarissa's bullying insensitivity would be death.

Those who knew Croyle agree that, in *Challenge to Clarissa*, Elizabeth lovingly painted a faithful portrait of her own house, decorated as she would like to have had the means to do. She bestows the house on a charming spinster lady, Miss Silver, who not only has created an elegant background for herself, but whose hospitality includes 'admirable coffee'. As far as coffee was concerned, Elizabeth was sadly conscious of her own deficiency, and in this she was not alone, after-luncheon coffee being notoriously a pale and unattractive brew in many English country houses.

The final challenge to Clarissa takes place when her son, Lucien, and Fitzmaurice's daughter, Sophie, insist that they can only love each other. Clarissa makes a terrible row about non-existent incest, but meets her match in Sophie's grandmother. The Princesse checkmates Clarissa by settling the money designed to support her own old age on Fitzmaurice. With the resource of an income of his own, Fitzmaurice threatens to leave Clarissa if she does not allow the marriage. Struck on her Achilles heel, represented in every sense by Fitzmaurice, Clarissa capitulates, and the fairy story, complete with wicked stepmother and benevolent grandmother, comes to a happy ending. Only Lucien and Sophie, the fairy-tale young couple, do not quite carry the weight that they should from a romantic point of view, finding it hard to face the idea of life without the cushion of Clarissa's money.

Besides describing her own home as she might wish it to be, Elizabeth also sketched in the wife of Clarissa's agent, who has a yearning to evoke 'a spirit of festivity and adventure' from the quiet and monotonous daily round of the perpetually hard-up. Young Mrs King has done her best to make her children fascinating by calling them Rosalind and Orlando, but their stolidity is a sad trial to their mother's fanciful spirit. Mrs King gets more excitement from consorting with her sister-in-law, Olivia, a reasonably successful novelist, who shares her home with a highly educated friend, Elinor Fish.

Miss Fish is a dynamo of energy in all local activities, and is slightly baffled that her friend's books should be consistently published while her own cultivated and witty efforts languish in a drawer. Otherwise, the couple's friendship has survived several years of a joint household. Equally, they have weathered, 'as Miss Fish resentfully observed, the fuss about *The Well of Loneliness*, that had put so many normal and respectable single women under the wholly unnecessary strain of being obliged to consider the breath of scandal with regard to relationships into which such a thing had not hitherto entered.'

Speaking, as it were, through the mouth of Miss Fish on the subject of *The Well of Loneliness*, Elizabeth was making a point of far more importance than the question as to whether this essentially dreary book should be widely distributed. Those who agitated for its suppression would have done far better to reflect that the greatest argument for or against a ban was not the possibility of corrupting the innocent, but the obvious inconvenience that the public fuss was bringing into many blameless lives. Elizabeth's women friends included Virginia Woolf, who published two of her books of literary criticism, and Kate O'Brien, who was to be a rock of support in the last hard years of her life. Both of these writers are known to have had lesbian relationships, but Elizabeth herself was always interested in men. Assuming that, throughout an American tour, Elizabeth suffered, as did the Provincial Lady, from perpetual questions as to what she thought about Women, American Women, all Women, the Provincial Lady's comment would apply to both herself and her creator: 'I have never taken the subject of Women seriously enough, the only problem about them in England being why there are so many.'

Towards the end of 1931, when a national crisis had rocked the country, Elizabeth achieved the liberation of a flat of her own in London. Doughty Street was the address, an area of Bloomsbury distinct from the Squares of Mecklenburgh and Gordon, where Stracheys and their subsidiaries lived as if behind a palisade of intellectual spikes. Elizabeth's immediate neighbourhood was, however, inhabited by creative artists in considerable numbers, among them Constant Lambert and Anthony Powell, who both began their married lives in flats round the corner from Doughty Street. St George the Martyr, Queen's Square, might be considered as the focal point of this subsection of Bloomsbury, so much so that when Frederick Ashton and three friends gave a Christmas Tree party the large guest list was limited to past and present Parishioners, the invitation reading 'R.S.V.P. or no present'.

Elizabeth's new independence seems to have been accompanied by a determination to free herself from domestic shackles. Cicely McCall, when staying in the flat, was almost outraged to find that it was Elizabeth's practice to go out for breakfast to the nearest Lyons tea-shop. Cicely firmly installed a kettle, but Elizabeth never became more than a tentative cook. From this new base she did, however, increase her circle of literary friends, and benefit professionally from her widening reputation.

In the meantime, back at Croyle, Paul was relieved from having to entertain people who, in the words of A. P. Herbert, 'If they're not reading or writing, they're painting or singing or acting.' Unfortunately there is no record of Paul's feelings when Leonard and Virginia

Woolf come to stay, presumably on one of the journeys to promote the books of the Hogarth Press, which often took them to the West of England. Rosamund, on the other hand, remembered the visit as a vivid disappointment. Devoted to animals, she had been delighted with the idea that Wolves were coming to stay. She found herself snubbed by Mrs Woolf, who was unattracted to children, and had no wish to make friends with such a lively extrovert as Rosamund.

Dorchester House, Park Lane, a sombre mansion only visible when the doors in its high walls were opened, had, by the summer of 1932, been replaced by the Dorchester Hotel. It was in this hostelry, still gleaming with newness, that *Time and Tide* gave a huge party for readers and contributors, with the offer of tea to be followed by a debate between distinguished *litterateurs*. It was an entertainment at which Elizabeth/E. M. Delafield/ the Provincial Lady made an arrival, as a troika, at 4 pm on 16 June and, in their triple capacity, were summoned to help Lady Rhondda receive the guests.

As Elizabeth not only gave an ecstatic account of the occasion in the Provincial Lady's Diary, but also wrote a report for *Time and Tide* itself, it is almost impossible to disentangle fact, reportage and fiction. The party was held in the Spanish Grill, which was actually more famous for sherry coplas than for tea, but to the Provincial Lady, 'Extraordinary and unsuitable association at once springs to mind here, with Tortures of the Inquisition.'

Among the guests was Bernard Shaw, but whether he remained for the debate is unrecorded though problematical. The debate itself, subject not mentioned, was approached by Elizabeth as she might have felt when faced by an actual Torture of the Inquisition. Harold Laski cleverly pre-empted the first speech by claiming that he had a train to catch. Assuming Elizabeth was describing her own feelings at having to speak after Rebecca West and Stephen Gwynn, it is pleasant to know that she was encouraged by catching the eye of an American publisher, presumably Cass Canfield to whom she was to dedicate the current volume of the Diary. With his support, she managed to survive the nightmare of any late speaker on an occasion when every possible aspect of a subject has already been covered.

This party in the Spanish Grill appears to have been the first time that Elizabeth met two friends who were, in different ways, to become important in her life. Lorna Lewis was lending a hand in the party's organization, and she rapidly came to lend a hand in many other phases of Elizabeth's life and home. According to Cicely McCall, Miss Lewis was really keen on being described by Elizabeth in her own character. Consquently, when she bobs up in a number of books and sketches it is safe to assume that the portrait is close to life. As will be seen, she was invaluable both as a secretary and a long-distance chauffeur, though her sudden storms of temperament made for crises at awkward moments.

Rosamund, when at her first boarding school, had enjoyed being petted as the clever little daughter of a famous mother, and a distinct asset to the establishment. Later, she came to the conclusion that there was another side to being the child of someone so much admired. Devoted as she and Lionel were to Cicely McCall, their feelings about Lorna Lewis were moderate, not to say tepid. The girl who bustled about the Spanish Grill, with no hat on her pretty hair, seemed to Elizabeth both charming and efficient. To Elizabeth's children she seemed, as time went on, to intervene too much in life at Croyle, and they suspected that their father felt the same. Possibly, they thought that to have someone frequently in the home who had created for herself the position of an honorary aunt, was superfluous to a family well supplied with the commodity. With the remorselessness of growing children they ignored Lorna Lewis's kindness in meeting them from school, and only knew that she had usurped a function that, in their eyes, belonged to their mother.

The other acquaintance made by Elizabeth at the *Time and Tide* party was reviewed very differently by Lionel and Rosamund, and remained to them a yardstick against which they measured worldly success and its enjoyment. Hamish Hamilton had recently become head of the publishing house of that name, which he had founded. Jamie Hamilton became deeply attached to Elizabeth, not only as a delightful guest for his luncheon parties, but as someone who was thoroughly at home in the literary and publishing circles in which their professional lives were spent. It was to Jamie that Elizabeth confided her belief that her writing came from the depth of an emotionally unsatisfied nature. She even went so far as to say that this was the spring of her creativity, and that, had her life been otherwise, she would have found the need to write far less imperative. Remembering her early career as a novelist, and her persistence through adverse circumstances, it is hard not to feel that Elizabeth was underestimating the force of her 'demon', as

Kipling has called the irresistible spirit which drives a writer forward.

If Elizabeth was fortunate in making two new friends on that June day at the Dorchester, she also had the pleasure of a talk with an old friend, to whom she had already dedicated a novel, *Jill*. Their friendship was affectionate, and Elizabeth did not hesitate to use the triple personality of the distinguished writer of crime stories as an opportunity for the Provincial Lady to find herself in the midst of surrealist speculation. Asked if Francis Iles is present, and having expressed ignorance, she is assured that Francis Iles is really Mr Aldous Huxley, only to have this information contradicted by a deluded know-all who insists that Francis Iles is really Miss Edith Sitwell.

It must now be explained that A. B. Cox, to whom *Jill* had been dedicated, wrote much enjoyed detective stories under the name of Anthony Berkeley, presumably his Christian names. It was, however, as Francis Iles that he won most fame as a writer of psychological thrillers. Thirty years later Rupert Hart-Davis, from whom no pen names were hid, enlightened George Lyttelton during one of their enjoyable exchanges on the subject of re-reading. After thirty years, Hart-Davis wrote, he had still found that *Malice Aforethought* by Francis Iles held his interest. Lyttelton replied that he had also thought *Malice Aforethought* 'awfully good', but added that he could never remember who Francis Iles might be.

Hart-Davis explained that there was a writer called A. B. Cox/Anthony Berkeley/Francis Iles, to which Lyttelton responded by quoting the opening sentence of *Malice Aforethought*, and asked if his former pupil was not impressed by this feat of memory. Hart-Davis responded that he was, indeed, impressed, and would have been even more so if his old preceptor had quoted the immortal sentence correctly: 'It was not until several weeks after he had decided to murder his wife that Doctor Bickleigh took any active steps in the matter.'

These exchanges show how much respected, in the world of criminological writing, Cox/Berkeley/Iles continued to be. Having received a dedication from Elizabeth, as A. B. Cox, Anthony Berkeley riposted with the dedication of *The Wychford Poisoning Case*, 'To E. M. Delafield, Most delightful of writers,' adding that this tribute was her due, as the book owed much to their discussions about the psychological roots of crime. Dedications, as will be seen, continued to be exchanged, though Elizabeth, except for a play for radio, *The*

Little Boy, which was based on the Crippen case, never again advanced into the shadow of murder. E. M. Delafield was, however, prepared to act on Francis Ile's advice as to how tension might be increased in a novel mostly concerned with adventurers and adulterers.

XII

THANK HEAVEN FASTING

At the *Time and Tide* party the official announcer punctuated the names of the guests by the refrain 'Lady Rhondda receiving', as it might be the response of a litany. Having shaken hands with the Editor, the guests then found themselves being greeted by Miss E. M. Delafield as the label she had been bidden to wear informed them. Many, if not all, of those attending the party would know of her as one of the magazine's most popular contributors. Many would recognize her as the author of *Thank Heaven Fasting*, a novel published less than a month before, and may even have noticed that the book had been dedicated to Lady Rhondda, the hostess who was, that afternoon, receiving them.

In a note attached to the dedication, Elizabeth explained to Margaret Rhondda that the idea of the novel had grown out of their many discussions on the fate of young girls with no future except matrimony, only to be achieved by meeting suitable *partis* in society. The agonies involved had given Margaret Rhondda an impetus towards a formidable feminism, after a marriage that had lacked happiness. Elizabeth had not married early, and looked back with a slightly neurotic horror at the years of her unsought girlhood.

The first section of *Thank Heaven Fasting* is called 'The Eaton Square Tradition', and conjures up the atmosphere of the oblong of cream-coloured stucco, perhaps the most regularly laid out among what *Muirhead's London* describes as 'the solemn squares' of Belgravia. The period of the book is contained strictly between the historical landmarks of the Boer War and 1914, though neither of these disturbances intrude on the story of Monica Ingram. Some Eaton Square houses could almost be considered as small palaces, notably a vast mansion long inhabited by the bachelor Mr Ferguson. This possessed not only a ballroom, but a conservatory reached by a marble staircase, to which a touch of informality had been added by a number of pennies set at random in the marble steps. The Ingrams' house is on a less pompous scale, but the social assurance of Mr and Mrs Ingram is equally solid.

In earlier books, Elizabeth had dealt with the tyranny of possessive parents, but by the time she came to write *Thank Heaven Fasting* she had learnt to pare inessentials away from her style. The two types of maternal tyrant, Mrs Ingram and her co-chaperone, Lady Marlowe, the former smothering her pretty daughter with over-anxious care, the latter bullying her plain daughters with good-natured contempt, are, in their individual ways, blood-chilling. Buying the book for her own mother's birthday, a girl up at Somerville College, Oxford, decided that it would be an impossible gift for a daughter to offer a mother. No obstacle had been placed in the progression of this particular daughter to the emancipation of Oxford, but she had the inescapable feeling that *Thank Heaven Fasting* would, as a birthday present, be both insensitive and unfilial.

From her earliest years, Monica Ingram has been instructed by her mother never to fall in love with anyone who is not 'quite, quite', her parents' circle being composed of people who are 'quite, quite', in every way like themselves. As Monica's debut comes nearer, Mrs Ingram's fears have something in common with those of that otherwise wildly dissimilar mother, Mrs Peachum, in *The Beggar's Opera*:

'In a very great passion,' Mrs Peachum sings,
    'I wonder any man alive will ever rear a daughter! . . .
    'And when she's drest with Care and Cost, all tempting fine and gay
    'As Men should serve a cucumber, she flings herself away.'

Mrs Ingram would never have expressed herself in such a forthright manner, but the same apprehension can be seen to be lurking at the back of her mind.

Monica's mother dictates that young men must be met with an agreeable show of interest, but not with an obvious exercise of come-hither. Girls should appear to be pleased, rather than be seen to be attempting to please. Inculcated with this point of view, Monica has also before her examples of two unhappy girls who have grown up to be unattractive to men. Mrs Ingram has cultivated Lady Marlowe, a rich widow with no difficulty in surrounding herself with attentive males. Her daughters, Frederica and Cicely, can only be called non-starters in the matrimonial stakes. Elizabeth had briefly examined the theme of a sister's overpowering possessiveness in a short story 'Oil Painting, 1890', but now she develops the idea, the obsessive protection of Cicely by Frederica almost driving the latter to the verge of insanity.

The account of Monica's coming-out ball, which her mother shares with Lady Marlowe, is a *tour de force*. Undressing for a rest beforehand Monica reveals that she does possess young, hot blood by a brief contemplation of the curves of her figure, and when she appears before her father dressed 'As Men should serve a cucumber', he begins to wonder if she will not soon be snapped up. At the dinner party before the ball, Monica struggles to follow her mother's instructions in making conversation. Elizabeth understood the difficulties. Her own mother's injunction, 'Be natural', had always had an unnerving effect on herself and Yoé. An even worse example of maternal fussing has been recorded of Mrs Adeane, one of the Three Graces in Sargent's famous group, who, on observing that a daughter was sitting tongue-tied, would hiss 'T.O.R.K.' down the length of a dinner table.

At the ball itself, the Marlowe sisters, dispirited veterans of several Seasons, droop their way through the evening, but to a certain extent the dew still lies on Monica. She has been told to dance only with young men approved by her parents, and at this ball she finds no difficulty in obeying orders. At the White City Fun Fair, however, she has the misfortune to meet Captain Christopher Lane, neither a suitable young man for her to know, nor one who abides by the rules of the Ingrams' world.

A ride down the water shute, famous as a frightening pleasure of the White City, gives Captain Lane an opportunity to put an arm round Monica. Thrilled by this tribute to her charm, she accepts that he has been awakened from a mood of disillusion by the delightful prettiness of the débutante Miss Ingram. Captain Lane makes an assignation to meet Monica at Ranelagh, but by this time her parents have been alerted to his unsuitability, even as a dancing partner, for the daughter on whom they have lavished such quantities of 'Scarfs and Stays, and Gloves and Lace', as Mrs Peachum so furiously sang.

Admonished to have nothing more to do with this detrimental, Monica's fancy is sufficiently smitten for her to write to Lane, giving him a list of places to which she will be going without her parents. The trysting place he chooses is the dentist's waiting room, and in this unusual setting for a romance Monica falls in love with an abandon due partly to her inexperience and partly to the excitement of being treated as a grown-up woman by a man of ambiguous background. Even the slight shock when Lane suggests that he might bribe her maid to keep silent about their meetings does not warn Monica that she has actually fallen in love with one of the 'not quite, quite'.

Monica's naïveté leads her to suppose that her admirer will propose marriage, and for one week she lives as a story-book heroine, contriving to meet her lover in such blameless surroundings as the National Gallery. At what will be for Lane and Monica the last ball of the Season, she promises to evade her mother. Monica is not much in demand, and she is even grateful to dance with Herbert Pelham, a dull 'spare man' of solid physique and uncertain age. Finally, she escapes with Christopher Lane onto the roof garden. Here they are alone, and with her senses stirred by Lane's kisses, Monica forgets Mrs Ingram, fidgeting in growing anxiety among her fellow chaperones.

A terrible scene follows, with Mrs Ingram in floods of tears. To quote Mrs Peachum yet again, 'Our [Monica's] a sad slut! Nor heeds what we have taught her,' practically expresses Mrs Ingram's feelings. She believes that Monica's flirtation will ruin the poor girl socially, almost as badly as if she had actually been seduced. Monica, submerged in waves of guilt, finds that she has made herself cheap with a cad and bounder. Captain Lane exits from the imbroglio with a masterly letter of vulgar side-stepping. 'Darling little Monica [he writes] I'm afraid I got you into trouble with your lady mother last night. . . .' At the age of eighteen the wretched Monica has been duped, with no reassurance from her parents that life will go on and that time will heal.

Gloomy years follow, while Monica, a defeated tortoise, sees contemporaries hareing ahead of her to the goal of matrimony. A new male friend does, at first, raise bruised hopes that he will have serious intentions, but Carol Anderson, in his wet way, turns out to be as much of a deceiver as Captain Lane. He represents himself to Monica as sensitive, rich with intuition, and with an unusual capacity for suffering. These imagined qualities enable him to talk of his devotion to an unattainable married woman, without apprehending his own self-deception. Monica, originally accepting his confidences as an honour, grows in disillusion, but her self-esteem clings desperately to someone who is, at least, a presentable escort.

The death in an accident of Mr Ingram, and the abandonment of his widow to an agony of grief, are further trials for Monica. Into the shadowed life of the Marlowes, however, a ray of light comes, temporarily, when a young doctor attempts to rescue Cicely, introverted, but with undeveloped intelligence, from the domination of the neurotic Frederica. Lady Marlowe, one of E. M. Delafield's fiercest portraits of domineering mothers, consents contemptuously to the marriage, merely disinheriting Cicely for accepting someone from a world remote from her own. Regarding her daughters as better left to themselves, Lady Marlowe refuses to interfere when, in a final victorious burst of possessiveness, Frederica rivets the fetters on Cicely and breaks off the engagement.

It should, perhaps, have been mentioned earlier that the title of *Thank Heaven Fasting* comes from Act III of *As You Like It*. In a scene of androgynous complication, Rosalind, who would, of course, have been played by a boy, is disguised as Ganymede. Phebe, who would also have been played by a boy, has fallen in love with the boy she supposes Ganymede to be. Rosalind, in a boy-meets-boy, boy-loses-boy situation, gives Phebe a tremendous bawling-out for spurning the love of the devoted Silvius. Possibly, Elizabeth felt that the novel was already too harrowing for her to insert, as an epigraph, the lines in which Rosalind/Ganymede abjures Phebe:

> But, mistress, know yourself: down on your knees,
> And thank heaven, fasting, for a good man's love:
> For I must tell you friendly in your ear,
> Sell when you can: you are not for all markets.

Although the market in which Monica might hope to sell seems to have disappeared, condemning her to life imprisonment with a widowed mother, painfully aware of Monica's unwed state, there is help at hand. Herbert Pelham, stout, prosy and middle-aged, has, during Monica's brief spell of success, lain hull-down below the horizon. To Monica, older and sadder, he now appears as a deliverer, instead of a barely tolerated dancing partner.

Thank Heaven Fasting is, on the whole, a harsh book. The humour is generally tart, but Mr Pelham's proposal of marriage takes place in a sudden burst of comedy. Wandering in the New Forest, under a starlit sky, Monica, accustomed to answering Herbert mechanically, suddenly hears the Order of Release: '". . . so that, having made my little confession, I ask you, Monica, most earnestly, if you will become my wife."' To what Mr Pelham has confessed Monica remains in ignorance, and so does the reader. On Monica's part, grateful acceptance leaves no room for curiosity. Rosalind would, undoubtedly, have applauded her decision.

The excitement of the engagement and the wedding plans revive the prettiness which had first attracted Mr Pelham to Monica. Between the bride and her mother discussions are kept on the surface, with the fiction that Herbert, so solid and 'quite, quite', represents the Real Thing for which Monica has been waiting. Only on the night before the wedding does Mrs Ingram let down her guard, with an appeal that Monica will promise her to be happy, even if this marriage is not the one of which mother and daughter had once dreamt. Monica assures her mother that she will be happy, and her feelings when she goes up the aisle to exchange vows with Mr Pelham confirm her new sense of security: 'There was no need to be afraid or ashamed or anxious any more.' She is watched by the Marlowe sisters, now forever prisoners of Frederica's possessiveness, but even the past derision with which the three girls have regarded the bridegroom cannot detract from the triumph of the bride.

Although the *Times Literary Supplement* put *Thank Heaven Fasting* below *Little Red Horses*, a rather creepy novel by G. B. Stern, E. M. Delafield was praised for her ability to sustain the reader's interest in characters leading a life of unrelieved tedium. There was some grumbling about the grimness of the story. Ralph Straus, in the *Sunday Times*, for example, used the word 'solemn' twice in his review. The blurb had perhaps laid too much emphasis on the Edwardian background of the story, for the *Daily Mail* objected with violence to this 'catchpenny talk about Edwardian', without which, the reviewer insisted, the story would be much more gripping. There was what the author herself might have called a 'General Impression' that the creator of the Provincial Lady had no business to unmask such powerful batteries.

XIII

THE HOTEL, THE SCHOOL,
THE STAGE

Of the places Elizabeth had visited along the Côte d'Azur, it was Agay, roughly half-way between St Raphaël and Cannes, which seems to have made the most appeal to her literary imagination. She used the seascape of red rocks, burning against the blue of the Mediterranean, in more than one story, and finally made it the background for one of her most carefully constructed novels. This book she was able, in 1933, to call *Gay Life*, without there being any question of ribald remarks. Compared with *Jill* (1926) not only is the style more tightly knit, but any leniency for a young couple living on their wits has disappeared. For the unemployed ex-officer in *Jill*, it was possible to feel that he deserved to be rescued. The young couple in *Gay Life* exist in a state of moral anarchy, surrounded by characters hardly less depraved than themselves, and Elizabeth felt no need to write of them with pity or kindness.

A number of novelists have found the unity imposed by setting the plot in an hotel a useful device for bringing diverse types together. Vicki Baum's *Grand Hotel* and Arnold Bennett's *Imperial Palace* are two which Elizabeth had certainly read. She represents the Provincial Lady as absorbed in *Grand Hotel* when she ought to have been doing several other things. Elizabeth herself wrote a take-off of *Imperial Palace* among the sketches which she called *The Sincerest Form*. . . . Capturing the style of one of Bennett's less meritorious works, she wrote; 'The night manager was at his post. He was an Italian, of French extraction, with a Polish father, no mother, and some Anglo-Indian cousins.' Elizabeth had obviously not neglected contemporary studies before she set herself to create the Hôtel d'Azur.

Gay Life opens on a raucous note which is sustained throughout. The son of *la patronne* shatters the peace of the hotel's siesta with a wild shriek, ' "*Maman, j'ai râté l'autobus!*" ' At the third repetition of this cry of disaster the hotel, its staff and its guests are thoroughly awakened, and the elements which lead to the final tragedy are already apparent. In a book which was dedicated to Francis Iles, and owed something to his advice, it is appropriate that some of the characters should be tottering on the edge of criminality, financial and moral. This establishment is a jungle, whose elemental savagery surpasses that of Vicki Baum's *Grand Hotel*.

New arrivals, the young Moons, have some money, earned by Hilary Moon as a *maquereau*, as their only immediate resource, and the beauty of Angie Moon as their only capital. Depending on an ability to cut a dash for the support of their frail credit, Hilary regards the acquisition of a motor-car and a speed-boat as practically an economic necessity, while Angie has eyes that can calculate the wealth and sexual potential of every male who crosses her range of vision. She immediately catches the attention of Buckland, himself a sexual adventurer, but just at the moment on velvet as holiday tutor to the son of Coral Romayne. Patrick Romayne has an almost visible hatred for Buckland, whose flirtatious behaviour with Patrick's mother, a fast-fading beauty, is edging its way towards an affair.

Patrick's only happy times are spent with the Morgan family from Monmouthshire, who are having a once-in-a-lifetime holiday. Mary Morgan has financed the excursion from a legacy, her husband only agreeing from a sense of justice. The elder Morgan children are perhaps slightly too idealized, but Gwennie, at nine years old, is one of Elizabeth's most successful portraits of a tough little girl. Sunburnt, chubby, and spoilt by visitors and staff, she collects general sympathy, particularly among the French, when her mother refuses to take her to Monte Carlo. Mary Morgan utters an appeal to her daughter to be a good child, but Gwennie is implacable.

'Everybody else is going. Dulcie is.'

'I thought you didn't much care for Dulcie.'

'I simply loathe her. That's why I don't like her to go, and me not.'

Confronted with this fresh evidence of Gwennie's lack of principle, Mary felt more helpless than ever.

The unpopular Dulcie lives the harried life of an hotel child, Mr Courtney, her father, being a courier and manager of recreations for the guests. This allows Dulcie free board, but also exposes her to the neglectful contempt of the waiters. To them she is a blank card in the game of jockeying for tips. Courtney, speaking perfect French, and playing the piano competently, makes his living by oiling the social wheels. There is a sinister side of his character, which appears when he recognizes Denis Waller as a young man whose unacknowledged, and seldom visited, wife lives opposite Courtney's London lodgings.

The relationship between Denis Waller and Chrissie Challoner, yet another reasonably successful novelist, is part of a secondary plot which Francis Iles thought might be expanded. Denis is a fantasist who poses as an accomplished man of the world but lacks the physique or stamina to carry off his pretentions. He is, temporarily, secretary to Mr Bolham, 'with a reputation as a savant in his own circles – London Library circles.' Mr Bolham, having engaged Denis out of laziness, makes little attempt to conceal his irritation with the unfortunate chap's mixture of incompetence and sycophancy.

The link between Chrissie Challoner, in her rented villa, and Coral Romayne, in the hotel, takes the form of Miss Challoner's secretary-housekeeper, Mrs Wolverton-Gush. Ageing, overweight, and perpetually hiding her feelings from those on whom her livelihood depends, Gushie is almost as pathetic a figure as Denis Waller. It is she who has persuaded Mrs Romayne to engage Buckland as a holiday tutor, and extracted a commission for fixing the job. She is thus in a position to tell him that he had better suppress his lust after Angie Moon, or he will find himself out on his ear. Gushie has also to repress her feelings on the subject of Denis Waller, to whom Chrissie Challoner has taken a capricious fancy. This situation was the one that Francis Iles thought might profitably be exploited, but Elizabeth went no further than to allow Denis to accept an adolescent but amorous advance from Dulcie Courtney. Her father surprises a feeble exchange of kisses, and reveals that the wretched Denis is a married man. Consequently, he loses both Chrissie and his job.

On the other hand, Elizabeth took up the challenge from Francis Iles when he asked if she would have the courage to send Buckland into Mrs Romayne's bedroom, Patrick, in the room next door, finding his suppressed fears to be realized. There has been a happy moment for Patrick when he has reason to believe that Buckland, stigmatized as 'terribly foul' by the Morgan children, is about to elope with Angie Moon. This indeed happens, Buckland having won enough at Monte Carlo to buy Angie from her husband. With *la patronne* remorselessly dunning him for the hotel bill, Hilary Moon has no choice but to agree to the transaction. Unfortunately, Buckland decides to lull Mrs Romayne's suspicions by a pacifying visit to her bedroom, and Patrick, monitoring the situation, cannot face further existence. After seeing the Morgan family start for home, he drives his mother's enormous Buick over the edge of a cliff and into the Mediterranean.

Both *The Times* and the *Times Literary Supplement* were rather condescending, almost perfunctory, about *Gay Life*. On the other hand, in *Time and Tide*, R. Ellis Roberts gave the book more consideration. He pointed out that Patrick, the tragic adolescent, might be thought to be the character most deserving of pity, but Denis and Dulcie should not be overlooked among the noisier visitors to the hotel. Denis, humiliated by Chrissie and by his employer, has to face the prospect of returning once again to his secreted wife, jobless, and with the knowledge that Courtney will be his opposite neighbour. Dulcie, beaten by her father for an ill-judged attempt to work up a romance with Denis, is now destined for some cheap school, where the hotel child can hardly fail to be a misfit. As R. Ellis Roberts wrote, it is hard for the reader not to feel any sympathy for such a couple of permanent losers.

When the Provincial Lady establishes herself in London, her son Robin is still a preparatory schoolboy, while his sister, Vicky, has only just bullied her mother into choosing a school which will emancipate her from Mademoiselle. The models for these children were in somewhat different situations, Rosamund having already passed on to Mickleham from the school where she had been the show specimen as the daughter of a famous mother. Lionel was on the point of following his father to Rugby, and an insight into his life there can be found in a collection of sketches, mostly from *Punch*, which appeared in 1937.

Reflections on the sad state of a man married to a writing wife, as seen by his male friends, and complaints about the furtive habits of the Directors of Banks, both occur in this collection, *As Others Hear Us*, but the liveliest essays concern *Charles, Laura and Another*. The Other is, of course, Elizabeth herself. Laura can be equated with Lorna Lewis, who was not only deeply embedded in Elizabeth's fiction, but also in the everyday life of the Dashwood family. Charles is a rather endearing projection of Paul Dashwood, in his role of Old Rugbean, visiting the Old School.

The party having found the son of Charles and Another, Charles proceeds to extract what pleasure he can from an occasion supposed to be a festival. He deplores any softening of traditional practices. He is particularly depressed to hear that boys are no longer tossed in a blanket, ritually, in the Headmaster's garden, though Charles is slightly cheered to be assured by his son that boys due to be beaten still ascend to their doom by a particularly gloomy staircase. The father's pleasure is, however, dampened by the boy's admission that he has not, himself, suffered this penalty.

After a wistful reminiscence of the agonies he had undergone in the School Sanatorium, when smitten by an outbreak of carbuncles, Charles catches sight of a contemporary, now a Bishop, for whom he expresses an unabated dislike. Time never reduces Charles's distaste for survivors from the Old School List. His *bêtes noires* remain untinged by grey, but such nostalgia as he has for Rugby as a school, rather unexpectedly surfaces in a joke, or rather in an ungrammatical pun. What, he inquires, is the name of that poem about a school? When Henry Newbolt's *Clifton Chapel* is put forward, Charles says, contentedly, 'He ought not to have said "Clifton for aye!" he ought to have said "Rugby for me!"' It can only be hoped that Lionel shared enough of this robust sentiment to support him through his school days.

Although Elizabeth had moments of insisting that the children of professional women should be raised by those who had graduated in the exacting school of child care, she was far from free of nervous agitation on behalf of her own. She obviously shared the Provincial Lady's habit of running at the sound of the telephone bell, convinced that the call will presage either wonderful good fortune or terrible accidents to her children. Perhaps it was to shed the load of these fears that Elizabeth engaged a holiday tutor for Lionel and Rosamund, and he accompanied the Dashwoods on a holiday in Brittany. Its rigours were such that, when Elizabeth was sitting to Arthur Watts for some Provincial Lady illustrations, all he had to do was ask her to imagine that she was on holiday with her family. The drawing of Robert and his wife, sitting on a sofa in the Casino at Dinard, showed that Watts got the expression he wanted. Elizabeth said that it was a totally accurate picture of an evening out of unrelieved horror. The holiday tutor was far from being such a sexual athlete as the loathsome Buckland in *Gay Life*. Using the language of a later generation, Rosamund described him as a wimp.

Ever since the triumph of *To See Ourselves*, Elizabeth had hoped for another success as a playwright. In February 1932 she did have a second chance, when *The Glass Wall* was produced at the Embassy Theatre, Swiss Cottage, but the play did not reach the West End. *The Glass Wall* was preceded by Strindberg's one-act play, *The Pariah*, a far from cheerful curtain-raiser. Uncheerful curtain-raisers were something of a policy at this theatre; *Genius at Home*, a play in which Thomas and Jane Carlyle struggled with their domestic difficulties, was introduced by a playlet in which a business man committed suicide only to find he had entered a life identical to the one he had left.

With *The Glass Wall*, Elizabeth turned yet again to the subject of a religious vocation. In her early novel, *Consequences*, and in her masterpiece, *Turn Back the Leaves*, she had examined the question from two different angles. Five years later she was to set down a factual account of the failure of her own vocation, but in writing *The Glass Wall* she obviously felt that there were dramatic possibilities in this past experience which might lead to another theatrical success. The nuns, who had assured her that they expected her return to the convent would be granted as an answer to their prayers, found, in time, that they had been mistaken. If *The Glass Wall* had ever come their way as a printed play, which is improbable, they might have thought it fortunate that a deaf ear had been turned to these particular petitions.

When Elizabeth left her convent she had only spent months under its discipline, but in *The Glass Wall*, an image of the barrier between the world and the Order, she dealt with a more poignant situation. Stella, child of a 'mixed marriage', has joined an enclosed order of nuns, partly to escape from an admirer, to whom she is drawn, and partly under the influence of the Reverend Mother. The young man presses for marriage, but refuses to agree that any children should be brought up as Catholics. The Reverend Mother's remarkable personality so impresses Stella that she convinces herself that she has a vocation, which is the end of the first act.

After ten years in a Brussels convent, Stella's dedication to the enclosed life is wearing ever thinner, and only her secret conviction that she is Reverend Mother's chosen child of her heart enables her to endure the hardships and petty jealousies among the sisters. The crisis comes when Reverend Mother is ordered to South America to found a new house of the Order, a sentence of exile for life. Stella breaks down at the prospect of separation, and in a terrible scene with Reverend Mother she confesses not only her loss of vocation, but her agony at the thought of losing the object of all her love. Reverend Mother admits her own mistake in allowing such a situation to have come about, but she also totally rejects Stella, having painted an intensely gloomy picture of Stella's homelessness, spiritual and physical, if she does return to the world.

Reverend Mother's assessment of Stella's predicament as a spoiled nun appears, at first, to be only too true. Stella's sister-in-law, piously priggish, has no place in her home for a conventual reject who has lost her bearings, and moves like a zombie in a state of mental paralysis. Stella only finds the affection she has come back into the world to seek when her father, previously a stumbling block in her religious life, and known to have lived in sin, comes to her rescue. The final curtain falls on father and daughter agreeing that they totally need each other.

From this outline it will be clear that there is one big part, that of the Reverend Mother, in *The Glass Wall*, and that the interest of the drama evaporates when she abandons Stella at the end of the second act. Reviewers agreed that Marda Vanne, much admired by Elizabeth, carried the play, but notices were respectful rather than enthusiastic. Elizabeth's hopes of another West End success petered out, although there were effective dramatic moments. Mary Casson, daughter of Sybil Thorndike, was said to have made a gallant, but not entirely convincing, attempt at the part of Stella. The chanting of an Office by the nuns as a background to the wrestling for Stella's soul would have been recognized as a theatrical gambit of respectable ancestry: the last scene of *Cyrano de Bergerac* comes easily to mind. Stella's brother, hen-pecked by a priest-pecked wife, cannot really have been worthy of the great comic talents of Max Adrian. As a writer for the live theatre, Elizabeth may be said to have reached a cul-de-sac, but her career as a writer for the blossoming medium of radio was shortly to give her a new outlet, well suited to her ability to make a quick verbal killing.

XIV

ACROSS THE ATLANTIC, THE
BRONTËS, *FASTER! FASTER!*

Besides the impression of immediacy which adds such force to the Provincial Lady's prose, Elizabeth was also a most cunning manipulator of the cliché. Nowhere is this gift more in evidence than in the reaction of the neighbours to the news that unknown powers in America are actually prepared to finance a lecture tour for such a familiar figure as the wife of Robert and mother of Robin and Vicky. The cliché, and its cousin, the Generally Received Opinion (as E. M. Delafield might have put it), appear as a cross-section of what a rural community in Devonshire thought about the United States in the year 1933.

Contradictory opinions abound, and take the form of advising the Provincial Lady that the Americans like the English, or that the Americans do not like the English at all. Even more frightening than the insistence that to go anywhere in Chicago without a revolver would be highly dangerous – she feels that to go out with a revolver would be even more so – are warnings about alcohol, Prohibition still prevailing. All alcohol in North America, the Provincial Lady is assured, would be wood alcohol, whose consumption will inevitably lead to death, blindness or raving madness. A final twitch is given to the fine-drawn thread of the Provincial Lady's nerves when she is told that, notwithstanding the dangers, it would be unforgivably bad manners ever to refuse a cocktail.

At last, after infinite agonies over domestic arrangements, children, and intermittent comments from Robert that 'this American plan is going to Upset Everything', the Provincial Lady sails. Actually, her journey started before it began by the difficulty of getting up her nerve sufficiently to break the news to Robert, though fate does this for her by arranging for Robert to take down a telegram that gives the show away. Guilt at leaving her family, even though doing so to win bread on their behalf, combines with sea-sickness to reduce the traveller to a sorry state of pulp, but the welcome of the New World assuages these pains.

Cass Canfield, to whom *The Provincial Lady Goes Further* was dedicated, must have had great confidence in the popularity of Elizabeth's voice from the English Provinces to support her in an American tour, at a time when echoes of the crash of 1929 were still reverberating through the economy of the United States. Canfield was, at that date, in his early thirties. He was the galvanizer of the firm of Harper's, subsequently Harper & Row. His faith in Elizabeth was justified. The Provincial Lady records that she met with the kind of welcome that made her wish she could inform her neighbours at home how high her stock stood in New York. Her complacency was checked by the conviction that the neighbours would reply in unison, 'Yes, they had always heard Americans were Like That.'

Interviews are continuous in the case of the Provincial Lady, and there is no reason to suppose that Elizabeth suffered from anything less intensive. There is a note of personal experience in exchanges with a female literary critic of considerable renown. Talking of books, the Provincial Lady praises Virginia Woolf's *Flush*, only to be told that to write a whole book about a dog is Simply Morbid. A reference to the possibility of lecturing in Chicago merely causes the critic, Miss Isabel Paterson, to look at the floor and mutter, 'Yes, Club-women, large women with marcelled hair, wearing reception gowns.'

It was not so much 'Clubwomen in reception gowns' who pursued the Provincial Lady throughout her tour, but the repeated inquiry as to her opinion of *Anthony Adverse*, the best-selling historical novel of 1933. Not having read this block-buster, the diarist's condition begins to approach nervous hysteria. She could not even have had the comfort of the clerihew composed a year or two later by Constant Lambert:

> *Anthony Adverse*
> May not be bad verse,
> But God knows,
> It's bad prose.

There is a tricky moment when, invited to meet a Mr Allen, the Provincial Lady assumes that she will have to explain her lonely position, as a non-reader of the mammoth novel, to its author, Hervey

Allen. Mercifully, the introduction is to a charming Frederick Lewis Allen, author of *American Procession*, a work of a very different calibre. Persecution on the subject of *Anthony Adverse* continues up to the moment of sailing, when it tops the pile of books given her for the voyage. She does not record that she threw this literary Hound of Heaven overboard, but the steward, formerly of the SS *Mentor* of the Blue Funnel Line, would surely have added this to his attentions had she requested it.

The itinerary which the Provincial Lady follows is both ferocious and labyrinthine. New York, Chicago, with the World's Fair, Cleveland, Ohio, a dart over the Canadian border to Toronto, with Niagara included, Buffalo, Boston, Mass., Washington DC, and a return to New York, are all breathlessly covered between 4 October and 2 December. It cannot be found surprising that many instalments were written in the early morning, E. M. Delafield sitting up in bed, her portable typewriter nursed like a baby on her lap.

Elizabeth had always had a devotion to children's books of the nineteenth century, regardless on which side of the Atlantic they had been written. Particularly attached to Louisa M. Alcott, she was also fascinated by the home life of the Alcott family. She gave to the Provincial Lady the triumph of overcoming obstacles put in her way when she demanded to visit the Alcott house at Concord. She might, indeed, have been defeated, had she not had the unexpected support of Alexander Woollcott. His patronage strikes as much awe into the promotors of her lecture tour as does the attentions of her friend the steward into her table companions on board the SS *Berengaria*.

It is at a Tea – cocktails and sandwiches – in Manhattan that the Provincial Lady meets Mr Woollcott, who was already a most respected figure in literary circles and on the radio. Although he had not yet played the lead in *The Man Who Came to Dinner*, which was based on his personality, and gave a new phrase to the language, he could pick and choose from the work humbly offered him. The Provincial Lady is much impressed by Woollcott briefly breaking off their conversation to take a telephone call, and even more impressed by his refusal to accept any more work, even on the highest terms. She must, herself, have made more than a transitory impression on the literary dictator, for in her revolt against being swept along on a wave of public relations, it is Woollcott who comes to her rescue.

A *leitmotif* of the Provincial Lady's tour is the frequency with which she is assured that, like all her fellow countrymen, she will adore Boston because it is so like England. On her arrival the City of Boston lies under thick snow, which is hardly the diarist's idea of England in November, although she does recollect that the heroine of a favourite book, *An Old Fashioned Girl*, goes tobogganing down the steep hill of the Common. On putting forward her wish to visit the Alcott House, the publicity manager of her publisher assures her that the arranged schedule allows no time for such frivolity. Without actually kicking and screaming, the Provincial Lady makes a tolerable shindy, which induces two young girl reporters for the *Boston Evening Transcript* to mention, in that journal, that the diarist's chief object in coming to America was to see the home of Louisa M. Alcott.

T. S. Eliot has remarked that 'The readers of the *Boston Evening Transcript* sway in the wind like a field of ripe corn.' Alexander Woollcott, if not among those who swayed, must certainly have been among the readers on that November evening. Learning of the Provincial Lady's laudable ambition, he announces that, if she will send him her reaction, he will 'Mention It in a Radio Talk'. At the prospect of this accolade, difficulties evaporate. The Alcott House at Concord, previously said to be hermetically sealed for the winter, opens with a flourish and proves to be all that could be hoped. Miss Alcott's surviving relation allows her visitor the full run of the shrine of *Little Women*, surrounded by silence and snow, with never a gasoline-station in sight. The Provincial Lady, to cite another classic, passes as easily into the world of the March family as Alice passed through the Looking Glass.

The Provincial Lady in America was the only book to be published by E. M. Delafield in 1934, after which the diarist went underground, only to emerge again at the outbreak of the war. The lecture tour of America can be read as a fairy story, and none the less enjoyable for that. The delicate balance by which Elizabeth manages to be grateful for the hospitality of kind and intelligent hosts without sacrificing her gift of sardonic comment, could be compared to dancing on eggs. The next assignment from Cass Canfield showed that he, at any rate, had not lost his enthusiasm for Elizabeth's potential, but in the meantime she contracted to write a book for a very different publishing house to either Harper & Row or Macmillan.

Although she had brought out no novel in 1934, Elizabeth had contributed more than fifty pieces to *Punch*, the temptation of relatively easy bread and butter probably slowing her production as a novelist. She was also working on one of two books which were to be published by Leonard and Virginia Woolf at the Hogarth Press, where a series of new biographies was in preparation 'on a system different from the usual. The life of the person concerned presented entirely through the eyes of his contemporaries.' This publisher's note laid down a principle for an enterprise in which the first volume on *Charles Lamb* was edited by the poet Edmund Blunden, and the second, *The Brontës*, was produced by E. M. Delafield.

The Preface, contributed by Elizabeth, is, like the compilation itself, well constructed, and deals with important points for which notes would have cluttered up the text. Mrs Gaskell's *Life of Charlotte Brontë* must always remain the main source for understanding the family at Haworth Vicarage, in spite of her omission of Charlotte's unhappy passion for M. Héger of the *pensionnât* in Brussels. Elizabeth, however, has assembled excellent quotations, which further illuminate Mrs Gaskell's story, or, in some cases, offer evidence of the limitation of her opinions.

On the subject of Branwell Brontë, and his possible share in the writing of *Wuthering Heights*, Elizabeth takes up an extremely sensible attitude. Branwell, a shiftless boaster and fantasist, would, she points out, have been most unlikely to have the staying power to write any book, although she concedes that he might have convinced himself that he had done so.

Mr Nicholls, the curate who became Charlotte's husband for less than a year, does not really appeal to Elizabeth, though she admits that, to a woman of that date, he stood for 'that supreme symbol of feminine achievement – a wedding ring'. Elizabeth also writes, rather pensively, that Mr Nicholls's position as a husband for genius is one that 'has never yet been filled with grace unalloyed'. With her entirely practical assessment of her own talent, it is hard to believe that she would have seriously claimed genius for herself, in the sense that she applied it to the Brontës. If she felt that there was a trace of Mr Nicholls in Paul, she had at least been allowed time to enjoy their reciprocal affection, their children and their home. Charlotte, on the other hand, died in the later months of her first pregnancy, her symptoms possibly suggestive of pernicious vomiting. With her the Brontë line became extinct, and the Reverend Patrick was left alone with his ghosts.

Forty years after the Hogarth Press brought out *The Brontës: Their Lives Recorded by their Contemporaries,* Jean Rhys emerged, from what had been supposed to be her actual tomb, to write *The Wide Sargasso Sea,* a book far removed from the largely autobiographical novels which had been admired in the 1930s. Whether Elizabeth would have accepted Jean Rhys's story of the career of mad Mrs Rochester, from her drowsy West Indian childhood to her salamander's end, cannot be known. With her fancy for take-offs of established reputations, she might have found the approach of the columnist Peter Simple to the Brontë family more to her taste. She would surely have enjoyed reading, in the *Daily Telegraph,* of the melancholy Julian Birdbath, who, together with his toad Amiel, sits at the bottom of a mine-shaft while he endeavours to trace 'Doreen, the missing Brontë sister'.

Faster! Faster! (1936) could be called a study in a self-deceiving woman, less abominable than the matriarch in *Challenge to Clarissa,* and more sympathetic than the calculating Lydia of *The Heel of Achilles.* Claudia Winsloe, a dynamo of energy, runs a business, London Universal Services, which solves domestic, secretarial and scholastic problems with an efficiency that might well have been the envy of the Provincial Lady, and, indeed, of her creator. Not content with acting Napoleonically in the office, Claudia runs everything in her home with an equal tyranny. Her husband, another unemployed ex-officer, remains in a state of disgruntled emasculation, while one daughter is being harried into a job for which she is unenthusiastic, and the other is prevented from spreading her wings. Their little brother, one of Elizabeth's poignant studies of a worried small boy, is chronically distressed at the sight of his mother over-working.

Faster! Faster! ('however fast they went, they never seemed to pass anything' – Lewis Carroll) might almost be considered as a warning from Elizabeth to herself not to allow the role of Atlas to distort her sense of proportion. One incident does, however, seem to be based on a paper and pencil game such as used to be played at Croyle. The Winsloe family play Qualities, always a tricky choice, in which the company gives each other marks for honesty, humour, sex-appeal, and so on. Claudia, who frequently stresses her total honesty, even against her own interest, is incensed that her average has been brought down by an unknown enemy, who has given her two out of ten for the quality on which she most prides herself.

At Croyle the same game was played, but it is remembered as

having had to be abandoned, for a rather different reason. Elizabeth scored highly for Intelligence, Humour, and other respectable qualities, but her chagrin at getting consistently low marks for sex-appeal was so obvious that her family thought it kinder to change to a game with less perilous implications. As an attractive woman, admired by a large circle, male and female, Elizabeth had good reason to feel annoyed. Few people, of either sex, can relish the knowledge that they are considered to be virtuous because they offer no temptation.

Elizabeth more than once solves the problems of her novels with the crash of a motor vehicle or even, on one occasion, of horse-drawn carriage. Pushing herself too hard, Claudia comes to her death in a collison between her motor-car and a tram. As might be expected, the family and the business get on very well without her. The fatal accident that ends *Faster! Faster!* is exceptionally opportune, and enables the survivors to arrange their lives along lines particularly deplored by Claudia. When the book appeared Elizabeth had, herself, moved with far more effect than Alice and the Red Queen. She had sailed for Russia in the first week of May 1936. If reviews were posted to her, and, even more problematically, if they arrived, they must have seemed messages from another planet at the Commune near Rostov-on-Don, where her persistence allowed her to spend some weeks of mixed discomfort and fascination.

STRAW WITHOUT BRICKS

No one could have had more belief in E. M. Delafield's ability to extract humour from the harshest circumstances than Cass Canfield, her American publisher. Taking Elizabeth out to luncheon at an expensive London restaurant, he laid a proposition before her which, at first hearing, appalled her. Canfield suggested that Elizabeth should go to Russia, stay for six months (a preposterous period) on a collective farm, and record the experience in a humorous book. No one, he insisted, had been funny about Russia, and while urging Elizabeth to assume the mantle, or at least the overcoat, of Gogol he softened his approach by ordering caviar and a bottle of champagne. Bleats of objection, that she would certainly not be allowed to join the workers on a collective farm, were brushed aside. Canfield was positive that the visit could be arranged, showing both a callous indifference for the comfort of one of his star authors, and a fine disregard for Soviet policy towards foreigners.

Canfield's technique of alternately bullying and coaxing was a shrewd tactic when dealing with someone whose convent education had left her with an ineradicable conviction that the thing which she did not want to do must be done. As it turned out some of Elizabeth's Russian experiences had echoes of the Brussels convent which she had left more than twenty years before, not least in the lesson of bearing hardships without murmuring. Her reward was the privilege of a prolonged close-up of Russian farm life, almost certainly a unique experience for someone of her nationality and social background.

Elizabeth felt both the need to respond professionally to this challenge and the pressure to help to keep her family afloat by her earnings. Neither she nor Canfield can have had a clear idea of the life she would be facing when she actually got down to the reality of her assignment. The previous year had seen the infliction of a man-made famine on the kulaks of the Ukraine, which had strengthened Stalin's grip on the USSR. The Revolution was set to devour not only its children but its parents, by political purges which did not spare the most loyal party members. The tightening of the bonds of tyranny was reflected in an increase in the difficulties foreign visitors had to face if they wished to stray beyond the limits laid down by the Intourist Bureau.

It was this obstructionism that Elizabeth found herself immediately confronting, having left her husband, her children and, it might almost be said, the Provincial Lady, in the rural peace of Devonshire. An application for a 'worker's visa' was flatly refused. She may have made the mistake of admitting that she knew some Russian, when filling in the requisite form. (Another visitor, taxed with a knowledge of Russian which he had denied in his original application, foxed the officials concerned by pointing out that the visa's issue had been so long delayed that he had had time to learn the language.)

In the summer of 1936, ships for Leningrad sailed from London Docks, under the upraised Tower Bridge, 'down Greenwich reach past the Isle of Dogs', as described in section 270 of *The Waste Land*. On board the SS *Jan Rutzutak*, Elizabeth was fortunate to find the Baltic calm. Later in the summer rough weather delayed the SS *Smolny*, making her last, leaking, voyage, for over twenty-four hours. Elizabeth would, however, have appreciated the *Smolny*'s library, or rather one volume that had found a most unexpected home among the works of Lenin and Stalin. Charlotte M. Yonge was, as will be seen, one of Elizabeth's favourite authors. She would certainly have been delighted to find on board any boat a copy of *The Heir of Redclyffe*. Whatever chance had deposited Miss Yonge's best-seller among works devoted to World Revolution, it can hardly have been due to the fact that Guy Morville, the hero, was descended from Hugo de Morville, a slayer of Thomas à Becket.

Elizabeth's own choice for reading on the voyage was *Bleak House*, which depressed her so deeply that she even wept at the death of the rather deplorable Rick. As an alternative to *Bleak House*, she had been given a variety of handbooks on the marvels of democratic progress she might expect to meet in the Union of Soviet Socialist Republics. One booklet, in particular, extolled the camaraderie to be found on board a Russian ship. Having imagined evenings when passengers joined with the captain and crew in singing the songs of their re-

spective countries, Elizabeth was disappointed to find no fraterniza-
tion. Only a lady from the Middle West, christened by Elizabeth with
the evocative name of Mrs Pansy Baker, attempted to exchange ideas
with the lower deck. Mrs Baker was an ardent upholder of Com-
munism, but her lack of Russian, and the crew's lack of English,
inhibited any fruitful exchanges.

Elizabeth's hopes that her suggested stay on a collective farm would
prove impracticable were strengthened when the Soviet official to
whom she had an introduction assured her that she was asking the
impossible. An untrained hand would be merely an encumbrance on
the farms which were now at their busiest. He did not add that the net
designed to contain foreign travellers was being increasingly tight-
ened, with the object of minimizing contacts with ordinary working
comrades. At each apparently insuperable obstacle, Elizabeth's heart
leapt up at the prospect of a liberating failure, but conscience forced
her to persist. Finally, she found herself slipping through an undetected hole in the fence that was supposed to keep Capitalist serp-
ents out of the Socialist Garden of Eden.

Directed to Rostov-on-Don, by a member of the United States
Embassy in Moscow, she was bidden to contact an American married
to a Russian wife. He had been a pioneer in establishing the Seattle
Commune twelve years previously. From Seattle he had led a group
of workers who, dissatisfied with conditions of employment, or the
lack of it, determined to set up their own commune. Tackling, yet
again, the problem of making contact, Elizabeth met with the stone-
walling technique immemorial in Russia: 'He is away', or 'There is
no reply', rebuffs which probably greeted the Mongol invaders in the
twelfth century when they demanded to see the Keeper of the Keys
of the State Treasury.

Under the knout of conscience, Elizabeth managed to meet the
Russian wife of the Seattle pioneer. She then found herself obliged to
be grateful for the blocking of her last escape route. With most un-
Russian celerity, her new acquaintance defeated the rearguard action
fought by the Intourist Bureau with its last-minute objection that
'They are all away at the farm'. The Seattle Commune agreed to
welcome Elizabeth the following day. It can be speculated that the
wife of the American pioneer had reasons of her own to wish that an
independent observer, with literary connections, should pay a visit to
the Commune. In the summer of 1936, visitors could still be taken to

inspect collective farms, under strict supervision. A single, untrammelled foreigner was a rare bird, and Elizabeth's account of life on the farm will explain why.

Following the tradition of indomitable British female travellers, Elizabeth set out 'hard class' from Rostov-on-Don. After seven hours she reached a tiny station whence a young man, speaking only Russian, drove her bumpily across limitless prairie. Arrived at the Commune, her driver showed her what was to be her room, and she realized that she would be left alone, with urgent needs, unless she acted speedily. Neither Russian nor English conveyed what these needs were, but the driver had the sense to find an Armenian who spoke recognizable American. In the accents of a New York taxi driver, the Armenian asked:

'How-d'you-do? What you want?' – I replied with equal brevity,
  'How-d'you-do? I want the W.C.'
  'Uh-uh?'
  'The water-closet.'
  'Oh, watter-closet! Sure. You see them two buildin's over there? The foist one men, the second one ladies. You'll find electric light, everythin' fine.'

Sensibly, Elizabeth had made a resolution to abandon all squeamishness when she entered the commune, but to be faced with a six-seater lavatory, sited over a cess pit and with no lock on the door, was, she felt, a harsh initiation.

No one, she found, seemed to object to this very public latrine, nor to the equally open plan of the laundry, and the wash house which led out of the latter. Elizabeth described the semi-darkness of the wash house as that of a Spanish Cathedral, and the atmosphere as thick as the Black Hole of Calcutta. She could not bring herself to join the communal washing, but used a bucket lent her by Eva, the most interesting friend she was to make in the Commune. As a contrast to the blocking tactics of the Intourist clerks, Elizabeth met with nothing but kindness and helpfulness from the comrades on whom she had imposed herself. Eva was, however, alone in having an occasionally critical approach to the Communist system. Unlike the comrades among whom she worked, she could concede that there were still imperfections to be removed before Utopia could be deemed to have arrived.

Eva, an Estonian by origin, was in charge of the dispensary, her husband being the Chairman of the Executive Board that supervised the daily working of the Commune. The 'Comradely Courts', which dealt with misdemeanours, were popular and always crowded with spectators, presumably enjoying a form of entertainment in a life of monotonous struggle. It was Eva's opinion that mostly the comrades were too exhausted to develop quarrels among themselves. Those who wished to leave the Commune would be obliged to forfeit a considerable sum paid as a deposit. Elizabeth also discovered that some, like novices in a religious order, as she well knew, were sent away as having no vocation for the life.

Tough on the surface, but essentially kind, Eva in her clinical technique showed a disregard for modern principles of hygiene more complete than that of the dispenser of the convent in Brussels. She gave injections ruthlessly, using potions compounded by herself, and with needles unsterilized. It was from Eva that Elizabeth learned of the terrible struggles in the early years of the Commune, before a desert prairie had been turned into a self-supporting community. Although the settlement had an American name, the inhabitants were really drawn from most Slavonic races, and had only been first-generation emigrants to the United States. One Russian woman had the distinction of having been married to an American for eighteen years without learning to speak, or understand, a word of English.

'Comrade Dashvood' found that, though there was a reluctance to assign her to a particular job, her help was accepted in any work of which she was capable. By this means, she learnt more about the Commune and the attitudes of the comrades. In the past, parties of tourists had come regularly for the day and were shown round the settlement. Elizabeth added the comment, 'I'll lay any wager they didn't inspect all of it.' No such visits, regarded as an interruption in the day's work, with a special meal to be cooked, had taken place for some years, from which Elizabeth, with what was probably correct intuition, deduced that a shadow of Governmental disfavour lay upon the Seattle Commune. This was a matter too delicate to be inquired into, as it might be a temptation to commit that most heinous of offences, 'to speak bad against the Government'.

The original settlers had existed largely on tinned food sent from the United States, but at the time of Elizabeth's visit the Commune was entirely self-supporting. She had decided that it would distort her purpose if she took with her a private supply of food, and she existed throughout on the diet of her hosts. Pasta, eggs, and the excellent bread, which she helped to knead in the bakery, made up for almost inedible chunks of meat. Her health, in spite of the absence of sugar in any form, remained surprisingly good, and she felt no evil effects as a result of drinking water from a tap said, rather dubiously, to be potable.

One of the friends that Elizabeth made in the bake-house admitted that she had, at first, suffered from nostalgia for America. Now that she was acclimatized to the hard life, she found a compensation in being free from the anxiety of finding, and keeping, a job that would enable her to pay her rent. Although Elizabeth, from lack of occupation and mental stimulus, often suffered from intense boredom, the reader is left with a suspicion that the relief of no meals to order and no cook to placate may have given her a slight feeling of holiday.

Inquiries into marital arrangements revealed a far from bureaucratic approach. A couple who wished to live together simply applied for married quarters, one room per family. No couple had more than three children, most only one, which in the cramped circumstances must have been a mercy. Elizabeth offered no reason for this surprisingly low rate of reproduction, beyond mentioning the frequency with which a proposal to repeal the legality of abortion was discussed. Some of the young people were promiscuous in the extreme, in particular the Armenian who had directed Elizabeth to the 'watter-closet' on the evening of her arrival. Eva, the Estonian dispenser, said that he had taken nearly all the girls behind the pig-house, '"not even a very nice place," Eva a added thoughtfully.' This Casanova of the Steppes had left the Commune two days after Elizabeth's advent, but she never learnt if his departure was the result of his sexual athleticism.

When the heavens opened, the Commune became a quagmire. Elizabeth's stoutest shoes were useless, and Eva sent her a pair of rubber boots. This was not a humanitarian action, Eva explained, but insurance against Comrade Dashvood falling ill, when Eva would be unable to look after her. Elizabeth respected Eva's determination not to appear as the kind friend which she was proving herself to be. Eva struggled to grow flowers in the unpropitious soil, but they shrivelled in the summer heat and the winter cold. Elizabeth suggested that Eva might be able to grow hyacinths indoors, and promised to send her some bulbs. It must have seemed a moment infinitely remote from the day when Elizabeth sat down to write, 'Plant the indoor bulbs. Just as I am in the middle of them, Lady Boxe calls.'

During the deluge the comrades, deprived of work, stood about in a silence which they often seemed to prefer to speech. Although she did not, herself, make the comparison, Elizabeth might be said to have arrived, like Gulliver, in a country where Houyhnhnms alone led a life of respected ease. Bred for the Red Army, the horses on the Commune were privileged and pampered. Only occasionally were they required to draw a cart in a dilettante manner. These fine animals were sired by a stallion of whom even the Comrade Groom, who had him in charge, was afraid. The Houyhnhnms were exercised at a gallop by one of the juniors in a work force of five hundred, while a crowd of fellow Yahoos watched enviously.

Smitten by an unexpected attack of toothache, Elizabeth was obliged to ask to be returned to Rostov. She concealed her reason, fearing that Eva would insist on giving her an injection of mysterious composition from an unsterilized syringe. News of the visitor's departure brought about a surge of the Slav creative spirit of entertainment. Eva, shrewdly judging that Elizabeth was used to public speaking, insisted that she should give an address to the comrades, to be followed by a discussion, and a farewell concert.

Grotesquely reminded of the many times she had addressed Women's Institutes at home, Elizabeth was glad to have the opportunity to thank her assembled hosts for their unfailing kindness, adding that, whenever she lost her way, she was much impressed by the helpfulness of Russians in this only too frequent dilemma. The flood of intelligent questions that followed had to be fielded as best she could through the interpretation of Eva. Comrade Dashwood had obviously stirred her audience out of the exhausted apathy into which they were liable to collapse after the day's work. Someone, with an endearing hankering after Royal gossip, inquired after King Edward VIII (then moving towards his Abdication). As if she had heard from him that morning, Elizabeth, with more attention to expediency than veracity, replied firmly that the future Duke of Windsor was 'Splendid'.

Inevitably, the question was asked as to what was thought, in England, on the subject of abortion, not, at that date, a topic acceptable for an address to Women's Institutes. Elizabeth found that the arguments for and against repealing the legality of abortion had taken the place in conversation held by the weather in England. A tram conductor in Rostov, for example, had asked her views when punching her ticket. Foreigners, extreme admirers of the Soviet system, were even known to support the theory that, in the Paradise of the USSR, there was now no reason, social or physical, why any woman should not wish to bear a child. The Russians themselves, Elizabeth concluded, 'found it an interesting subject, well-calculated to promote the social amenities.'

Although Elizabeth had sensed that there was currently some official disapproval of the Seattle Commune, she had never been conscious of any supervision of her movements as she wandered about the farm. A last question put to her at the farewell meeting may, however, have indicated that she had been kept under closer observation than she supposed. A comrade who, she thought, spoke rather aggressively, asked which way Comrade Dashwood intended to vote when the Revolution reached England. By this time Elizabeth had enough Russian to be pretty certain that he had said 'when' and that Eva had tactfully translated 'when' as 'if'. Elizabeth assured the aggressive comrade that a Revolution in England would take a very different form than in Russia, adding that the Communist Party in England was a negligible political force, and that her own sympathies were with the Labour Party, a view she found unwise to express at home.

Eva's translation of question and answer showed her diplomatic skills at their highest level. (It is to be hoped that these skills carried her through the Great Terror, which was looming.) She translated Elizabeth's opening remark, skipped the reference to the Communist Party, and rendered Elizabeth's sympathy with the Labour Party as support for 'the workers'. As Soviet Russia had only 'workers' among its citizens, this was greeted with loud applause as an expression of Communist convictions. The concert that followed was dominated by Ukrainians, who sang part songs in a minor key. Eva, conceding that this was a foretaste of eternity, whispered to Elizabeth, 'Very nice . . . but have no end.'

The next day Elizabeth was chaperoned back to the Rostov train by an elderly comrade, David, who treated her as a piece of delicate china. He, also, was from the Ukraine, and sometimes thought of returning there to surprise people who had long thought him to be dead, not considering, Elizabeth thought, that there might be few people left to be surprised at his resurrection. With the usual warning not to leave her luggage unwatched, David dispatched Comrade Dash-vood back to her own life, after an experience as separate as that of the days when she aspired to be a Bride of Heaven.

After her life at the Commune, the Intourist Hotel, not previously regarded as a lap of luxury, welcomed Elizabeth with a hot bath, a soft bed, and a menu that seemed positively Lucullan after the diet on which she had been subsisting. The Intourist employees gave her a greeting which combined curiosity about the Commune and awe that Elizabeth not only got there but had showed more endurance than a fellow countryman, an Englishman, who had succumbed to illness after two weeks. Above all, she was implored not to encourage anyone else to ask for a privileged visit, which, she was assured, would cer-tainly be refused. It is likely that Comrade Dashwood remained as a legend of the Steppes, without rival, as the owner of a lipstick and a tiny looking glass.

After visiting other collective farms as a conducted tourist, Eliza-beth became convinced that the Seattle Commune was far from typical, in fact that each collective varied in circumstances and ef-ficiency. As far as what might be called her own Commune was con-cerned, she balanced the deadening effect on the intellect from lack of privacy and primitive habits at table against a strong feeling of 'civic pride'. In spite of a limited diet, she had found the standard of health reasonably high, though she had, at first, been concerned that the children were never seen to be drinking milk. After she had seen the conditions in which the cows were milked, Elizabeth felt that this was no loss to the children. Back at home, she found difficulty in believing that life on the Seattle Commune was continuing as she had known it, a life of heavy work lightened by few pleasures. Considering the terrors of the next decade in the USSR, it is to be hoped that her friends suffered no worse hardships than the ones she had shared with them.

Straw Without Bricks opened with the chapter which Elizabeth called 'Commune', and it stands alone in the book as an account of a unique experience. The following chapters do, however, give a consistently truthful picture of the visual splendours and physical miseries en-countered by travellers to the USSR in the 1930s. Interminable waits for food to be served, even in the less bad hotels, were matched by the blocking tactics of every Intourist Bureau. The standard replies, when Elizabeth strove to get in touch with those to whom she had an introduction, were monotonous in their reiteration that the party was called away or did not answer the telephone.

This obstructiveness was, of course, a simple means of keeping potentially dangerous foreigners under supervision. A tourist, however incensed by delays, was neutralized if he was contained in the hall of his hotel, unable to get into mischief which might not only subvert the state, but get the bureau itself into trouble from higher authorities. Even to take a morning off from a sightseeing programme would bring regular telephone calls to ascertain that the truant had not strayed from the allotted bedroom.

On a morning's sightseeing of beautiful, decaying, Leningrad, Elizabeth's party only started after a wait, almost regulation, for the Intourist guide. The tour included a halt outside what had been, until 1917, the British Embassy, and an exchange between Elizabeth and the guide took place:

> 'At that window,' says the guide, pointing to a little iron balcony, 'Sir Buchanan (sic), the British Ambassador spoke to the workers of the October Revolution.'
>
> I ask what he said.
>
> 'I do not know.'

Intourist guides of that date were notoriously obdurate in refusing to accept any correction of the facts they dispensed to their captive audience, however well informed the interrupter might obviously be. The reference to 'Sir Buchanan' may have been an exception to this rule, owing to an episode known to have taken place in the summer before Elizabeth's visit. This same balcony had then been pointed out to a party of tourists as the spot from whence 'Lord Buchanan' had addressed the workers. One of the group, the indomitable Charlotte, Lady Bonham-Carter, felt compelled to make a protest. Exclaiming, 'I must tell her, I must tell her,' she broke into the guide's discourse. 'Please forgive me, it was not *Lord* Buchanan. It was *Sir George* Buchanan.' At the next halt, probably the Finland Station, the guide hit back. 'It was here', she said, 'that Lenin, who was not *Lord* Lenin, nor *Sir George* Lenin, but just *Lenin*, addressed the workers.' The attractive idea of supposing Lenin to have been a peer, a Baronet, or even a knight, was not pursued farther, but Charlotte Bonham-Carter's correction seems, at least, to have turned a gross inaccuracy into a mere solecism.

It was in Leningrad that Elizabeth, sympathizer of the Labour Party as she claimed to be, found herself thinking painful thoughts about the dead or exiled owners of the Imperial palaces. Her fellow traveller, Mrs Pansy Baker, the well dressed lady from the Middle West, did not share her feelings. Seeing everything Russian through a golden haze, Mrs Baker even refused to accept that the flea she had caught on the *Jan Rutzutak* could have been of Russian origin. Insisting that the highest standard of cleanliness prevailed throughout the USSR, she obviously suspected that her flea was British, come aboard at London Docks.

The lady from the Middle West reached her nadir in Elizabeth's eyes when talking of the horror of the amount of blood shed in the course of the Revolution. Mrs Baker said that in her view to achieve the Revolution the blood-letting had also been necessary. Elizabeth pressed her further, giving details of the murder of the Imperial family, husband, wife, four daughters and an invalid son, together with members of their household.

'Was that so?' . . .' [Mrs Pansy Baker] is silent for a moment, and then, with an agreeable smile, sums up the whole thing.

'I guess,' she remarks tolerantly, 'that it was done as kindly as possible.'

Although depressed by Moscow, Elizabeth at least had the support of Peter Stucley, both a neighbour from Devonshire and a contact at BBC Bristol. Assisted by Stucley's comforting solidity, she struggled on and off trams, whose frequent derailments were such a feature of the Moscow rush hour. Together they were able to express their loathing for the guide allotted to them, christening her the Little Monster. Waiting long hours for meals, they not only settled the dishes they would order once they got home, but discussed the titles they would choose for their books on Russia. Elizabeth favoured 'Harper's Surprise', on the grounds that the publishers who had commissioned the book would find it, whether funny or not, innocent of the columns of facts and figures under which, for example, the books of Sidney and Beatrice Webb buckled at the knees.

Having escaped from the unloved Mrs Pansy Baker, in Rostov Elizabeth collected a French *agronome*, whom she called the Savoyard, after his native province. Finding Elizabeth to be fluent in French, he made her his confidante in his perpetual suspicion of the mendacity of the Intourist guides. '*On nous cache assurement quelque chose*,' he reiterated, not without reason. He fought, and won, a dogged battle over the cancellation by Intourist of a visit to a farm of special interest, overriding the stock excuses of absence, sickness and no answer from the telephone. Trailing round the farm behind the Savoyard, Elizabeth's only contribution was to point out that rats were eating, in a comradely manner, from the pigs' troughs. As a country dweller, she was somewhat insulted when her friend asked her if she was sure that they were not mice, but she parted from the Savoyard on the kindest terms, promising impossibilities of meeting again.

During this interlude an English woman, a lecturer in economics already met in Moscow, had held aloof from Elizabeth. Her rather governessy attitude may have been due to distrust of someone who could so easily pick up a French escort. At the departure of the Savoyard, however, she resumed relations by suggesting that they should see what he had written in the visitor's book, which the Intourist staff was apt to secrete if they thought visitors were likely to be less than laudatory.

The Savoyard's comment was poignant in raising a matter of extreme discontent. He had written: '*Pourquoi pas de vases de nuit – cependent bien necessaire?*' Elizabeth suggested that this lack was possibly a labour-saving measure, and a question of hygiene. The lecturer in economics took a different view. She said that she had always supposed that all the *vases de nuit* had been broken in the Revolution.

Odessa was the port from which Elizabeth was to sail out of Russia to Istanbul. The charming town with its tree-lined boulevards was the city in Russia which she liked best. Its layout commemorates the spirit of the emigré Duc de Richelieu, appointed Governor of Odessa after fleeing from the French Revolution. (The preceding Duc de Richelieu had closed a career of gallantry by a well timed death in 1788, at the age of ninety-two.) Although Elizabeth does not seem to have seen Eisenstein's film *Battleship Potemkin*, with its renowned sequence of the pram bumping down the steps, two hundred in all, which fall in a beautiful cascade to the harbour, she could still appreciate the prospect, although exercised by a problem of her own.

Packing for the last time in Russia, Elizabeth was faced with the question of how to export, undetected, a manuscript of thirty thousand words, written in pencil. This was to be the foundation of the humorous book, commissioned light years before by Cass Canfield, and customs officers were known to examine all writing for subversive matter, even if ignorant of the language in which it was written. Books were, in any case, suspect, because currency could be smuggled between their pages, and confiscation would follow only too frequently even if search revealed nothing.

Finally, Elizabeth stripped the manuscript from its cardboard cover and managed to fix it, in just bearable agony, between her spine and her suspender belt. As the customs officer made an upside-down examination of her diary, and ruffled through the pages of a book, with Russian text, devoted to the Museum of Western Art in Moscow, Elizabeth felt that she had been wise to inflict such discomfort on herself. Then she was suddenly smitten with the physical symptoms against which all returning travellers from Russia warned those about to set forth to the USSR.

The warning was unequivocal: 'In Russia you will get diarrhoea. Everybody does.' The suggested cause varied from black bread to 'salad grown in drains'. Brandy was the remedy most recommended, and at least would tend to numb the victim's suffering. More exotic was the offer, presumably made to Elizabeth, of 'A special prescription . . . given me by a Russian ballet dancer before the war.' Having survived the diet of the Seattle Commune, Elizabeth succumbed on the dock at Odessa. Waves of nausea caused her to break out into a heavy sweat, with the additional worry that the pencilled manuscript, clamped to her spine, must be becoming ever more illegible.

Barely conscious, she was yet able to register the final drama which she was to see in Russia. A family of five or six, including a baby screaming from its swaddling of shawls, and a bundle of rags that turned out to be a grandmother, were in trouble. The father's passport was not in order. He could not leave. His family might not stay. Only at the very last moment was the wretched chap hustled up the gangway. It might be speculated that the Comrade Douanier had used this simple stratagem to augment his probably meagre wages.

Next to the ship, by a wild coincidence, lay the SS *Jan Rutzutak*, in which, it seemed months and months before, Elizabeth had sailed from London Docks to Leningrad. Convinced that she was at the point of death, this dog-like fidelity on the part of the vessel of the Soviet Mercantile Marine hardly raised her spirits, but it was a relief to find her manuscript was less obliterated by sweat than she had feared. The ship began to move. Seeking the sleep of gastric exhaustion, Elizabeth blocked from her consciousness the blaring jazz from the loudspeaker, and the voices of the comrades inevitably engaged on the question of whether abortion, as in capitalist countries, should be made illegal. After long weeks of travel, crossing Russia-in-Europe from the Baltic to the Black Sea, Elizabeth was on her way home.

The manuscript smuggled out on the author's person became, in due course, one of the most remarkable books ever written by E. M. Delafield. In England it appeared as *Straw Without Bricks: I visit Soviet Russia*, with a note that 'straws, in their frail, irresponsible fashion, are sometimes thought to show which way the wind blows'. This note would have been inappropriate for the American edition, which appeared under a title less fraught with symbolism. *I Visit the Soviets: The Provincial Lady in Russia*, was obviously designed to catch the attention of the audiences who had crowded to the Provincial Lady's lectures.

Elizabeth had found the lady from the Middle West to be highly untypical of her compatriots, in unassailable pro-Communism and total lack of imagination. She had concealed from her fellow traveller, a fellow traveller in every sense, that it was an American publisher who had commissioned her to write a funny book about the Soviet Union. Elizabeth was also disguised under her married name, easily handled, as has been seen, as Dashwood in Russian. If, back in the Middle West, the original of the egregious Mrs Pansy Baker did happen on a copy of *I Visit the Soviets*, she would certainly have been confirmed in the opinion she had expressed on board the *Jan Rutzutak*. Kindly, but firmly, she had assured her British fellow passengers that she found them to be wanting in 'vitality, uplift, culture and the wider outlook'.

When the reviews came out both *The Times* and the *Literary Supplement* wrote of *Straw Without Bricks* in the manner of a nervous bather testing the water with one toe. It seemed out of line that a famous comic writer should have become an authoritative reporter on conditions in Russia. The *Literary Supplement* barely mentioned the author's unique experience at the Seattle Commune, but dwelt on the fact that, although a professed sympathizer with the Labour Party, she had experienced a revulsion from certain aspects of proletarian life. This, the reviewer wrote, had brought it home to E. M. Delafield that she was 'what communists would call a snob', hardly the word that communists, it might be thought, would use when attacking class enemies.

Neither of these anonymous reviewers could claim to have visited Russia, but the review in *Time and Tide* was written by an expert, who had been purged, by actual experience, of any communist sympathies he had once possessed. Malcolm Muggeridge had been Moscow correspondent of the *Manchester Guardian* in the early 1930s. He had seen the implementation of Stalin's genocidal policy of a man-made famine in the Ukraine, a tragedy from which sympathizers with the Russian experiment were still prepared to avert their eyes. Muggeridge found Miss Delafield to be a most truthful reporter, with an indomitable humour. He particularly enjoyed the plea from the Savoyard for *des vases de nuit*. When Malcolm Muggeridge described Miss Delafield as sincere, and *Straw Without Bricks* as both exceptionally entertaining and authentic, he was paying her the compliment of being sincere himself.

XVI

AT HOME, WITH A FAR FROM
UNLUCKY FAMILY

The family to which Elizabeth returned after her Russian journey
was always a devoted one. If Paul found the more literary of his
wife's friends hard to bear, he had a great affection for her. Among
those who knew him, and frequented Croyle, he was remembered as
distinctly milder than the husbands in his wife's novels, and not nearly
such an oaf as Freddie in her play *To See Ourselves*. Nor were the
animals at Croyle under the constant threat of extermination which
hangs over those in Elizabeth's novels. When not protecting their
children from the irritation caused to their male parent by bad behaviour at meals, E. M. Delafield's heroines, major and minor, are
frequently occupied by the effort to create the impression that cats
and dogs are merely temporary lodgers.

Family photographs taken at Croyle show Paul Dashwood as much
submerged by puppies and kittens as his wife, his children and the
stranger within his gates. When the stranger was Cicely McCall her
Cairn terrier càme with her, and together Cicely and Nelleigh became
constant visitors. In most of the snapshots that have been preserved
the subjects are dressed for the rough and tumble of the countryside.
Paul, in particular, looks as if it would be a life's work to smarten
him up.

One photograph is an exception to the general untidiness of the
Dashwood family when faced by a camera. Elizabeth and Paul were
recorded on a visit to Lady Clifford, at the Villa Rosa, St Marychurch,
on the edge of Torquay. Although the unreliability of the family
automobile was often stressed by Elizabeth, the journey of over thirty
miles does not seem to have ruffled the fine feathers put on for the
occasion. Elizabeth's clothes are in the high fashion of the moment,
and almost over-emphasize her thread paper silhouette. Paul, wearing
a suit with a waistcoat, and with a hat on the back of his head, gives

more of an idea than usual of the charm that had attracted Lady
Clifford towards him, both as an honorary ADC and a potential son-
in-law.

If Lady Clifford's grandchildren found her to be a source of lavish
treats, and, on occasion, a support against the edicts of their parents,
to her daughter she remained an Olympian figure, difficult to propitiate. When a maid, found for her locally by Elizabeth, eventually left
when she realized that her youth and the prospect of a home of her
own were slipping away, Elizabeth expressed grateful surprise that
the kind woman had stuck by Lady Clifford for so long. Sir Hugh
was, by this time, sequestered in a convent at Roehampton. His wife
paid him regular visits, and continued to do so when war had doubled
the time of the journey. The end to Sir Hugh's ruined life came in
1941, by which time a more dreadful blow had struck his step-
daughter.

Another recurrent problem that the Dashwoods had to face was
the difficulties created by the erratic personality of Elizabeth's sister
Yoé. Paul, his daughter Rosamund remembered, groaned and cast up
his eyes when it seemed likely that Yoé would be visiting Croyle.
Rosamund suspected that this was an exaggerated reaction, as he appeared to her to have a weakness for his sister-in-law. To Lionel and
Rosamund her weirdness, intelligence and streak of stupidity combined to make her attractive, in spite of selfishness which obliged
frequent inconvenient sacrifices to be made to Miss de la Pasture's
high principles.

Yoé had remained unmarried, but in the summer of 1936 Elizabeth,
at Odessa, received startling news from Vienna, where Yoé's 'rather
sporadic medical career', to quote Rosamund, had caused her to be.
Elizabeth wrote to Mrs Milton, who worked at Croyle, that she felt
very far from home, but Mrs Milton might be interested to hear a
piece of family news. Her sister Yoé had married an Austrian gentleman in Vienna. Her name was now Mme Friedl, and Elizabeth wrote,
firmly, that her sister seemed to be very happy. Subsequently it turned
out that Yoé's condition had been misrepresented. The idea that, in
her forties, she was finally settled as a married woman proved an
illusion. With that strange prevision which is far from uncommon in
novelists, Elizabeth had, long ago, in *Humbug*, written of a similar
situation to the one that was to confront Yoé. The bohemian Aunt
Clo is disappointed and deserted by a weakling who allows his wife

to extricate him from an entanglement with Clotilde. This sad predicament, as recounted in *Humbug*, can be compared with the one in which Yoé was to find herself in Vienna more than fifteen years later.

To return to Croyle, Cicely McCall had a prolonged stay in the household and great opportunities for observation, when she was taken in as a convalescent, after overstrain in her work. She had, at short notice, been appointed head of an Approved School for disturbed and delinquent girls. Her dedication was such that she had taken forty of these tough customers to camp in a barn, and taught the whole party to swim. It is hardly surprising that, when she reached Croyle, with orders to shun stairs, she needed to be carried up and down in an improvised sling, between Lionel and a helplessly giggling Rosamund. To Cicely the Dashwoods' home was always an oasis, filled with sunshine and rippling with jokes, nor did the threat of any maid giving notice loom as largely as in the writings of the mistress of the house.

Straw Without Bricks was published in February 1937, to be followed, in June, by the almost simultaneous appearance of *Nothing is Safe* and *Ladies and Gentlemen in Victorian Fiction*. *Nothing is Safe*, an impressive, even harrowing, study of child psychology, will be considered in a later chapter. *Ladies and Gentlemen in Victorian Fiction* gave Elizabeth the excuse to flex her literary muscles on the nineteenth-century novels which had meant so much to her in her growing-up years. This was the second book by E. M. Delafield to be published by Leonard and Virginia Woolf at the Hogarth Press, and Virginia Woolf's *Diary* for 1937 provides a brief note on Elizabeth's relationship with the Press and its proprietors.

On 23 January 1937 Virginia Woolf recorded in her diary that she and her husband had been to the cremation, at Golders Green, of Margaret West, 'far and away the best manager' that the Hogarth Press had had. Mrs Woolf complained that the mourners had been forced to wail their way through 'hymn 478, or some such number; about saints receiving their due; alleluia.' To the unbaptized daughter of Sir Leslie Stephen, this was obviously an uncongenial and unfamiliar exercise, the hymn probably being 'For all the Saints, who from their labours rest', actually number 437 in the contemporary edition of *Hymns Ancient and Modern*.

Although Mrs Woolf registered, in herself, a disconcerting lack of feeling for Margaret West's death – 'had she been a kitten or a puppy

I think one would have felt as much' – as a novelist she took a warmer view. There had been, she recorded, something of cheerful virtue in the basement room where Miss West had sat, among what might be called her properties, 'a spotted horse; a carved wooden flower and a piece of green linoleum. Miss L. [Lorna Lewis] came up and said she was left executor of what little money belonged to Margaret . . . Miss Delafield was there.' Two years earlier, when the Hogarth Press published Elizabeth's compilation of the Brontës as seen by their contemporaries, she must have consulted with Margaret West in the basement room with the piece of green linoleum on the floor. She had now come to say good-bye to a friend who had not lived to see the publication of Elizabeth's next book.

If it was through Lorna Lewis's friendship with Margaret West that Elizabeth was introduced to the Hogarth Press, the owners would obviously have been pleased to add the successful E. M. Delafield to their list. So many extracts from the novels of Charlotte M. Yonge were included in *Ladies and Gentlemen in Victorian Fiction* that, in the Introduction, Elizabeth excused what might be considered an excess, on the entirely reasonable grounds that Miss Yonge's works are a peculiarly rich mine for students of Victorian attitudes and habits. Even the most austere minds can sometimes find comfort in reading the favourites of their early years. Virginia Woolf probably welcomed an opportunity to glance again at selections from books that, as a child of the late Victorian age, she can hardly have failed to have read in her schoolroom.

Elizabeth did not, unhappily, live to see the foundation of the Charlotte M. Yonge Society in 1961, but she would certainly have been glad to know that, after twenty-five years, there was still a waiting list for membership. (Nowadays apologies for quoting too freely from Miss Yonge would be much less necessary than they were in 1937.) Besides extracts from the well loved *Daisy Chain* and *The Heir of Redcliffe*, Elizabeth included some samples from *Heartsease or the Brother's Wife*, a novel which had many contemporary admirers.

Among the readers who read *Heartsease* through to the end was Queen Victoria, who wrote to say she had finished 'Violet' – the name of the heroine rather than the book – in a letter to her daughter the Princess Royal. From the bohemian world of the arts, Maria Ellen Peacock, the first wife of George Meredith, made notes from *Heartsease* in a commonplace book. The example of the heroine's wifely endurance seems, however, to have made little impression on the first Mrs Meredith. She eloped with Henry Wallis, painter of the well-known *Death of Chatterton*, for which, incidentally George Meredith had posed. In modern fiction, Joyce Cary endowed the maltreated cook, Sara Munday, heroine of *Herself Surprised*, with a great admiration for Miss Yonge's works, and a special respect for the character of Violet, the brother's wife in *Heartsease*.

Skilfully as Elizabeth analysed Miss Yonge's novels in *Ladies and Gentlemen in Victorian Fiction*, she reserved a special place for *The Fairchild Family* by Mrs Sherwood. Published in 1818, this intensely moral story could hardly be described as Victorian, but it certainly had a considerable influence over succeeding generations. At a period superficially thought to have been dominated by Regency rakes, Mrs Sherwood wished to preach a sermon to children that they should submit unquestionably to parents, as representatives of the Almighty, and custodians of the keys of Heaven and Hell. Mrs Sherwood must have been gratified at the success of her book. She could not know that the continued fame of *The Fairchild Family* was to depend on how wildly funny the doings of Mr and Mrs Fairchild would appear to future generations.

The longest episode which Elizabeth chose concerned the deplorable rebellion of Henry, aged seven, when his father proposed to teach him Latin. Naturally, Mr Fairchild wins in the end, but only after Henry has been beaten, nearly starved and sent to Coventry. Elizabeth's fascination concerning Mr Fairchild led her to write regretfully that, after he had inherited 'a handsome property in the vicinity of Reading', he fades out of the later volumes. Possibly Mrs Sherwood herself lost her nerve about the monster she had created. In the first edition of the original *Fairchild Family*, besides the famous scene when Mr Fairchild tries to cure his children of strife among themselves by taking them to see a rotting corpse on a gibbet, he also walked the children to a cottage where a corpse lay unburied. 'The stink was extremely powerful even before they reached the door', but this moral lesson was dropped from the second edition.

That *The Fairchild Family* had a far-flung influence into Queen Victoria's reign, and beyond her dominions, came to Elizabeth's notice when she discovered the second and third volumes in the 1847 edition among dusty textbooks in a Moscow bookshop, good clean copies, as second-hand book catalogues say. 'Inside each cover is a bookplate, a crest, and a motto beneath a crown and "Graf Lamsdorf" in Russian lettering.' Elizabeth, for a few roubles, rescued these relics of the days when English governesses were an important item in the trade between England and Russia. Her pleasure was augmented by the speculation as to what would have been Mr Fairchild's fate had he visited Moscow, either under the Tsars or the Soviet. As he would have obviously disapproved of both regimes, and as, with Mr Fairchild to think was to rebuke, she could only conclude that he would certainly have found himself in the dungeons of the Kremlin or their modern equivalent.

Finally, in November 1937, Elizabeth brought her bumper year of production to a close with *As Others Hear Us*, a collection of pieces from *Punch* and *Time and Tide*. In this anthology can be found Elizabeth's bitter comments on the habits of the Directors of Banks. These skulking executives, she complained, for ever sheltered behind their branch managers, and 'never came out into the open in a manly, straightforward spirit.' Here also are collected the sketches *Charles, Laura and Another*, already quoted from in connection with Charles/Paul's visit to his old school. Among Elizabeth's portraits of husbands, a subject to which she usually applied a well sharpened scalpel, Charles appears as only reasonably querulous, and has moments when his charm breaks through the clouds of disapprobation of the circumstances in which he habitually finds himself.

Lorna Lewis, 'Miss L.' in Virginia Woolf's *Diary*, had by this time become an important figure in Elizabeth's professional and private life. *Faster! Faster!* had been dedicated to 'Lorna with love and gratitude', and in 1937 Lorna was even more helpful than usual as a chauffeur. Elizabeth then needed to be driven to the film studio, where Pall Mall Productions had engaged her to work on a script of strange, almost eccentric, composition. E. M. Delafield was eventually to be given a credit as a script-writer in second place to Edward Knoblock, well known as a dramatist, and for collaboration in the plays of Arnold Bennett, J. B. Priestley and Beverley Nichols.

When filming had been completed, the billing announced that Pall Mall Productions presented Ignace Jan PADEREWSKI in MOON-LIGHT SONATA. Smaller letters gave the starring performers as Charles Farrell, Marie Tempest, Barbara Greene and Eric Portman. Paderewski was obviously the biggest plum in this particular pudding, being not only famous throughout the world as a pianist, but also as the first President of Poland when the independent state was set up in 1919.

Among the theatrical stars Charles Farrell and Barbara Greene, both Americans, have probably faded from the public memory. Marie Tempest, at least in England, has retained her own legend. She was said to have been the original of the famous actress in Somerset Maugham's novel *Theatre*, whose determination not to be outshone leads her to annihilate an inexperienced fellow actress. The girl had also made the elementary mistake of appropriating the leading lady's young lover.

It is to be hoped that Eric Portman has not been entirely forgotten, an excellent actor with a strong line in caddish parts. Nine years earlier he had played Edmund in *King Lear* at the Old Vic, undoubtedly one of Shakespeare's most formidable cads. Eric Portman's appearance, a wig of flowing black curls above bare limbs disclosed by an exiguous costume, evoked a rapturous response from an audience of schoolgirls, studying *Lear* in readiness for the Cambridge School Certificate, and too entranced to reflect on the enormity of Edmund's behaviour.

Rosamund Dashwood remembers the period when her mother set off at dawn for the film studios, with Lorna Lewis at the wheel, paid by the film bosses to bring Miss Delafield to her work as a scriptwriter. Soon they found that the early clock-in merely resulted in long hours with nothing to do, which might almost be called the industrial malady of writers for the cinema. Elizabeth did, however, collect material for a sketch, *OK for Story*. Its light-heartedness is a refreshing change from the many works which have been devoted to showing the film industry in all the inconsequent tortures it inflicts on sensitive artists.

The young man who, in *OK for Story*, has hung around the studio for weeks in total neglect, suddenly gets the opportunity to rescue a half-finished picture out of which the leading lady has incontinently stormed. With a flash of brilliance, he manages to sell the producer a new Christmas fantasy devised by himself. The producer and his underlings are ravished by the piquant originality of the plot of *Loud Rings Noël*. From that moment the young man's future also rings loudly with promise. All have failed to recognize the *Merchant of Venice*, adroitly brought up to date.

Moonlight Sonata had a hardly less preposterous plot, and the Knoblock/Delafield dialogue was bland rather than sparking. Paderewski had the advantage of playing himself, and Rosamund remembers that her mother thought him to be wonderful. He was old and frail, but the magic he put into the ripples of the 'Moonlight Sonata' succeeded in composing a broken love affair. Marie Tempest was cast as a Swedish baroness, grandmother of the heroine, but this venerable rôle did not prevent her from making trouble on the set. She also appeared at dinner in a dress so flagrantly decolleté that it was a miracle that she did not succumb to pneumonia.

Elizabeth, her daughter says, not only worshipped Paderewski, but lost her heart to Eric Portman, playing the part of an archetypal Delafield cad. Portman represents himself as a figure familiar with High Society, although he is, in reality, a Chilian adventurer, earning a precarious living as an itinerant conjuror. He accounts for his appearance in professional white tie and tails by claiming to have lost his luggage in the air crash which brings a disparate company together. He fascinates the heroine, but disillusion sets in when she finds that he has not only been bought off, but has signed a receipt for the sum he has accepted.

Critics were distinctly scathing about the film, but as Paderewski played Brahms and Liszt, as well as Beethoven's 'Moonlight Sonata', it was suggested that the sight of Paderewski at the piano would always have a certain value in the history of recorded music. Nearly half a century after its original production *Moonlight Sonata* was shown on television (Channel 4). It was hard, then, not to agree with earlier critics, but for Elizabeth the experience had been both profitable and emotionally enjoyable.

XVII

NOTHING IS SAFE

During her Russian tour, Elizabeth had had frequent reason to doubt the reliability of the information offered by the Intourist guides. For example, in Kharkov she had visited a school, and being, as a magistrate, experienced in such matters, asked what was done about 'problem' children. She was assured by the Intourist young lady that, in the Soviet state, there were no difficult, nervous children. No children had what, in the West, were called complexes.

'No complexes? Not any at all, ever?' [inquired Mrs Dashwood JP]
'Never.'
Naturally, this simplifies the problem of dealing with them.

Friends staying at Croyle were impressed by Elizabeth's calm in the midst of constant interruption to her writing. Paul searching for something, calls from the secretary of the Women's Institute, business to do with the magistrate's court, were all handled without complaint. Elizabeth never laid down that she was to have an uninterrupted hour, and it seems that she seldom did. She treated everything that came her way as raw material, including the relationship between the gentle, introvert Lionel and the ebullient Rosamund. If complexes were non-existent in the USSR, they were matters to be tackled at Croyle.

When *Nothing is Safe* appeared in 1937, the Dashwood children were, respectively, sixteen and thirteen. Lionel was approaching the end of his career at Rugby, while Rosamund, following the rather erratic line of education laid down by her mother, was finally settled at Queen Margaret's School, Scarborough. (Elizabeth seems to have forgotten the disruptive effect of the change from school to school inflicted on her in her own youth.) Her mother's worry that Rosamund's puppy fat was a sign that she would develop into a big-boned Dashwood, rather than follow the slender de la Pasture line, turned out to be unjustified. The problems of Lionel's diffident temperament were more troubling, and increased as he grew older.

Nothing is Safe has two principal characters, Julia, a plump little girl of ten, and her brother Terry, who is about thirteen. The action of the story is seen entirely from Julia's point of view. Not only is the conception of the children's opposed dispositions faultlessly carried out, but the book is a perspicacious study of the pain that remorselessly selfish parents can, by a divorce, inflict on their children. Although separated by their boarding schools, Terry and Julia resume a devoted companionship in the holidays. Julia finds Terry's imaginative games deeply satisfying, and tries to protect him from the misery caused by his frequent failure to cope with the simple physical problems of everyday life.

Children, before they reach an age to question their parents' behaviour, notoriously accept it as natural, if inexplicable. When Daphne, the mother of Terry and Julia, explains that she and their father, being no longer happy together, have separated, Julia's main anxiety is not to whom she and Terry will belong, but who will have custody of Chang the chow. For the moment the children, and Chang, are lodged for the Easter holidays in the neighbourhood of Chepstow with their maternal grandparents. Elizabeth used the Monmouthshire countryside in which she had herself grown up as a background for adolescent pains in more than one of her books.

The sense of disruption grows for Julia when her father takes her out from school in the company of Petah, an arty girl of twenty-two, whom he plans to marry. Still finding this news indigestible, Julia reels from another shock when she learns that her mother is now the wife of Captain Tom Pretyman, a beefy type, with a small head on wide shoulders and the nickname of 'Tiger'.

It is obvious, from their second choices, that Daphne and Mark (rather oddly called Alec by Petah later in the book) may well have been incompatible. Financial difficulties follow the divorce, and the first, inexorable separation between Terry and Julia comes when there is not room for both in the mews flat inhabited by Mark and his young bohemian wife. The earache theme, which made the first chapters of *Humbug* so agonizing, recurs, but Julia is made of tougher stuff than the unhappy Vonnie.

Far more painful is the intolerance shown by Daphne's second husband for her son's neurotic temperament. After each hysterical scene, when Captain Pretyman fails to instil his ideas of manliness into the gentle, dreamy boy, there is a crisis, in which Julia's protectiveness loses yet more of its force. After an evening in a cornfield when rabbits, isolated in the last standing corn, are bloodily massacred and Terry collapses into physical sickness, Julia begins to realize that the grown-ups are almost in despair about her brother's incapacity. Even her grandmother, disapproving of divorce and barely acknowledging the second marriages which have wrought such havoc, manages to convey to Julia that her loving efforts to shield Terry from upsets may be an obstacle to his development.

Throughout the summer holidays, which cover the major part of the novel, matters get steadily worse, Julia's happiness depending on whether Terry is green with misery or in a state when he can enjoy eating and shopping. Terry is sent for sessions with a psychotherapist, but, though Julia overhears such phrases as 'infant fixation' and 'the dependence must be broken', it is not until the last day of the holidays that she realizes that the plan to separate her from Terry is likely to be permanent. Only as Terry says good-bye to her as the school train is leaving does Julia absorb her grandmother's hints that brother and sister will not be together at Christmas. Although E. M. Delafield has recorded that she mistrusted her powers of ending a book with an appropriate flourish, and she is known to have rewritten the end of *Nothing is Safe*, never did she leave a more harrowing impression of shattered victims than when she parted Terry and Julia at the railway station.

If *The Way Things Are* could be called the dark side of *The Diary of a Provincial Lady*, the portraits of Terry and Julia might be called an unhappy reflection of Robin and Vicky, the Provincial Lady's own children. Tackled by her daughter, Rosamund, Elizabeth admitted that she and Lionel were, with some exaggeration, Terry and Julia, though at an earlier stage of their lives. Rosamund thought that Terry's ineffectiveness was overdone, but was impressed by the perception shown in some aspects of Julia's character. Anxious to see what is happening to Terry, on the night of a hideous scene, Julia empties her water-bottle, so that it will not be an absolute lie that she has gone downstairs in search of a drink.

There are other perceptive passages, as when, for example, Julia feels shy at the idea of finding Captain Pretyman in the twin bed in

her mother's bedroom. 'Tiger' Pretyman is a splendidly vulgar character, with whom it is possible to feel some sympathy when the children
giggle behind his back at the joke that his remarkably small head has
grown no larger. If he finds Terry's nervous incompetence positively
repulsive, Pretyman admires Julia's guts, even when she attacks him
with teeth and fists in outrage at his efforts to exact obedience from
her brother. He sums up his step-daughter's character by remarking,
'"God help the fellow you decide to marry, one of these days".'

Over Terry's future there hangs a more ominous question mark.
Their father's new wife exists in a disgruntled haze, exacerbated, as
Julia is sharp enough to recognize, by her husband's attentions to
another bohemian girl. There is little prospect that the separate lives
of their parents will not continue to be disrupting for Terry and
Julia. The reader is left with the impression that the author must
have thought with some nostalgia of the Fairchild Family, who at
least stuck together.

Most of Elizabeth's correspondence with the firm of Macmillan was
professionally routine, discussions of book jackets, inquiries as to sales,
lists of people to whom books were to be sent, this last being sometimes
generously longer than the six of a usual contract. This calm relationship
was disturbed when Elizabeth received a reader's report from Macmillan before the publication of *Nothing is Safe*. There was a curiously
uneasy feeling in the reader's comments. He, or she, almost showed
disapproval of the whole story, complained that there was too much of
Chang the chow, and called Julia an uninteresting little girl. This 'study
of childhood' was also condemned for its lack of beauty.

On reading this report, obviously written by one whose childhood
was long forgotten, Elizabeth, to use a later colloquialism, exploded.
She had had, she wrote, no intention of making a study of the beauty
of childhood. Neither could she accept the criticism that the author's
attitude was left in doubt. When the storm had blown over she was,
however, pleased to find that Captain Macmillan, eventually Prime
Minister and Earl of Stockton, had liked *Nothing is Safe*. 'It is a good
many years,' she wrote, 'since I have written anything about which I
feel as strongly as I do about *Nothing is Safe*, and, indeed, the book
almost wrote itself.' Looking back on the earlier childhood of her
own children, Elizabeth's imagination had only needed the stimula-
tion of thinking in terms of the break-up of a family home.

Nothing is Safe was dedicated to 'Cicely who doesn't need convincing'. Cicely may well have not needed to be convinced of the fragility of the human condition, but she was also doubtful that the portraits of Terry and Julia were not too close to the originals for comfort. When the book appeared in America the *New Yorker* carried a review written by someone almost as uneasy in his reaction as Macmillan's reader. Besides a complaint that too much agony had been piled on, there was the hint of an uneasy conscience in the reviewer's inquiry if divorce need always be so bad for the children of separating parents.

The Times Literary Supplement found the study of wrecked childhood to be impressive, though raising the question as to why Terry should be such a mess if his parents had originally been happy together. The answer might well be that Terry's neuroticism was ingrained, and a major factor in the split between his father and mother. More pertinently, the reviewer referred to the story as a descendant of *What Maisie Knew*. It does not require much effort of visual imagination to picture the solid figure of Henry James walking beside the slender E. M. Delafield along a road whose signpost should read 'This Way To Desolation'.

XVIII

ON AND OFF THE AIR

Among the numbers at the Gate Theatre off the Strand, where in the 1930s intimate revues were produced, was a sketch in which four players faced the audience. Seated on park chairs, they commented on four shiny society weekly papers which they passed from hand to hand. One quatrain was personal to the never-flagging Hermione Gingold. Casually examining a photograph, Miss Gingold remarked in a detached voice,

> 'Here's Mr Eric Maschwitz,
> Who's at the BBC.
> He's married to some actress,
> Oh, I quite forgot – it's ME.'

This was the period when Elizabeth had added writing for radio to her other commitments. With a high reputation as a writer of comedy, she was apt to be torn between the wish to please the Directors of Drama and Light Entertainment, and the wish to be given her head over something more serious.

Eric Maschwitz, then the husband of the absent-minded Miss Gingold, was directing Light Entertainment programmes. He was keen to employ E. M. Delafield, although he turned down a monologue, 'Cousin Louisa Speaking'. Hermione Gingold herself was to be murdered in *The Little Boy*, Elizabeth's best known play for radio. Others who crossed her path, and who were later to be well known on the heights of the BBC, included Cecil Madden and Harman Grisewood, but Elizabeth worked most closely with Val Gielgud, novelist and playwright, in his capacity as Director of Drama.

Elizabeth's West End success *To See Ourselves* was quickly snapped up by the BBC and produced in September 1931, soon after the end of its London run. It was in this production that the young actor

Harman Grisewood played Owen, the Welshman who gives his fevered hostess a brief glimpse of romance. A new producer, in 1944, cast Cathleen Nesbit as Caroline. Miss Nesbit was a gifted actress who had been loved by Rupert Brooke thirty years before, but she was possibly rather mature to play, even on the air, the part of a frustrated housewife still under middle age.

The *Radio Times* gave *To See Ourselves* an encouraging puff on its first BBC production. The play's success in the West End was attributed to the 'sympathetic irony' with which the author had discussed whether marriage kills romance. Skilful presentation of this problem had, the *Radio Times* continued, overcome the play's handicap of the total absence of cocktails (a side-swipe at Noël Coward), gangsters (an obvious hit at Edgar Wallace) and precocious schoolboys. It should be explained that 'precocious schoolboys' lunges at John van Druten's *Young Woodley*, in which a schoolboy falls into reciprocated love with a master's wife. This play had a *succès de scandale* as a daring study in the difficulties of puberty. (Incidentally, when translated to the French stage, Young Woodley's youth was emphasized by the *jeune premier* appearing in shorts.)

From 1933 onwards, exchanges between Elizabeth and Val Gielgud were frequent, friendly, almost affectionate, although in letters they remained 'Dear Miss Delafield' and 'Dear Mr Gielgud'. She met him for luncheon at the Ivy, a restaurant where the theatrical clientele went to see and be seen. In her novel *Return I Dare Not*, Margaret Kennedy has left a wonderfully comic description of a character based on Noël Coward who, with a train to catch, can only escape from the Ivy by promising everyone who hails him that he will ring up in the morning.

One of the subjects Val Gielgud wished to discuss with Elizabeth was her adaptation for radio of her short story 'The Gesture' in which the heroine is won by the devotion of an admirer. He follows her, secretly, across the Channel, because he knows that she will arrive at Dover prostrated by sea-sickness. This drama of extreme romantic devotion was produced in 1934, the year in which Elizabeth made her most ambitious foray into criminology since building *A Messalina of the Suburbs* round the Thompson/Bywater murder.

The Little Boy has its foundation in Crippen's murder of his wife, and his burial of the body in the cellar of his house in Hilldrop Crescent. A small boy, Sonnie, replaces Ethel le Neve with whom, in real life, Crippen fled to America. Having accidentally killed his drunken wife, Edgar, the father of Sonnie, bumps her down the cellar steps and buries her under the bricks. A police inspector working on the case has a shrewd idea of what has happened from some nervous remarks made by Sonnie, but lets the mystery go unsolved so that father and son can escape to the New World. Hermione Gingold played the drunken harridan of a wife, a challenge well suited to her talents.

With the craggy shadow of Sir John Reith lying over the BBC, dramatic offerings which dealt with sexual matters had to be sifted through a moral riddle, a process also applied to the Corporation's employees. No objection was made to Edgar, father of Sonnie in *The Little Boy*, getting away with the killing of his terrible wife, but there were difficulties when Elizabeth put forward the outline of a courtroom drama with a distinctly immoral twist in its tail. Gielgud was, he told Elizabeth, apprehensive that higher authorities would prove obdurate.

The plot of *Case for the Defence* concerned a murder trial, the accused having hit and killed a chap who, he claimed, had been 'annoying his girl'. The plea of self-defence was thin, but a verdict of 'not guilty' was returned on the grounds that the accused had had no intention of killing his man. The twist came when a few words between Counsel made it clear that the acquitted was a married man carrying on an intrigue, rather than a simple chap defending 'his girl' from annoyance. There was no objection to getting away with murder, but, as Val Gielgud explained, this development brought up the eternal problem of a sexually guilty party being unpunished for his sin. Although Gielgud was gallantly prepared to risk wrath from Jove/Reith if the play would work dramatically, he must have been relieved when it was considered to lack the necessary punch.

Elizabeth, who declared that she knew the book by heart, suggested that she should dramatize *Vice Versa*, F. Anstey's classic, in which a father and his schoolboy son change places. She also asked if she could not turn *Treasure Island* into dramatic form. Both suggestions were accepted, but the results were not entirely satisfactory from the BBC point of view. Perhaps over-familiarity with *Vice Versa* was a handicap. Certainly Barbara Burnham, the producer, went so far as to say that had she not cast the versatile Cyril Maude as Mr Bultitude in *Vice Versa*, the adaptation would have fallen flat.

On Elizabeth's side matters did not work smoothly, and she felt compelled to write an indignant letter to Gielgud in his capacity as Director of Drama. She complained that not only had she had no acknowledgment for her treatment of *Vice Versa*, but her script for *Treasure Island* had been shuffled between Bristol and London; nor had she been sent payment for this work. If she continued to be treated so churlishly she would, she wrote, consider ceasing to contribute to the Drama Department. She asked for an explanation before calling out her reserves by passing the correspondence to the Society of Authors.

Elizabeth softened this hoity-toity attack by a private note to Val Gielgud, hoping that he would not take the matter personally, as she felt their relationship had always been of the friendliest. Gielgud apologized profoundly for any discourtesy which Elizabeth felt she had suffered. He was able to offer a unique and wonderful excuse for an unusual neglect of his office work. It seemed that the Corporation had been like an overturned bee-hive, with the death and funeral of King George V superseding all other business.

Although she stood on her dignity when she felt that she had been treated impolitely, Elizabeth did not take the BBC as seriously as it habitually took itself. Ragging the Corporation had early become a feature of its existence, and, to be fair, there had been occasions when the BBC had countenanced fun at its own expense. In 1926, Father Ronald Knox put out a broadcast that described revolution as breaking out in London, which was accepted as the truth in homes where scepticism was undeveloped. Even an apology, in the conventional BBC formula, that there had been a mistake as to whether the Home Secretary had been hung from a lamp post or a tramway standard, failed to allay the terrified fear that London was in the hands of a savage mob.

Elizabeth did her own ragging of the BBC in *Time and Tide* with a series of sketches called *Home Life Relayed*. The reporter, with the attractive name of Clarion Vox, spends a bewildered day giving an hour-by-hour commentary on the vicissitudes of a family, living in Highgate but surely lineal descendants of *The Unlucky Family* created by Elizabeth's mother.

'As I was saying, the weather is most unfortunate, and Grandmama is laying sheets of newspaper over the linoleum in the hall . . .it is quite impossible for me to give [listeners] the actual names of the newspapers. The BBC has to make very stringent rules as to anything of that sort. . . . Very well, then, Grandmama – as I was saying – is laying sheets of anonymous newspaper over the linoleum.'

The last sketch ends with an appeal to the relations of Mr Clarion Vox to go to Hanwell Asylum, where – Home Life in Highgate having been too much for him – he is lying dangerously ill.

A complication of Elizabeth's dealings with the BBC arose from an unevenness of the scripts she offered, compounded by the fact that she was not thought to be more than passable as a broadcaster. Over the air the charm of her appearance was naturally lost, together with the highly personal appeal to audiences which made her much sought after as a speaker. Such points were, of course, only indicated to her indirectly, if at all, but there was an internal argument between Val Gielgud in London and Cyril Wood in Bristol, as to whether she should be considered a regional writer, and therefore the property of West Country Broadcasting. This argument, which was to be revived, comically, a few years later, was settled by Val Gielgud refusing to accept that E. M. Delafield should be contained in the West Country limits that applied, for example, to Eden Philpotts. Elizabeth's scope was certainly far wider than that of Philpotts, a prolific writer of novels and plays, who had not allowed his birth in India to be a handicap in becoming an interpreter of Devonshire folk at home and at sea.

Compared to *Home Life Relayed*, in *Time and Tide*, Elizabeth's three radio talks, *Home Is Like That*, given in the winter of 1938, were almost emollient, with only occasional thorns to scratch the skin of the unwary. Elizabeth's authentic voice rang out at its clearest when she assured her listeners that, while she did not wish disasters on her neighbours, when they did occur she liked to hear every detail, and be in a position to supply details of her own.

Elizabeth would certainly have endorsed the dictum 'that good news seldom comes in a buff envelope', when she was describing with distaste 'those unalluring communications in long buff envelopes that adorn the breakfast table', from which, as her listeners well knew, no home can claim immunity. To Elizabeth the unalluring communications, if not accounts rendered in ever more threatening tones, were apt to be signals that the schools to which her children had been confided were flying the yellow flag of quarantine for measles or mumps. When printed in *The Listener*, these sidelights on Home Life were given some rather inadequate illustrations. Arthur Watts, unhappily killed in an air crash in 1935, stood alone in his brilliant interpretation of Elizabeth's overall view of the human predicament.

When the first series of *The Diary of a Provincial Lady* came to an end a howl of complaint had arisen from readers of *Time and Tide* who had totally identified themselves with the Diarist. The flow of appreciative letters had come from such essentially unprovincial places as California and Patagonia. 'Robert' might be valued as a lifelike portrait of a typical English husband in his particular walk of life, but it was the Provincial Lady's own struggle with daily existence that brought letters of almost tearful sympathy. Elizabeth must have been additionally gratified when the radio talks *Home is Like That* induced a number of listeners to write and tell the speaker that, in their experience, home was, indeed, Exactly Like That.

In spite of the feeling among the directors of programmes that some of Elizabeth's offerings were not 'good Delafield', in the first three months of 1935 Felix Greene invited her to review fiction, alternately with G. K. Chesterton. Her reviews seem to have fallen rather flat with Greene and his colleagues. Elizabeth had obviously enjoyed taking off contemporary novelists in *The Sincerest Form* . . . but she possibly lacked the objectivity so desirable among reviewers. G. K. Chesterton's reviews were printed in full in *The Listener* while those of the less widely famous E. M. Delafield were edited down to half a column. That she did not, perhaps, take her work as a reviewer with sufficient seriousness may be guessed from her distinctly disingenuous request to review *The Bazalgettes*. This anonymous novel of the years 1870–6 was described by Hamish Hamilton, its publisher, as 'a literary conundrum'. Elizabeth backed up her wish to review *The Bazalgettes* by explaining that she was 'very much interested in Victorian novels'.

Elizabeth was, indeed, so much interested in Victorian novels that *The Bazalgettes* had been written by herself as a pastiche, the only book of hers which Jamie Hamilton was to publish. The spoof did not take in many readers, though there were some rather wild guesses as to the author. Rosamund Dashwood claimed to have been responsible for an incident in which a ten-year-old child, having ingratiated herself by slipping a hand into her stepmother's during a church service, spoils the effect by demanding to know the meaning of the word adultery, as it is thundered forth in the Ten Commandments. Elizabeth well knew that childhood's innocence invariably asks for enlightenment at the most inconvenient moments. It does not seem that the author's dead-pan appeal to be given her own book for review was granted. Elizabeth had at one time suggested to the BBC a series, *Speeches that Never Happened*, and though one had been broadcast the idea had gone no further. It was not entirely inappropriate that her career as a literary critic on radio should end with a Review that Had never been Written.

XIX

HARD WORK, GOOD FRIENDS

Although some of the Dashwood family viewed her with a certain lack of enthusiasm, Lorna Lewis continued to be a very necessary helper to Elizabeth. There were, however, a number of secretarial jobs which Elizabeth came to see might best be done by a part-time, non-resident assistant. She was fortunate in finding locally a girl of eighteen, competent to deal with correspondence and able to bicycle to Croyle from Uffculme, where her father kept the chemist's shop. By coincidence, Miss Mesney, later Mrs Waite, also bore the Christian name of Lorna, and the diary she kept of her days working for Mrs Dashwood gives a fresh and charming picture of Croyle as it appeared to a young girl eager for a new experience.

Starting work on 3 February 1938, Lorna Mesney found Mrs Dashwood kind and informal. When she stayed to luncheon, nothing could have been less like the meals that the guests of the Provincial Lady were apt to be offered. 'Marvellously served,' was the young secretary's comment. As she could, and did, write anywhere, Elizabeth had no need to be stationary. Almost at once she left for Holland, and as the work piled up in her absence the new helper was seen to be ever more necessary. The school holidays were due to start, and, from the dignity of her eighteen years, Lorna Mesney expected that those referred to as 'The Children' would actually be children. She liked the looks of Rosamund and Lionel, but was startled to find Rosamund as big as herself, and Lionel even bigger.

After six months at Croyle, Miss Mesney found herself swept into Elizabeth's public life. She travelled to London for the Annual General Meeting of the National Federation of Women's Institutes, an organization to which Mrs Dashwood gave her support at national as well as local level. This meeting, at the Royal Albert Hall, has remained an impressive occasion, when eight thousand voices raised in

Blake's *Jerusalem,* to the music of Parry, still stirs all but the most sluggish blood. Lorna Mesney's blood was far from sluggish, and she responded whole-heartedly not only to the Meeting but to the supper party which Elizabeth arranged for the evening. Lyons Corner House, sadly now defunct, may not sound to have been a Lucullan haunt, but in fact the food was excellent and the wine list far from despicable. It was there that Elizabeth entertained Lorna Mesney, together with the namesake Lorna Lewis and Cicely McCall. 'Perfectly lovely people,' Miss Mesney wrote in her diary, 'Wonderful supper and marvellous drinks, and a drive round London to see the sights.' The exhilaration of this trip is far removed from what would usually be accepted as a traditional Women's Institute outing.

Life at Croyle, as the young secretary knew it, was very different from the Provincial Lady's crisis-torn home. As Kate O'Brien emphasized in a later broadcast, 'Surely it is obvious that if [E. M. Delafield] had been the Provincial Lady she'd never have written her.' Grammatically awkward this sentence may be, but it contains a truth seldom acknowledged by readers (but only too well known to writers). Speaking of Elizabeth's physical appearance, Lorna Mesney thought her an example of fine breeding, as it might be a greyhound. The elegance of her bone structure was a contrast to the sturdy build of Mrs Adams.

As it happened 1938, the year in which Lorna Mesney came to Croyle, was a blank year in Elizabeth's steady productivity. After the bumper crop of 1937, and the strain of writing two books of such high quality as *Nothing is Safe* and *Straw Without Bricks,* a fallow period was hardly surprising. Elizabeth's next book, *Three Marriages* (1939), has one exceptionally harrowing story, 'We Meant to be Happy', with an unrelentingly bleak ending. 'The Wedding of Rose Barlow' is also far from cheerful, although Rose, the heroine, surviving the perils of the Indian Mutiny, eventually marries the man she loves. The happy ending has the coda, 'A clear shining after the rain', which, in a very few years, was to become a footnote to Elizabeth's own life. 'The Girl of the Period', the oddest story in *Three Marriages,* has its climax in a physical fight between two girl cousins as to which shall marry a vulgar and rather caddish major. He is engaged to the plainer cousin, but has made a pass at the prettier one. Had this story been dramatized, Eric Portman would have played the caddish major to perfection.

The *Times Literary Supplement* thought *Three Marriages* well up to Miss Delafield's standard. The *Western Morning News*, on the other hand, could hardly have been more scathing at such a disappointing offering from what the reviewer called 'this Cullompton woman author'. Few authors could truthfully swear that they followed Joseph Conrad's declared practice of measuring reviews rather than reading them, nor to being indifferent to adverse criticism that the reviews may contain. Elizabeth might have created the Provincial Lady, but, much travelled and with a transatlantic reputation, this sternly local label can hardly have failed to have caused more amusement than chagrin.

A year earlier the *Church Times*, long ago critical of *The Optimist*, nearly gibbered at Elizabeth's Introduction to *The British Character* by 'Pont', the *Punch* artist, who died young and much lamented. Elizabeth, suffering from romantic ideas about the Celts, wrote that she wished 'Pont' had called this collection of drawings the English Character, but it was other remarks that aroused the indignation of the *Church Times*. Grave exception was taken to the suggestion that most Englishmen, if required to analyse their own creed, would be convinced that 'God is an Englishman, probably educated at Eton'. The reviewer (possibly educated at Harrow) found it strange that 'a clever woman should write such offensive banality'. The displeasure of the *Church Times* may well have been increased by Elizabeth having quoted a schoolboy's definition of faith, 'believing what you know to be untrue'.

Although 'Pont's' sense of colour was attractively delicate, *The British Character* was an album of black and white drawings, with many written inserts that sharpened the point of the joke. Elizabeth did not choose a favourite, but from her knowledge of France, and her interest in fashion, it is possible to suggest what her choice might have been. The appalled expressions on the faces of an impeccably dressed French couple as they unbelievingly study the clearly legible menu in a smart English hotel dining room, would not have been out of place as an illustration to one of Elizabeth's attacks on the unpalatable side of English cooking.

The acknowledgements of the stories in the last of Elizabeth's prewar books, *Love has no Resurrection*, show the range of her market: *Time and Tide*, *Good Housekeeping*, the *Radio Times* and other periodicals. In this collection 'OK for Story', the result of Elizabeth's experience as a script-writer, is enjoyably knockabout, but most of the dramas deal with painfully racked emotions. Husbands or lovers ride away, leaving wives or mistresses to react with pious long-suffering, a fainting fit, or the slow comprehension that the tug of love is slack compared to the grip of the habit of home.

With the final story, 'They Don't Wear Labels', Elizabeth returned to a situation when criminal intent is working in the most ordinary circumstances. Mrs Fuller, unlike some E. M. Delafield boarding-house keepers, is a shrewd, kind-hearted soul, prepared to help any unfortunate lodging in her house. She feels all the more uncomfortable that the semi-invalid wife of Mr Prevelli should be obsessed with the idea that her husband is trying to poison her, as only by her death can he get his hands on his wife's money. Whenever he realizes that she has confided her fears to another person, Mrs Prevelli explains to Mrs Fuller, her husband changes their lodgings. Although pooh-poohing the idea of such a nice, kind gentleman plotting to poison his wife, Mrs Fuller finds herself preventing Mr Prevelli from mixing his wife's evening drink. At the signal that his behaviour is again suspect, Mr Prevelli promptly removes his wife, leaving no address. Afterwards Mrs Fuller finds in the vacated bedroom some traces of broken glass from a Christmas Tree decoration, but although she makes a careful search she never finds the rest of the pulverized glass ball.

On 7 September 1938 Lorna Mesney had written in her diary, 'Oh my stars and garters! Mrs D. rang and wants me to work for the Archbishop of York.' This charmingly surrealist comment was brought out by the prospect of working for Doctor Temple, a Rugby contemporary of Paul Dashwood, but not, apparently, under the blanket disapproval that Paul's avatars, 'Robert' and 'Charles' spread over their old school chums. Elizabeth warned Lorna Mesney that the war scare would be likely to cause the job at Croyle to evaporate, but this pessimism was premature. The household at Croyle found it difficult to get on without Miss Mesney, and even when, a year later, Mars had opened what Charlotte M. Yonge called 'his gloomy school of geography', she was still found to be indispensable.

Undeterred by the first of a series of winters matching the harshness of the fate in store for the human race, Elizabeth started 1939 with a Northern lecture tour. Unsurprisingly, she returned in a state of near collapse. Two months later she was smitten with chicken-pox, a complaint of childhood which always inflicts its fiercest outbreaks of pustules on those in middle life. Remembering the grisly saga of the Provincial Lady's antiquated kitchen, it is to be hoped that the new cooker and the newly painted kitchen recorded in June by Lorna Mesney were a tonic for the mistress of the house.

It was only too easy to feel in July 1939 that the international situation could hardly be blacker, and that the last opportunity for a Continental holiday must be snatched. Elizabeth and Cicely McCall joined the crowd swarming across the Channel. Pausing in Paris, where Elizabeth defied the future by buying a hat, they stopped to visit Lionel, in France for the summer holidays, and travelled on to Corsica.

As always their spirits were high in each other's company, and on one expedition they withdrew from an uncongenial group, finding themselves an eating place free from tourists. The restaurant turned out to be of an extreme unsophistication. Corsica remained a French possession in which the French language was still accepted with reluctance, as Elizabeth found when she asked to be shown to a lavatory. A variety of euphemisms, produced by her good command of French, were met for a while with incomprehension. There was no Armenian interpreter to clarify her request as there had been at the Seattle commune, but eventually her need was recognized, though still unaccommodated. Such conveniences as Elizabeth had asked for were only, she was told, to be found 'on the mainland'.

Communication with the mainland, for any purpose, was frequently irregular. Newspapers arrived at the Corsican hotel sporadically, and many days after publication. The first sign of bad trouble impending was the sudden disappearance of the hotel waiters, 'leur fascule était appelé'. Joining a flood of holiday-makers heading for home, and conscripts heading for their call-up depôts, Elizabeth and Cicely struggled back to England, Elizabeth cherishing the last Paris hat she was ever to buy. For someone of her generation there was ghastly repetition in the crisis, with the inescapable threat that once more, in the words of George Macdonald's poem, 'And there follows a mist and a weeping rain, And life is never the same again'. Many cruel blows were to rain on the undeserving during the next six years. Elizabeth's share took from her a great part of her happiness and, finally, her life.

On 6 September 1939, three days after the declaration of war, Elizabeth summoned Lorna Mesney, who was shocked by Mrs Dashwood's ravaged appearance and state of distress. The young girl had become much attached to an employer who treated her as an intelligent friend, admired her ability to wash fine chamois leather gloves, and brought back for her secretary presents of sweets from Switzerland and Scotland. On amiable terms with Lionel and Rosamund, it is possible that Lorna Mesney's youthful imagination was not immediately perceptive of the anxiety that war had brought to the mother of a gentle, maladroit son whose age would inevitably make him liable for military service.

There was also the 'bombshell' announcement that Mrs Dashwood would be going to London, with the idea of finding a job in the Ministry of Information or the Women's Voluntary Services. Once again Lorna was told that her own job had come to an end, but three months later she was asked back to lend a hand in coping with a sudden spate of letters. The last entry in her diary of her life at Croyle may be quoted in full: 'December 4th. Very strange to be back. E.M.D. very sweet. She had written to *The Times*. 80 replies to do.'

The letter which had drawn such a number of replies had appeared in *The Times* on 30 November 1939. The eighty letters already received by 4 December were, as will be seen, merely the first wave of a flood tide. Elizabeth's letter was a reply to one from a male correspondent in which he had, with an air of patronage, recommended the works of Charlotte M. Yonge as 'escapist literature' in war time. Elizabeth was unwilling to tolerate such denigration of Miss Yonge as a literary force. She could support her claim that Charlotte M. Yonge was still read with enthusiasm, and not 'with a pitying smile', by writing of her own experience in lecturing to a Cambridge University Extension School. A large audience attended her lecture on Charlotte M. Yonge, and at the mention of the well loved name of Doctor May (*Daisy Chain*) broke into spontaneous clapping. Elizabeth's letter also reproved Sir Hugh Walpole, considered by himself to be a Yonge expert, for the shocking slip of referring to Flora, daughter of Doctor May, as 'Florence'.

One of the effects of Elizabeth's letter was to bring an olive branch from the *Church Times* for past criticisms. Miss Delafield was quoted with approval, and congratulated on the number of letters she had received from those who agreed with her about the consolation of reading Charlotte M. Yonge under the increasing strain of war. The *Church Times* recorded Elizabeth as writing, 'How glad [Miss Yonge] would be to know it, and how much I hope she does.'

If Elizabeth and Cicely had a struggle to keep their feet in the crowds battling to get home, they did at least arrive with some days in hand. Yoé's not exactly welcome return to England had a smaller margin before the deadline of war, and the uncertainty of her nationality was a further complication. A complimentary copy of *Straw Without Bricks* had been sent, in December 1936, to Doctor Yolande Friedl, Wien 8, Josefstadterstrasse 81, an address that must have seemed remote from the Chester Square gardens where Elizabeth and Yoé had shared imaginary adventures. After the Anschluss, which in March 1938 merged Austria with the German Reich, living in Vienna became ever more perilous for someone of British birth, though supposedly Austrian by marriage.

Although Elizabeth was prepared to send her books to 'Doctor' Yolande Friedl, she must have known that a period spent studying psychology in the United States hardly gave her sister the right to use a professional style. With the outbreak of war, it became clear that Yoé's right to the name of wife was equally nebulous, the ceremony that had preceded the adoption of the name of Friedl having been, to put it mildly, irregular. Vows had been exchanged, in a church, between Yolande de la Pasture and Julius Friedl, but beyond the witness of some friends that the couple wished to share their lives, no legal or religious sanction had been obtained. As in the great love of Aunt Clotilde in *Humbug*, there was a wife in the background unable, or unwilling, to grant a divorce.

Obliged as she had been to travel back from Vienna on her British passport, Yoé was not prepared to revert to the status of a British spinster, a convenience beyond dispute in wartime. Doctor Yolande Friedl was above what she regarded as a base subterfuge, and insisted on registering as an enemy alien. Consequently, she brought on herself the harrassing inconvenience of having to clear any journey of more than a few miles with the local police. Rosamund remembered also that her aunt's vegetarianism complicated the housekeeping. Elizabeth can hardly have failed to have been reminded of some of her own scathing sketches about people who had developed Food Fads.

Twenty years earlier, William Heinemann had urged Miss de la Pasture not to let an opportunity slip, when she had the absolutely topical material for *The War Workers* immediately to hand. Elizabeth found that she had described a circle when Harold Macmillan, with an equally strong grasp of the mood of the moment, urged her to resurrect the Provincial Lady, firmly buried in an interview her creator had given only a year before. Harold Macmillan sensed that, through the eyes of the Provincial Lady, the mixture of confusion, apprehension and plain boredom which made the first months of the Second World War so trying would find a unique expression.

Except for a moment's displeasure with a reader who, she felt, had missed the point of *Nothing is Safe*, Elizabeth had always had the happiest relationship with the firm and family of Macmillan. She confirmed this when she wrote to Captain Macmillan, in January 1940, to thank him for persuading her to write *The Provincial Lady in Wartime*. She added the wish that the book might be a success, not only for her own sake, 'but for the sake of the kindest and most helpful publishing house with which any writer ever had to deal'. This was surely as handsome a bouquet as any publisher could ever wish to be presented with by any writer.

The Provincial Lady in Wartime begins, on 1 September 1939, with Robert's concern that Cook has been allocated a gas mask too small to contain her countenance. It is difficult now to make credible the enormous importance which was attached to the possibility of an attack of gas from the air. This dominated Air Raid Precautions between the Munich Agreement and the outbreak of war. Courses in the identification of gases and the steps needed to neutralize their effects were obligatory for all branches of all Services. Tags in acrostic style were devised to fix the characteristics of these airborne enemies in minds not scientifically trained. 'Pretty People in Dainty Uniforms' was suggested as a way to remember the properties of a gas ferociously Persistent, Penetrating and so on. In a more practically phrased sentence, it was taught that a gas which affected the NASAL passages could be recognized by Neuralgic pains in the jaw, Aching of the frontal bone of the head, Sneezing, and sometimes vomiting, Acute depression, and most important to guard against, Loss of faith in respirator. From these particulars, it is obvious that Robert would need to be sure that Cook was protected by a respirator so well fitting that her faith would remain intact.

Gas masks, which the Provincial Lady describes as 'Frightful . . . with a snout projecting below a little talc window', were obligatory, often lost, burdens throughout the first years of the Second World War. There was even a rumour that camels in the Western Desert would have to be so equipped. It was only when it became clear that neither side would risk the retaliation which would follow an initial gas attack that the square boxes holding the snouted masks ceased to be compulsory luggage.

Not infrequently in the game of Spillikins there comes a moment when the slivers of ivory are so delicately poised that no further extraction of a piece appears possible without causing movement among the others. To get the game out of the doldrums, a public-spirited player, usually one whose skill has won a lead over the other competitors, may disregard the usual constraints and create new opportunities for all by giving a General Stir. At the beginning of September 1939 something of the same dispersion had taken place throughout the British Isles, and the Provincial Lady finds herself at the receiving end of the mass evacuation from the cities.

The General Stir had as its spearhead mothers, actual and prospective, babies and children of school age. Air raids were confidently expected, and rumours went round with astonishing speed that they had actually taken place. When, however, bombs did not immediately fall, many mothers from the East End of London found their first experience of country living to be intolerable, and fled, with their young, back to the comfort of familiar streets. Many left because they had been totally dependent on their own mothers for cooking and child care, while others disliked the idea of husbands left footloose and a prey to any passing fancy.

The families that decided to endure their exile brought with them problems of different social habits, of which the most immediate trouble was the treatment of head lice. This infliction was regarded by the mothers of the sufferers as something it was more important not to mention than to eradicate. 'Not a nice thing to have said about one,' was a resentful comment sometimes heard. Outbreaks of *Pediculus capitus* were by no means unknown in homes whose cleanliness might have been expected to preclude such infestation, but the General Stir of wartime spread the nits over cottage and castle. As early in the war as 12 September the Provincial Lady records being told by the local chemist that if he had been asked what to do about a lousy head once in the last few days, he had been asked the question twenty times. Lively customers, the nits proliferated throughout the war, seeming actually to flourish on the better known brands of disinfectants.

Shortly after this stimulating conversation with the chemist, the

Provincial Lady is represented as having fixed her household, including a second wave of well conducted evacuees, so that she can leave for London, with the idea of filling the void left by those who had quitted London by public edict or from private apprehension. By this time the Provincial Lady had given up the fiction that, to use her own phrase, 'a minute and unpretentious literary effort' had been a shot fired from an otherwise empty locker. As she wins bread for her family, she feels justified professionally in keeping an eye on agents and publishers. Additionally, the Provincial Lady feels that she had a contribution to make on the propaganda front which will excuse her from facing the war permanently chained to the domestic treadmill.

Although there were those who refused to spend a night in London, even before a single bomb had been dropped on the capital, there were also those who declared that no attack by Hitler would induce them to leave a top-floor apartment. The flat offered to the Provincial Lady was, indeed, on the attic floor of a house in Buckingham Street, Strand. Thinly disguised for purposes of fiction, this rooms were under the roof of the building which housed the firm of A. D. Peters, called by E. M. Delafield in a dedication 'the most patient of literary agents'. Although prepared to make her nest in this eyrie, the Provincial Lady is not exactly reassured when the owner tells her that the building is three hundred years old and will burn like tinder 'if – am not sure he did not say when – incendiary bomb falls on roof'. As Buckingham Street is one of the pattern of four streets – George, Villiers, Duke and Of Alley, now changed to something inappropriate – all called after the handsome favourite of James I, the estimate of the house's age had historical backing.

All over London, the Provincial Lady discovers, telephones are ringing as friends, and even enemies, canvas each other for a job, any job, that might be considered to help the war effort, only to be told to Stand By. Lowering her sights, the Provincial Lady finally gets taken on as a voluntary, unpaid worker in the canteen of an ARP station under the Adelphi, a location with an atmosphere reminiscent of Avernus on a bad day. The alarms and excursions approach the Shakespearean in theatricality, though actual fighting is limited to a private battle, when an ambulance man gets bitten to the bone while trying to separate two chaps from other services, heavily locked in combat.

When Elizabeth wrote *The War Workers*, she allowed Charmian

Vivian, who directed the Supply Depôt, a few rather prickly virtues, which were some compensation for her bullying of her subordinates. The Commandant of Dis-below-the-Adelphi has the same frenetic attitude towards her work, but possesses no redeeming features. 'Have seldom met a more unendearing personality,' is the Provincial Lady's judgment on her boss, but her lowly position at least gives her an excuse for remaining in London. Her imagination gets to work on the composition to be called Women in Authority. This, she feels, could take the form of a trenchant leaflet to be dropped by the RAF, not on the enemy, but on Women's Organizations at home, from whom themselves was sent forth a flood of advice and exhortation, only to be reduced to a trickle when the rationing of paper was imposed.

Besides the exigence of the Commandant, the Provincial Lady has to suffer the high spirits of Mrs Pussy Winter-Gammon, a tiny, ancient lady, christened, on account of her mop of grey curls and girlish manner, Granny Bo-Peep, Sunshine of the Adelphi. As in all under-employed emergency services, 'Have you heard the latest?' is the question most often asked. Granny Bo-Peep is too busy spreading gratifying stories about her past to spread rumours, but the Provincial Lady has a struggle to keep her countenance when the question is put to her by a ginger-haired stretcher-bearer.

Indignantly, the stretcher-bearer announces that the Underworld (rather appropriately) has now been issued with shrouds, which are to be kept in each vehicle:

> Stretcher-bearer then reveals that his chief feeling at this innovation is one of resentment. He was, he declares, in the last war, and nobody had shrouds then, but he supposes that this is to be a regular Gentleman's Business.

Presumably he has a vision of gentlemen in bowler hats, umbrellas in their hands, being wrapped in the shrouds he considers to be so effete.

This wartime diary was to be the last of the four which had given Elizabeth fame, and what the Provincial Lady would have called a Thoroughly Exciting Time. Throughout her service in the Underworld, the latter has created an impression that she was only filling in time before being called up for work of national importance, ignoring the fact that the Ministry of Information was under siege from an army of writers, each confident that they could do better than the Ministry seemed to be doing on its own. Suddenly Elizabeth, with a gasp of surprise, was obliged to bring the Diary to an end. The Ministry of Information offered her the job of going to France, where her knowledge of the language would allow her to report on how the women of France were facing yet another war.

Consequently the *Diary*, which closes on 21 November 1939, comes to an end before the terrible cold of the winter of 1939-40 had gripped the country, until, to quote Christina Rossetti, 'Earth stood hard as iron, Water like a stone.' London, and Elsewhere, as metropolitan letter boxes were then labelled, became an arctic jungle of frozen pipes and unpullable lavatory plugs. Even such an expert in handling domestic disaster as the Provincial Lady had always shown herself to be would have been tested to the utmost.

XX

THE HORROR OF WAR

The proposed excursion in propaganda, sponsored by the Ministry of Information, was planned to take Elizabeth to France early in 1940. At about the same time *The Provincial Lady in Wartime* appeared, with an affectionate dedication to Peter Stucley, 'Because of our long friendship, and as a tribute to many shared recollections of Moscow, London, Edinburgh and the West Country'. The Stucleys had belonged to the West Country for many generations, Peter being the son of a father killed in 1914. His brother died on active service in 1943, but Peter was to survive as a Captain in the Grenadier Guards, though by then the friend with whom he had toured Moscow under the guidance of the Little Monster was no longer alive to share further adventures.

Stucley had himself written in the previous December from Radio Bristol to another BBC executive to inquire, on Elizabeth's behalf, about possible broadcasting contacts in Paris. Stucley was slightly guarded about Elizabeth's performance on the air, indicating that it was her reputation that carried off a rather inadequate delivery. Having travelled with her, he was, however, able to declare that she spoke good French, so that there was some sense in sending her on a mission of inquiry into the morale of French housewives.

On her return from France Elizabeth gave an interview to the *Western Morning News*, somewhat padded with explanations of the attitude of French housewives towards the cooking and serving of a meal, which she found to be unaffected by the war. She explained that the practice of waiting until the guests had arrived before the most important dishes were actually cooked was made less tedious, even if an hour and a half passed, by the animation of the conversation. Seated on a stiff circle of chairs, internal and international affairs were discussed with an intensity unknown, Elizabeth implied, in

Devonshire. Delicious as the meal might well be when it finally appeared, it is hard to feel that Robert's temper, for example, would have survived such a famished hiatus.

It does not appear that Elizabeth made any broadcasts from her experiences. Even to the *Western Morning News* she could do little more than repeat how frequently she had been told, 'Cette fois-çi il faut en finir.' This was the catchword of the moment, reported by many other inquirers into the feelings of the French. The way to its consummation was to be far longer and harder than could have been visualized by those who had, early in 1940, entertained Elizabeth.

Professional opinion that Elizabeth's charm as a public speaker did not transfer to the air was shared by more than her old friend Peter Stucley. Geoffrey Grigson, poet, critic and wartime employee of BBC Bristol, was to complain in 1942 that E. M. Delafield had been poached from Bristol for a talk going out from London. He added that Bristol could have told London of Miss Delafield's inadequacies as a broadcaster, not improved after many rehearsals. Grigson was well known for displays of resentment, which were apt to lead him into untenable situations. The assumption that E. M. Delafield was, as it were, a regional property, was quickly deflated yet again, in this case by the Empire Talks Manager. On the contrary, this official pointed out, she was a writer of international reputation, whose level of ability as a broadcaster was as well known to London as it was to Bristol. It was only her last illness that was to close Elizabeth's career with the BBC.

As a public speaker Elizabeth had served her apprenticeship by addressing many meetings of Women's Institutes, an undeniably tough breed of audience. Her delivery was so engaging that she was always welcomed, no matter on what subject she had decided to talk. She had learnt to measure the receptivity of her listeners, and so was spared the depressing experience suffered by her contemporary, the novelist Margaret Kennedy. Miss Kennedy, after giving a carefully researched talk on a tour of Sweden, learnt later that the highest praise awarded for her effort had been the lukewarm comment 'quite interesting'.

A rare complaint about Elizabeth as a speaker at meetings did, however, appear in *The Times* of 22 August 1940. France had fallen, and air raids were an immediate threat, no longer only a matter for precautionary exercises, in such places as the Underworld below the

Adelphi. The correspondent reported complaints from a woman in a Somerset village on which bombs had already fallen. It was not a protest about death falling from the air, but rather that a well-known novelist had been sent, by the Ministry of Information, to give an inspiriting lecture. 'The idea was for the well-known novelist to go about cheering women up and improving their moral (sic)'. Both the writer to *The Times*, and the encapsulated correspondent, not only disapproved of Elizabeth, but were obviously characters escaped from a novel by E. M. Delafield, particularly so in the closing sentence of the letter. 'Can nothing be done to curb this foolish procedure of the (miscalled) Ministry of Information?'

To someone of Elizabeth's generation the first casualties of the Second World War must have brought harrowing recollections of the losses of the First. Like a cloud that had never lifted, there lay across the landscape of the past the deaths of Paul's three brothers, Sir Hugh Clifford's young son, and Algernon Thynne, husband of Elizabeth's Aunt Constance. More cruel than the casualties of twenty odd years ago was the blow which fell on the Dashwoods in the autumn of 1940.

Rosamund was still a schoolgirl at Queen Margaret's, Scarborough, where, if Vicky's letters to the Provincial Lady were drawn from real life, she actively hoped for the kind of German bombardment which battered Scarborough in the First World War. (This attack not only gave Osbert Sitwell the title for a novel, but convinced his father, Sir George, that he and Lady Ida Sitwell had been under far heavier enemy fire than any to be met with in Flanders.) At Croyle, the question of Lionel's military service had become inescapable. He had been destined to go up to Oxford, and had been staying in France. Presumably this was what Anthony Powell has called 'the solution to that urgent problem . . . the disposal of the body of one of those uneasy, stranded beings, no longer a boy and hardly yet a man.'

While waiting to be called up to the Infantry Training Company of the King's Own Shropshire Light Infantry at Shrewsbury, Lionel joined the Home Guard, among men of all ages known to him since he had, as an infant, been brought to Devonshire from Malaya. On his last leave he drove what his mother called 'his awful little car', along the Taunton road. As they bucketed along Lionel remarked on the stretch of road where Jamie Hamilton had driven him at eighty miles an hour. If Elizabeth felt uneasiness at the roadworthiness of

Lionel's automobile, it is likely that she felt even more apprehensive about the tough life that would face her son at the Infantry Training Company of the KSLI. Her estimate of his temperament had appeared not infrequently in her writings, mostly in the shape of a boy who is anxiously dependent on his mother for reassurance and moral support.

The bright aspect of Lionel can be found in the charming portrait of the Provincial Lady's son Robin, the darker side in the near martyrdom of Terry in *Nothing is Safe*, though Terry would never, unlike Lionel, have survived a career at Rugby. Rosamund, looking back, thought that Lionel himself was anxious not to distress his father, an ex-soldier and one of a family of soldier brothers, by seeking to serve in some non-combatant capacity. On 3 November 1940 Lionel's mother received what she called a happy letter from him. The next day, 4 November, the Dashwoods were given the shattering news that Lionel had met with a fatal accident, and had died from gunshot wounds in the armoury of the Infantry Training Centre.

Sometimes the family of a war casualty have had the added bitterness that their loss is the result of a bungled operation, but Lionel's death had not even the justification of supposed military necessity. As there had been no witnesses, an open verdict was returned at the inquest, and Lionel was brought home to be buried at Kentisbeare with military honours. His coffin was borne by his comrades of the Home Guard, and his grave was under a yew tree which Elizabeth had pointed out to Lionel as the spot where she wished to be buried. When she wrote to tell her publisher, Daniel Macmillan, of Lionel's death, she assured him that she intended to go on writing, but now that Robin, of the Provincial Lady, had gone it would be impossible for her to continue in the vein which had made her famous.

If Lionel's death had effectively killed the Provincial Lady, there were those who thought that the blow to his mother was hardly less mortal. Although Paul and Rosamund supported her through their own suffering, Elizabeth's letters to her friends were written from a brave but broken heart. In thanking Jamie Hamilton for his messages of love and understanding, Elizabeth wrote that at least Lionel was spared the horrors which war might have brought upon him. Jamie had left happy memories of his kindness to both her children, so that even through her grief Elizabeth had the courage to write of Rosamund's earlier decision to work in the Hamish Hamilton office on leaving school. She even made the joke that she did not know if the advent of Yvonne, the new Mrs Jamie Hamilton, had in any way altered Rosamund's plans.

To Marjorie Watts, widow of Arthur Watts, Elizabeth wrote immediately to try to forestall the shock to her friend of reading of the tragedy in the newspapers. Elizabeth felt sure of Mrs Watts's fellow feeling, as they had been much together at the time of Arthur Watts's death in an air-crash. Elizabeth told Mrs Watts that she was sure that the accident had been due to Lionel's clumsiness with his hands, a lack of co-ordination he had never been able to conquer. To both these dear friends she wrote that she was sure that Lionel had passed to a life far less full of difficulties than the one which he had left.

Six months later, Elizabeth wrote to Marjorie Watts that Rosamund would soon be leaving school and that she planned to join the Women's Auxiliary Air Force. This would bring twenty years of happiness at Croyle to an end. The painfully empty nest had seen Elizabeth's children growing up, and had been the background of her professional success. There was, however, no element of surrender in Elizabeth's nature. She wrote as diligently as ever, never failing in her commitment to produce pieces for *Punch*, which she would send in clusters to be used as the editor saw fit. Paul was working seven days a week at ARP, the importance of his job increasing as bombs began to fall on Exeter and Plymouth. At Croyle, in the all too brief time left to Elizabeth, shortages were overcome, and friends continued to find it a sanctuary. To their relief nothing came of a threat that soldiers might be billeted on a household already overfull of refugees from the bombed cities.

No One Now Will Know, the penultimate novel by E. M. Delafield, appeared in June 1941. This was Elizabeth's last opportunity to add to her gallery of tyrannical mothers in Cecilia Lemprière, the widowed mother of two adored sons and a disregarded daughter. Cecilia returns from Barbados, where her husband has owned a slowly decaying sugar plantation. The family are of Creole origin, but, though she had no links with Barbados and had never been there, Elizabeth knew enough to make it plain that the designation Creole does not signify an inheritance of coloured blood. Settled in a large house overlooking Tintern and the loops of the River Wye, Cecilia marries again, and gives birth to a second daughter, Kate. Being attractive, this daughter is treated with less neglect than her half-sister Fanny. However, Cecilia's second husband is polished off with some ruthlessness, and the matriarch once again reigns unhindered.

Cecilia concentrates her affection on her son Fred, with a certain amount to spare for Lucien, known as Lucy. Kate, their half-sister, grows up loving Lucy as her favourite brother, but is shattered when Lucy becomes engaged to her girl friend, the beautiful, portionless Rosalie. Fred's return creates a triangular crisis, but does not prevent the marriage of Lucy and Rosalie. A sun-dew for absorbing admiration, Rosalie is unable to resist Fred, before and after her marriage. The final tragedy is brought about by Fred's second seduction of Rosalie, and her death in an accident, more or less the fault of Lucy, her husband. 'No one now will know' is a quotation from the Irish poem, *The Glens of Antrim*. The following line, 'Which of them loved her most', applies not only to the passion of Fred and Lucy for Rosalie, but to the question as to which is the father of Rosalie's daughter Callie.

Callie grows up to be the most attractive character in a novel which, like a film run backwards, begins with Callie's own children, poised on the brink of the Second World War, and works its way back to the 1870s. The devotion of Kate for Rosalie is repeated in Callie's love for a charming contemporary, Elizabeth. This time the disaster is on an emotional level. Elizabeth annexes an admirer of Callie's, being unable to allow admiration for anyone except herself. Callie marries a cousin, lamed in the First World War, and settles down to keeping a Devonshire estate from insolvency. Both the Devonshire manor house and the grander mansion overlooking the Wye come alive, in many respects, more vividly than some of their inhabitants.

No One Now Will Know appeared at a moment when the fortunes of the Allies in the Second World War were about to receive a jolt from Germany's invasion of Russia. The *Times Literary Supplement* wrote patronizingly that the novel 'had not much of a story, but was readable enough in its way'. The reviewer's interest seems to have been only moderately stirred by seduction of a sister-in-law, a suggestion of incest, incipient lesbianism, and a fatal carriage accident.

Earlier in 1941 Hugh Thomas, of the BBC, had written to Elizabeth asking if she would take part in a programme to go out on the Forces Wave-Length. Members of all units of the Forces were to be asked to send in questions which would be put to a panel of men and women, people possessed of wide knowledge. The *Encyclopaedia Britannica* would be held in reserve as umpire, should there be disagreement. The programme was to be called 'Any Questions?' Forty-six years later, to hear of such a title being suggested for the first time is a strange sensation. It is as if one Ancient Greek had been heard saying to another, 'I say, have you heard? That blind fellow Homer is thinking he might write something about the Trojan War.'

Elizabeth did agree to appear on the 'Any Questions?' programme, but with the reservation that her specialist subjects were Victorian fiction and juvenilia, with a capacity to bat back questions on the works of Dickens. She was not good, she wrote, on poetry and general literature. This self-assessment, if possibly too modest, is admirably clear-sighted. It would be agreeable to know if, from any unit of the Forces, there came a question on Mr Fairchild's attitude towards the upbringing of children, a question no one, on any panel, could have answered more competently than Elizabeth.

Speaking jobs were still taking up much of Elizabeth's time, entailing dreary hours of travelling in crowded trains to stations whose names had been reduced to illegibly small letters. This precaution was taken so that invaders by parachute would not immediately see whether they were dropping on, for example, St Neots or St Ives. One of her journeys took Elizabeth to stay near Witney with Kate O'Brien, a friend who now became increasingly important to her. It was from Kate O'Brien's house that she corresponded with the BBC about a proposed talk on Country Life in Wartime. The title was to be 'A Quiet Life', not a condition often experienced by Elizabeth. She was to have broadcast this talk on 8 November 1941, but returned her contract to the BBC as she was 'indisposed'. With the good manners that were a part of her character, she gave permission for the script to be read by a substitute, who in this case was the News Announcer.

The term 'indisposed' was inadequate to describe the illness that had attacked Elizabeth. On 5 November she had been sent into a nursing home for an operation which had resulted in a colostomy. It was not until 10 January 1942 that she was able to write to Marjorie Watts that her plans for convalescence would mean a visit to Bude, where her Aunt Constance once again provided a refuge for one of her sister's daughters. It was thirty years since a failed Bride of Heaven had gone to recuperate with Mrs Thynne, but the need for loving care was now far greater.

Elizabeth took the disabilities and occasional embarrassments caused by her operation with a calculated mixture of courage and ribaldry which disarmed the anxiety of her friends about her condition. She is said positively to have relished the repetition of a story which involved a ride in a taxi after some accident of miscalculation had obliged her to strip off most of her clothes. She enjoyed speculating as to the reaction of the taxi-driver had he suddenly realized that only an overcoat covered the nakedness of his passenger. A very poor impression will have been given of Elizabeth's unflagging zeal as a writer if there is surprise at learning that, on 20 January, ten days after she described herself as proposing to start her convalescence at Bude, she began another novel, to be called *Late and Soon*. This was to bring to an end a career which had begun in a VAD's off-duty hours long ago in Exeter.

The dedication of the last of E. M. Delafield's novels was to Kate O'Brien, who had had her first success in 1931 with a semi-historical family saga, *Without My Cloak*. The title's derivation from Shakespeare's 34th Sonnet does not seem, perhaps, entirely relevant to the fortunes of a Catholic family settled in business in Miss O'Brien's native town of Limerick, but it was an inspired title for a book which became a best-seller. An entirely historical novel, *That Lady*, was a more original work, being an account of the relationship between Philip II of Spain and the fascinating Princess of Eboli. In spite of wearing a black patch over an empty eye-socket, the Princess continued to hold the King's admiration, until he took against her so violently that he condemned her to be walled up in a room from which only death released her.

According to a talk given eighteen months after Elizabeth's death, it was early in 1941 that Kate O'Brien began to know Elizabeth as a friend, someone who previously had only been an acquaintance, a fellow author of exceptionally charming looks and manners. She also came to know Elizabeth's home, her husband, her daughter, and the family's sorrow for the vanished son. Having reached a rebellious age, Rosamund's immediate reaction was that here was yet another of her mother's admiring female friends. She was almost surprised to find herself liking and respecting Kate O'Brien as much as any of the writers and artists who came to Croyle.

According to Rosamund, her mother's favourite photograph of herself was a snapshot in which Elizabeth stands tall and slim, in an open shirt worn above neat slacks. Rosamund's own favourite photograph was one in which Elizabeth struggles in a tangle of dogs and cats, Yo-Yo, the keeshond, making no objection to being mixed up with a pair of kittens. These kittens were called Antony and Cleopatrick, the latter rechristened after his sex had been misdiagnosed. It is not difficult to understand that Rosamund felt more warmly sympathetic to the mother so obviously enjoying a romp among her pets, than to the author treated as a brilliant phenomenon by a circle of other talented writers, both men and women.

Undeterred by her physical state, Elizabeth carried on with her professional engagements, and, above all, she continued to write. *Late and Soon*, begun on 20 January 1942, was finished on 27 September. The novel opens in a large, cold country house, in the grip of the third icy winter of the Second World War. Valentine Arbell, the widowed chatelaine, struggles with her routine of village duties. Her rather dull husband has been killed in a hunting accident ten years or more ago, Elizabeth's perhaps too frequent way of disposing of a husband superfluous to a story. Once, as a very young girl in Rome, Valentine has had an essentially innocent romance with Rory Lonergan, who had the disadvantage of being both an Irish boy of twenty, and a penniless art student. Her marriage has left Valentine in the unawakened condition which Elizabeth inflicted on more than one of her virtuous women characters. On the other hand, her daughter, Primrose, has taken to living an almost undisguisedly loose life in London. Jess, the younger daughter, is waiting to be called up into the WAAF. Cheerfully extrovert, Jess might be a grown-up version of Julia (*Nothing is Safe*).

Primrose, the last of E. M. Delafield's slender, vicious blondes, arrives for an unexpected visit. As a hell-raiser she has points in common with Pamela Flitton from Anthony Powell's *Dance to the Music of Time*, but even Pamela Flitton never revealed publicly, as Primrose does, that she has been having an affair with Rory Lonergan, her mother's former sweetheart and now Primrose's prospective stepfather. Rory Lonergan has had a successful career as an artist and, as a Colonel, is in command of a unit stationed locally. He is billeted at Coombe, his presence accounting for the sudden appearance of Primrose. Rory and Valentine have surprisingly little difficulty in picking up where they left off in the Pincio Gardens.

If Primrose Arbell is the last of Elizabeth's blonde sluts, and

Valentine the last of a number of unawakened wives, Rory Lonergan might almost be called the last in a long line of cads. It is possible that Kate O'Brien, more or less in permanent residence at Croyle, may have supplied material on which Elizabeth built up a portrait of an Irishman from a middle-class Catholic background. Unfortunately, neither novelist realized that an essentially Kate O'Brien character would not be convincing when transplanted into an E. M. Delafield novel.

Lonergan, having fallen in love once again with Valentine, rightly goes on about what a low hound he is, as he wriggles out of his affair with Primrose. In spite of protests from Valentine's brother Reggie, a crippled General, and her sister-in-law, a last portrait of a beautiful, brassy woman, Lonergan and Valentine walk out into the snow to be married by special licence. Although largely activated by snobbery, there is something to be said for the objections raised against Valentine's marriage by her brother and sister-in-law. The reader is left with a suspicion that, after years of sedate behaviour, Valentine may find it difficult to join her life to that of an almost too consciously stage Irishman. Primrose, on the other hand, gives the union her blessing, and takes up with a tough, ambitious, young captain. Jess is called up into the WAAF, and Valentine has at least escaped from Coombe, the house that has stolen her youth.

Late and Soon was published in April 1943, and reviewed in a manner that can only be called mixed. A younger generation of reviewers had begun to make their mark, some finding the plot preposterous, others praising the comedy that sparkled through the gloom of war. The *Times Literary Supplement* thought Colonel Lonergan to be 'a complacent and humbugging bounder of a man', hardly better than the monstrous Primrose. Little attention appears to have been paid to the strictures of reviewers. *Late and Soon* went into a second reprint within the month of publication, not only showing a strong demand, but an indication of Macmillan's willingness to live up to their reputation for kindness and helpfulness in allocating scarce paper to their grateful author.

XXI

'A CLEAR SHINING AFTER THE RAIN'

The admirers of Charlotte M. Yonge, who had responded in such numbers to Elizabeth's letter to *The Times* on the subject of Miss Yonge's books as wartime reading, had even more cause for enthusiasm in 1943. That was the year in which *Charlotte M. Yonge* by Georgina Battiscombe appeared. Admirers had long been anxious for a full biography, previous attempts having been hampered by a conviction that Miss Yonge herself would have regarded any such book as an attack on the privacy of a remarkably blameless life.

Books published in this time of restrictions on paper were swiftly snatched from bookshops, and Mrs Battiscombe's *Charlotte M. Yonge* had the additional tribute of an Introduction by E. M. Delafield. As this was one of Elizabeth's last appearances in a book, she must surely have been glad that she could record her gratitude and affection for the works of an author whom she had loved for so long. Georgina Battiscombe has well expressed this feeling when she explained that admirers of Miss Yonge have their own answer when reproved for not preferring 'works of genius'. 'They don't want works of art, they whimper, they want Ethel and dear Doctor May.'

Even in Miss Yonge's lifetime there were, however, those, possibly mostly male, who found her admirers to be inexplicably obsessed. Oscar Wilde, in the 1880s, when Miss Yonge was still at work on her later 'linked' novels, happened to be shown round a prison in Nebraska. He asked, with pity, what a man in the condemned cell was reading to pass the time before his execution. When Wilde found the book to be *The Heir of Redclyffe*, he decided that it was right that the law should take its course, an opinion he subsequently revised when himself in Reading Gaol. In more modern times, T. S. Eliot found that to read *The Pillars of the House* aloud to the ladies of the Mirrlees family, all ardent fans, was beyond the bounds of his kindly tolerance.

As Elizabeth sat writing before the shelves of Charlotte M. Yonge which she had so sedulously collected, she would certainly not have approved of the attitude of either Wilde or Eliot, but she had nothing but praise for Georgina Battiscombe's biography. Of the staggering number of letters which she had herself received after her letter to *The Times* in 1939, she had only to criticize those who claimed that they possessed everything, over two hundred and fifty works, that Charlotte M. Yonge had written. She knew that her own collection of two hundred volumes was a feat unlikely to be equalled, and certainly not surpassed. Elizabeth ended her Introduction to *Charlotte M. Yonge* with a reminder of the blows war had inflicted on literature. 'Art is long,' she wrote, 'time is fleeting, and paper, at this date is rationed.' She had, once again, arrived full circle at the point when William Heinemann had pleaded a shortage of paper for his proposed delay in publishing *Zella Sees Herself*.

Increasingly, after her operation at the end of 1941, Elizabeth's friends were distressed by the bouts of pain from which she suffered, though admiring her capacity for rallying when pain had abated. After six weeks in bed in the spring of 1943, she came to London in July for X-ray treatment at Bart's Hospital. Although the medical report was encouraging, she was left in unusually low spirits. With Kate O'Brien, she returned to Croyle, the old schoolroom being made over to Miss O'Brien as a workroom. This was a privilege never attained by the mistress of the house.

Occupied now full-time by ARP, Paul had ceased some time previously to be the agent for the Bradfield estate, but the spectacle of Mrs Adams parading in the uniform of a Commandant reminded the neighbourhood that Bradfield was now a hospital. There was a rumour that Mrs Adams's position was the price she had exacted for the use of the house, though she had stopped short of Lady Boxe's insistence on 'Officers Only'. This was a stipulation which the Provincial Lady sardonically recorded.

Mrs Adams was most unfortunate, it seems, in only being able to show her least endearing side to her near neighbours. During the war, Bradfield Hall was visited by James Lees-Milne on behalf of the National Trust, of which he was, according to his own description, 'an unqualified historic buildings secretary'. He found Bradfield, in January 1943, to be as bitterly cold as on any evening when Lady Boxe entertained Robert and his wife. Otherwise James Lees-Milne found Mrs Adams to be 'simple and sweet', with a broad Scotch, or even Glasgow, accent. She said that she quite realized that she was a tradesman's daughter, married into the squirearchy, and finding different ethical standards to which she had had to adapt. This disarming confidence, had it been more widely known, might have softened local opinion and resulted in a gentler, if less entertaining, portrait of Lady Boxe.

The Milton family were, perhaps, the closest of Elizabeth's allies in the village of Kentisbeare, Richard Milton and Lionel Dashwood having been friendly contemporaries. Mrs Milton gave the kind of help at Croyle for which the Provincial Lady would have been immensely grateful, as indeed her creator was. It happened that Richard Milton, as a young soldier, had a unique opportunity of observing Mrs Adams's very real awe of Mrs Dashwood when he went into hospital at Bradfield for an operation.

On the subject of E. M. Delafield, it was believed that Mrs Adams was in the habit of fulminating, 'That woman . . . I'd like to get at that woman', until the day her bluff was called. She was not aware that Richard Milton knew the Dashwoods of Croyle, and it was with deep respect that she came to tell him to expect a visit from Mrs Dashwood. She was even more shaken when she was told that the young man's mother had already said that Mrs Dashwood might be his next visitor. Nothing, including the use of the Commandant's private study, was then too good to be lavished on a patient so honoured.

To those from the Home Counties, it sometimes seemed that west of Salisbury, the King's Writ as to food rationing considerably relaxed its grip. Certainly grateful visitors to Croyle, seeking brief holidays from war work, agreed that the standard of living never sank as low as that described in *Late and Soon*. On the other hand, troubles with Income Tax had crept up on Elizabeth unawares, and obliged her to appeal to the Secretary of the Society of Authors for advice in settling claims beyond the resources of a visit to the familiar Plymouth pawnbroker. After some haggling for a reduced demand, it seems possible that this was met by the sale of a field or a piece of furniture, and certainly either step would have been in keeping with the less serious side of Elizabeth's character.

It was late in August 1943 that Elizabeth returned to Croyle. Having only known her hostess well since her fiftieth birthday, Kate

O'Brien was surprised to find that Elizabeth could still run with a fair turn of speed, and could, if occasion arose, jump a tennis net at full stretch. Her hair had turned to a silvery grey, but she kept up all the attention to her appearance which, transmuted into her books, had given a particular distinction to her portraits of both heroines and villainesses. When she climbed into a fig tree to gather the fruit for which she had a passion, Kate O'Brien found it impossible to believe the medical opinion, known to them both, of the short time that lay before Elizabeth. Kate O'Brien wrote later that she believed that she had accepted the inevitable end, but the golden autumn days insidiously undermined her defences.

At the begining of November Paul's sister, Muriel Dashwood, was appealed to for help in getting Elizabeth from Oxford station to the Nuffield Clinic for a consultation with a neurological surgeon. The Great Western Railway provided a massive wheelchair, covered in black and red rep and probably designed, Muriel thought, by Isambard Kingdom Brunel. When the train came in Muriel was appalled at the sight of Elizabeth's white, shrunken face and black circled eyes. It was no surprise when the surgeon told Paul that he should take his wife home to her own surroundings, and make the days she had left as painless as possible.

Already almost a ghost, Elizabeth managed to welcome a visit from Jamie Hamilton, whose sympathy at the time of Lionel's death had been of much comfort to her. Ever since they had met at the *Time and Tide* party at the Dorchester, Jamie Hamilton had had such enjoyment in their friendship that, long afterwards, he had no hesitation in saying that he had 'loved her passionately'. He could remember many meals when Elizabeth had shone in such company as Rose Macaulay and her friend and illustrator Arthur Watts. He could also remember Paul's good-natured acceptance of the ribald portrait of his domestic habits in *To See Ourselves*.

At Croyle he found Kate O'Brien alone at luncheon. Afterwards he was taken up to Elizabeth's darkened room. He realized that she did not wish to show her ravaged face, to spoil her memory to an old friend who had known her in days of radiance. When he kissed her in a last good-bye, Elizabeth told him that he would pass the churchyard where Lionel lay buried under the big yew tree. 'Give him my love,' she said, and when Jamie did so it was with streaming eyes.

From 16 November onwards, *The Times* recorded, among 'Invalids', the inexorable decline of E. M. Delafield (Mrs Paul Dashwood). At about this time the last contribution to *Punch* to be signed E.M.D. appeared, bringing to an end the writing career that had begun in the spare time of a VAD. Rosamund, on compassionate leave from the WAAF, found that her mother still kept up a brave pretence of making plans for things to be done after the War should have ended. Yo-Yo, the devoted, much photographed keeshond, lay in Elizabeth's room until 1 December when he went out into the garden and died among the bushes. On 2 December 1943 Elizabeth died. Her last words were murmured in French, 'Ne pas mourir', perhaps an exhortation, in the language of her ancestors, to those she was leaving behind. At some moment during the day of her death, a robin, a frequent visitor to the window-sill, flew into the room and perched on the end of Elizabeth's bed, a messenger of farewell from the Devonshire countryside which she had loved since childhood.

Although in Elizabeth's writings husbands are sometimes shown to be unappreciative of their wives, at her death her own husband's feelings were beyond immediate comfort. A friend who met Paul Dashwood on local business in February 1944 at first thought him to be cheerful, even his usual self. It was only when they separated, and the hope was expressed that Paul would be fairly happy in the guest house where he was to lodge, that the surface cracked. Paul said he was not sure, because he wished he would not be in sight of Kentisbeare.

Having sold Croyle, disadvantageously, Rosamund thought, Paul eventually returned to Oxfordshire, where, in 1964, he ended his days among the Dashwood clan. After the exhilaration of life with Elizabeth, his later years may have had an echo of a story his wife had called 'Fauntleroy' and dedicated to A.P.D. (Arthur Paul Dashwood). Fauntleroy had been a cat at Croyle, but in fiction he is represented as becoming the companion of a widower, who has consistently threatened to banish him from bed and board when his wife was alive to share both. Elizabeth's portraits of cats are affectionate, but without illusion. Fauntleroy is a creature supremely uncaring of the impression he may be making, provided he attains his objective. It is to be hoped that some such companion comforted Paul in his last years.

Rosamund, after rising to be a sergeant in the WAAF (her mother lived long enough to boast of her child instructing others), married in 1948. She followed her husband, Doctor Harold Truelove, from a stint in the Antipodes to an appointment in Manitoba, and became the mother of four sons. Although she was often far away from her mother's friends, she always knew that Elizabeth's memory was unfading among those who had known her whether in Devonshire or in wider literary circles. Elizabeth had never hoarded her gift of friendship within a limited group. When the Kentisbeare Women's Institute stood in silent remembrance of 'their beloved President', it was no formality but a tribute from the hearts of the members.

Not very long before her own death, Elizabeth happened to listen to the obituary of another writer on the Six O'Clock News, and wondered if she might herself merit such a mention. Only too soon came the announcement of the death of E. M. Delafield, to sadden the hearts of a multitude of listening readers. Elizabeth herself is said to have believed that she might have written better had she written less, but writers can only obey the inexorable propulsion of their 'daemon'. Elizabeth's 'daemon' sat on her shoulder wherever she might be. In trains, at mealtimes, crossing the Atlantic, touring the steppes of Russia, her writing had been, physically, her unfailing companion. Her reward was not only to have been the financial buttress of her family, but to have made numberless, if unseen, friends.

Elizabeth was buried on 6 December 1943 in Kentisbeare churchyard under the big yew tree. This was the spot that she had long ago chosen for herself, and here she now joined Lionel. Already carved on Lionel's gravestone was the coda of his mother's novella 'The Wedding of Rose Barlow', a story which ends when troubles are past and there is a gleam of future happiness in the sky. Believing deeply that Lionel had gone to a life happier than the one which he had left, Elizabeth had chosen for him the encouragement of words which fortified her belief, 'A Clear Shining after the Rain'. This now became Elizabeth's own epitaph, a memorial profoundly in harmony with both her life and her works.

Extracts from the following works by E. M. Delafield are reprinted by permission of A. D. Peters & Co Ltd: *Humbug, Thank Heaven Fasting, The Way Things Are, The Suburban Young Man, The Diary of a Provincial Lady, Turn Back the Leaves, Gay Life, Straw Without Bricks, Home Life Relayed, The Provincial Lady in Wartime.*

The extract entitled 'Brides of Heaven' is reprinted by permission of Rosamund Dashwood.

INDEX

Adams, Honourable Mrs, 55,
   159, 181–2
Adeane, Mrs, 105
Adrian, Max, 115
Alcott, Louisa M., 118–19
Allingham, William, 39
Allen, Frederick Lewis, 118
Allen, Hervey, 117
Annesley, Honourable Caryl, 42
Anstey, F. A., 153
Anthony, C. L. (Dodie Smith), 92
Arnim, Elizabeth von, 70
Ashton, Frederick, 98
Asquith, Prime Minister, 8
Asquith, Margot, 8
Austen, Jane, 69

Balfour, Arthur, 8
Bane, Mrs, xiv
Battiscombe, Georgina, 180–1
Baum, Vicki, 109
Belloc, Hilaire, 76
Bennett, Arnold, 109, 143
Besier, Robert, 92
Betjeman, John, 1, 73
Blunden, Edmund, 120
Bonham, Constance, see Thynne
Bonham, Elizabeth Lydia
   Rosabelle, see Lady Clifford

Bonham-Carter, Charlotte, Lady,
   132
Brunel, Isambard Kingdom, 183
Buchanan, Sir George, 132
Buller, Dame Georgiana, 31
Buller, Sir Redvers, 31
Bullough, Sir George, 5
Bullough, Monica, 5
Burnham, Barbara, 153
Butler, Samuel, 4, 6
Bywaters, 5, 7

Canfield, Cass, 69, 117, 119, 123
Carey, Joyce, 142
Casson, Mary, 115
Charrington, Dorothea, 5
Charrington, Monica, see
   Bullough
Chesterton, G. K., 156
Clifford of Chudleigh, Lord, 9
Clifford, Sir Hugh, 9, 10, 31, 42,
   89, 139
Clifford, Lady, 1, 3 *passim*, 10, 12,
   31, 41–2, 59, 139
Clifford, Mary, 42
Compton, Fay, 92
Conrad, Joseph, 10, 89
Constable, Elizabeth, 9
Coward, Noël, 89, 152